4115
Budaya
2295

W9-BYF-277

basic
Indonesian

Sari lahir di Jakarta.

Keluarga Sari tinggal di Pasar Minggu.

...ampus UI di Dépok.

basic
Indonesian

An Introductory Coursebook

Stuart Robson and Yacinta Kurniasih

TUTTLE Publishing

Tokyo | Rutland, Vermont | Singapore

The Tuttle Story: "Books to Span the East and West"

Many people are surprised to learn that the world's largest publisher of books on Asia had its humble beginnings in the tiny American state of Vermont. The company's founder, Charles E. Tuttle, belonged to a New England family steeped in publishing. And his first love was naturally books—especially old and rare editions.

Immediately after WW II, Tuttle served in Tokyo under General Douglas MacArthur and was tasked with reviving the Japanese publishing industry. He later founded the Charles E. Tuttle Publishing Company, which thrives today as one of the world's leading independent publishers.

Though a westerner, Tuttle was hugely instrumental in bringing a knowledge of Japan and Asia to a world hungry for information about the East. By the time of his death in 1993, Tuttle had published over 6,000 books on Asian culture, history and art—a legacy honored by the Japanese emperor with the "Order of the Sacred Treasure," the highest tribute Japan can bestow upon a non-Japanese.

With a backlist of 1,500 titles, Tuttle Publishing is more active today than at any time in its past—inspired by Charles Tuttle's core mission to publish fine books to span the East and West and provide a greater understanding of each.

Published by Tuttle Publishing, an imprint of Periplus Editions (HK) Ltd.

www.tuttlepublishing.com

Copyright © 2010 by Periplus Editions (HK) Ltd.

Illustrator: Cleiffy Leonard

All rights reserved. No part of this publication may be reproduced or utilized in any form or by any means, electronic or mechanical, including photocopying, recording, or by any information storage and retrieval system, without prior written permission from the publisher.

Library of Congress Control Number: 2010922245

ISBN 978-0-8048-3896-2

Distributed by:

North America, Latin America & Europe
Tuttle Publishing
364 Innovation Drive, North Clarendon,
VT 05759-9436 U.S.A
Tel: 1 (802) 773 8930; Fax: 1 (802) 773 6993
info@tuttlepublishing.com
www.tuttlepublishing.com

Asia-Pacific
Berkeley Books Pte Ltd
61 Tai Seng Avenue #02-12, Singapore 534167
Tel: (65) 6280-3320; Fax: (65) 6280-6290
inquiries@periplus.com.sg
www.periplus.com

Japan
Tuttle Publishing
Yaekari Building, 3rd Floor, 5-4-12 Osaki,
Shinagawa-ku, Tokyo 141 0032
Tel: (81) 3 5437-0171; Fax: (81) 3 5437-0755
sales@tuttle.co.jp
www.tuttle.co.jp

Indonesia
PT Java Books Indonesia
Kawasan Industri Pulogadung
Jl Rawa Gelam IV No 9
Jakarta 13930
Tel: (62) 21 4682-1088; Fax: (62) 21 461-0206
crm@periplus.co.id
www.periplus.com

First edition
17 16 15 14   10 9 8 7 6 5 4   1403HP

Cover photo © Altrendo Images, Getty Images.

Printed in Singapore

TUTTLE PUBLISHING® is a registered trademark of Tuttle Publishing, a division of Periplus Editions (HK) Ltd.

Contents

Foreword

Basic Indonesian is an entirely new book. It has been made to fill the need for a one-volume coursebook which can be used for either self-study or classroom use by those who are keen to make a start on mastering the Indonesian language. The users we have in mind might be students in universities or schools outside Indonesia, or expatriates living in Indonesia.

The **Stories** are set in Jakarta (apart from an excursion to Yogyakarta), are original and describe realistic situations, contain some interesting cultural sidelights, and display a lively mix of narrative and dialogue. Bearing in mind that our readers will be adult learners, we have also included clear **Language notes**, which, we hope, will explain the grammar and build a solid foundation for further steps forward in the study of Indonesian.

The authors are Stuart Robson, Adjunct Associate Professor of Indonesian at Monash University (Melbourne, Australia), and Yacinta Kurniasih, a native speaker with very extensive experience in teaching Indonesian, now at Monash University. These two have a vision of language as a means of bringing people closer together, by enabling them to communicate — this isn't just a matter of exchanging information, but also a means of exploring our common humanity, by including some of the thoughts and feelings we share. Language should, we believe, help us to understand "what makes people tick".

The photos were taken by Benedicta Kuspartini in Jakarta. We are very grateful to her for all her efforts to get them right. **Terima kasih banyak, Tini!**

Most importantly, thanks to Eric Oey (CEO of Periplus/Tuttle), for patiently enduring the delays in the writing process and encouraging us to continue, and to Nancy Goh for formatting and editing the final product.

Introduction

If you decide to study a language, your study will be all the more meaningful if you know something about it, beyond memorizing vocabulary and analyzing sentence structures. You will certainly want to know where the language came from, and what it is related to. So at the beginning of our journey we offer a little information to whet your appetite.

In Indonesian, the Indonesian language is called **Bahasa Indonesia**, which means "the language of Indonesia". It has this name because it possesses the official status, under the Constitution, of national language of the Republic of Indonesia. In other words, this language is taught and used from one end of the country to the other, and in this way serves as the "language of unity". So it has an important political as well as practical function, providing a means of communication between all the various groups within the country.

As you will probably know, Indonesia consists of a large number of islands, located in Southeast Asia (see Map). Each of these islands is home to different ethnic groups, large and small, and each of these has its own language. These are separate languages, not dialects of Indonesian. They represent the vehicle of valuable cultural traditions, and form part of an individual's identity. So these languages are people's "home" language, and exist alongside the national language, which children learn at school. It is worth noting the interesting relationship between these two, and the way bilingualism works.

MAP: The islands of Indonesia

So where did Indonesian come from, and how did it achieve its present position? Indonesian is a variety of the Malay language, that is, it is Malay which has been adopted and adapted for a special purpose, namely to serve as the national language of Indonesia, a nation which only declared its independence on 17 August 1945. This shows clearly that there must have been some important historical developments prior to this time, and suggests that a knowledge of the history of the region will be useful.

Malay is a language used in various parts of Southeast Asia in different forms. It is the daily language of the inhabitants of parts of Sumatra and Kalimantan, as well as the Riau Archipelago, for example, and the Malay inhabitants of West Malaysia, and also the sultanate of Brunei and the Malays of Singapore. In view of these connections, a knowledge of Indonesian is useful for learning Malaysian, and vice versa, although they are by no means identical and display significant differences, despite the similarities and shared spelling system.

From its beginnings in the western part of the Archipelago, Malay became a trade language, and as such was used by the first Europeans, the Portuguese, who came in search of spices in the 16th century, soon followed by the Dutch. From their headquarters at Batavia, the present capital of Indonesia, Jakarta, the Dutch gradually extended their control over what now constitutes the territory of Indonesia, and for administrative purposes they used Malay for contacts with the "natives". In this way, Malay was already fulfilling a function as a language of unity in the 19th century, and was being regulated by Dutch administrators and scholars.

The early 20th century saw the rise of the nationalist movement in Indonesia and a desire for independence from the Dutch colonial power. In 1928 a declaration was made to recognize "one country, Indonesia", and "one people, the Indonesian people", who "uphold the language of unity, Indonesian". As a further boost, during the Japanese occupation (1942–45) Dutch was not allowed to be used, and so Indonesian (at that time still called Malay) was used, and a start was made on developing it to fulfil all the functions of a modern language, capable of being used not only for trade and administration, but also for all branches of education and science.

Indonesian has continued to be cultivated and developed since the end of the colonial period, and today it is the task of a government office, the National Language Development Centre, to promote the use of "good and correct" Indonesian. Modern Indonesian is the result of the convergence of several streams, for example the variety used by the print media and in government offices, "school" Malay as promoted by the government printing house Balai Pustaka, and the colloquial of the streets and markets as used in inter-ethnic communication. It is a lively language, and we see innovations being introduced by journalists, as well as the influence of the "Jakarta colloquial" in speech.

Malay, and hence also Indonesian, is a member of the Austronesian language-family, more specifically the western Malayo-Polynesian sub-branch of this family. This means that it is related to all the other (regional) languages of western Indonesia, as well as to other members of the family, found in the Philippines, in Melanesia and Polynesia, Madagascar, and even the aboriginal languages of Taiwan. But it is not related to important languages of mainland Southeast Asia, such as Thai, Cambodian, Vietnamese or Burmese, and also not to the East Asian languages Chinese, Japanese or Korean, or any Indian language. This gives an idea of its place among the languages of Asia.

However, as one would expect, we do find large numbers of loanwords in Indonesian. Ones which we readily recognize are the result of the process of modernization and globalization, and are likely to come from Dutch and English. It is curious that a number of terms in Indonesian (in contrast to Malaysian) are "loan-translations" from Dutch, that is, can be traced to a Dutch original by a process of translation, instead of literal borrowing. An example is the word for "vacuum cleaner", **pengisap debu**, "dust-sucker", which corresponds to Dutch *stofzuiger* — it doesn't look the same, but also means "dust-sucker".

Malay and Indonesian also contain many loanwords from Arabic, the language of Islam, which provided terms introduced as part of Islamic culture, and at an even deeper level there are loans from Sanskrit (the ancient language of India), some dating from the pre-Islamic period, and others very recent. Indonesian has also absorbed a large number of words from Javanese, some colloquial and others constructed from elements of classical Javanese, on the one hand because of the preponderance of speakers with Javanese as a first language, and on the other from a need to create new words or euphemisms. An example of the latter is **tuna netra**, which means "whose eyes are inadequate", and sounds better than the more basic **buta** "blind". Taking an interest in the origins and particular meanings of words makes them easier to remember.

Somebody who is approaching the study of Indonesian "from the outside", either as a visitor or student, or as an expatriate working in a business or similar environment, will want to communicate effectively and to have access to various channels such as the print media and TV. In particular, the active use of the language, speaking and writing, will require you to develop a "feeling" for what is right or appropriate in a certain setting: people will appreciate your efforts if you use correct grammar, and can also adjust your style to take account of who you are speaking or writing to, what the context is, and how they feel. In short, getting the words, pronunciation and constructions right shows that you value the language and its speakers, and your cultural sensitivity will admit you to people's hearts and homes.

The Development of Modern Indonesian

From the moment in 1928 when the Indonesian youth movement took its oath to uphold the Indonesian language, the leading figures began thinking about ways in which they could translate this into action. The first Language Congress was held in Solo (Central Java) on 25–28 June 1938, and after hearing a paper given by Amir Sjarifoeddin on "Accommodating foreign words and concepts into the Indonesian language" the congress passed a resolution to adopt foreign words for sciences, and that this work should be done carefully, by submitting it to a body.

Although the formulation is still fairly vague, under this point we can already see what was to become a preoccupation of language planners and practitioners, namely the best way to prepare the Indonesian language for its function as a language capable of being used in all branches of science. Obviously there was an assumption that Malay was not yet developed enough to be able to do this—an idea that may seem odd from the perspective of the 21st century. There was an assumption that foreign words would need to be borrowed in order to create the new terms; it would be Dutch words that the intellectuals turned to, as these were considered appropriate for anything modern or scientific.

Nothing more could be done for the time being, until the period of the Japanese Occupation. At the request of the Indonesians, the Japanese Army's Office of Education set up a Language Committee on 20 October 1942, chaired by Sutan Takdir Alisjahbana. The Committee had three sections: Grammar, Testing new words, and Terms. Takdir and his friends worked away at these projects undisturbed, till they were closed down on 30 April 1945 because of nationalist activities. However, the results of their work were published shortly after the Occupation, in the form of two small volumes. The first appeared in 1945 as the *Kamoes Istilah I Asing-Indonesia (Dictionary of Terms I: Foreign-Indonesian)*, and the second in 1947 as *Kamoes Istilah II Indonesia-Asing (Dictionary of Terms II: Indonesian-Foreign)*.

In this context, "foreign" meant Dutch, and the new terms that were discussed and approved by the Committee were sought first in Malay, and after that in other Indonesian languages, and finally in Sanskrit or Arabic. The total number was 7,000, and the terms were very technical.

Following the capitulation of the Japanese and the proclamation of the Republic two days later on 17 August 1945, a period of chaos ensued. The work of the committee was taken up again but it had the opportunity to meet only once, on 21 July 1947, before returning Dutch forces seized its offices, and the Republic moved its capital to Yogyakarta, where it held off the Dutch for some time, during the period known as the Revolution.

As a Dutch scholar, G.W.J. Drewes, remarked in 1948, Malay was teeming with new words that could not be found in the dictionaries, but were to be read in the daily newspapers. They did not come from the **Kamoes Istilah**, but most likely could be found in the Javanese dictionary, as either colloquial or literary terms. If before the war there was a Sumatran period in the development of Malay, then after the war it went through a Javanese period. This was attributed to the removal of the seat of the Republic from Batavia to Yogyakarta and the spread of terms via the press of Central Java.

The system of spelling was the one inherited from the colonial period, but the first Minister of Education, Soewandi, initiated an improvement as early as 19 March 1948, with the replacement of the digraph **oe** with **u**. It was more efficient to use one letter for one sound, and the letter **u** had not been used in the previous system; furthermore, it was a nationalistic step. However, many people still use **oe** instead of **u** in the spelling of their name.

A **Balai Bahasa** (Language Centre) was set up by the Republican administration in Yogyakarta in March 1948, under the Minister of Education and Culture (and the building still exists). This would be the first in a series of several institutions, all with the aim of cultivating and developing language, leading up to the one that exists in Jakarta today. After the Transfer of Sovereignty from the Netherlands to Indonesia at the end of 1949, and the takeover by the Republic in Jakarta, the **Balai Bahasa** now came under a new institute, the **Lembaga Bahasa dan Budaya** (Institute of Language and Culture), which was set up in 1952 as part of the **Fakultas Sastra** (Faculty of Arts) at the University of Indonesia in Jakarta.

In 1959 this was changed to become the **Lembaga Bahasa dan Kesusasteraan** (Institute of Language and Literature), under the Department of Education and Culture. Then on 3 November 1966 it was changed again, to become the **Direktorat Bahasa dan Kesusasteraan** (Directorate of Language and Literature). In 1969 it became the **Lembaga Bahasa Nasional** (National Language Institute), and finally, on 1 April 1975, it became the **Pusat Pembinaan dan Pengembangan Bahasa**, or **Pusat Bahasa** for short, normally translated as "National Language Development Centre", under the Director-General of Culture. This has grown and flourished, and today continues to fulfil an important function in the cultivation and development of language in Indonesia.

Alongside the institutional developments, there were also important publications in the field of language. Again going back to 1948, a monthly magazine appeared, founded and edited by Sutan Takdir Alisjahbana, called ***Pembina Bahasa Indonesia*** (*Cultivator of Indonesian*). This contained articles on questions of language for the information of readers on such matters as grammar, correct usage of words, questions from readers, general articles, and even language exercises. A proportion of the articles seems to have been written by Takdir himself. In September 1950 it had a print run of 15,000 copies, suggesting that it was widely read. It ceased publication around 1957. Takdir had been writing essays on the Indonesian language since the founding of the independent literary journal ***Pujangga Baru*** (*New Poet*) in 1933, as well as fiction, the novel ***Layar Terkembang*** (*With Sails Unfurled*, 1939) being the best known (see Figure). In 1957 Takdir's articles were collected and published as a useful volume under the title ***Dari Perjuangan dan Pertumbuhan Bahasa Indonesia*** (*On the Struggle and Growth of Indonesian*, reprinted in 1988).

Meanwhile, a more substantial journal, ***Bahasa dan Budaya*** (*Language and Culture*), was being published by the **Lembaga Bahasa dan Budaya**, commencing when this was still attached to the **Fakultas Sastra** of the University of Indonesia, beginning in 1952, and continuing up to the present day as a publication of the **Pusat Bahasa**. In the 1950s a **Komisi Istilah** (Terminology Committee) was again set up, probably inspired by the one that existed during the Japanese Occupation. Its results were listed as regular appendices to **Bahasa dan Budaya**. All these lists are from Dutch to Indonesian; the intention was to ensure that there existed Indonesian equivalents for every kind of technical term. The words were divided into sections, for example animal husbandry, military matters, mathematics and physics, education, aviation, agriculture and engineering. Apart from terminology, another matter that continued to occupy the minds of Indonesians during the 1950s was spelling. The Language Congress held in Medan in 1954 urged changes, and ideas began to be exchanged with scholars of Malay in Malaya and Singapore. The Federation of Malaya became independent from the British on 31 August 1957, and in April 1959 a cultural agreement between Indonesia and Malaya was signed, to include matters of language such as spelling. A delegation went to Jakarta and met Sukarno. A joint system of spelling would be created, to be called the **Ejaan Melindo**, but no details were ever announced. Instead, history intervened in the form of Confrontation, when Malaysia

A novel by Sutan Takdir Alisjahbana

became the enemy. Furthermore, politically and economically the early 1960s were extremely difficult years for Indonesia, and people had little time or inclination to think about little things like spelling.

The question only arose again in 1966, after the establishment of the **Orde Baru** (New Order) by Suharto. A spelling commission, chaired by Anton Moeliono then of the **Lembaga Bahasa dan Kesusasteraan**, was set up in May 1966, and a draft proposal was ready by August. This was submitted to the Malaysians, and was agreed and published in 1967. After much debate, it became official on 17 August 1972, and a similar proclamation was made by the Malaysian government, so that both countries would now use the same system of spelling. This new spelling is called the *ejaan yang disempurnakan* ("perfected spelling"), and the details were set out in a little guide called *Ejaan Baru*. The main effect was that in Indonesia the former **dj**, **j** and **tj** became **j**, **y** and **c** respectively, while in Malaysia only the former **ch** became **c**.

At this point, it is interesting to look at Malaysia, as there has been a similar concern with language development there, although this arose at a somewhat later date due to the historical circumstances. An institution called the **Dewan Bahasa dan Pustaka** was established in June 1956 as a small government bureau under the Department of Education in the pre-independence Federation of Malaya. After Independence in August 1957, the new Federal Constitution declared Malay as the National and Official Language, and in 1959 the Dewan Bahasa dan Pustaka Ordinance was enacted, making the **Dewan** an autonomous statutory body under the Ministry of Education. Exactly ten years after independence an Act of Parliament, called the National Language Act 1967, was passed, naming the National Language the sole official language of the country, replacing English. The **Dewan** has had many activities, including an extensive publication program. For example, it published a monthly magazine, called *Dewan Bahasa*. This contains lists of new technical terms, translated from English into Malay. These were formulated by terminology committees in various fields.

The **Pusat Bahasa**, which has its headquarters at Rawamangun in Jakarta, also engages in a wide range of activities. These cover both the Indonesian and regional languages, literature in Indonesian and regional languages, lexicography and terminology. In order to implement this program, it has an extensive program of publications, and provides information to the public on the correct use of Indonesian. An important example of its work in the field of lexicography is the great monolingual Indonesian dictionary, **Kamus Besar Bahasa Indonesia**, a very complete and reliable work produced by a large team and first published by **Balai Pustaka** in 1988.

An example of a publication in the area of terminology is the **Pedoman Pengindonesiaan Nama dan Kata Asing** (*Guide to the Indonesianization of Names and Foreign Words*, 1995), which lists English terms with an Indonesian equivalent, divided into seven sections, for business and finance, industry, sport and art, tourism, communications and telecommunications, personal appurtenances, and property.

It is interesting to make a comparison with other Southeast Asian languages. In the Philippines an Institute of National Language was set up in 1937, when President Quezon declared Tagalog to be the national language. But much has happened since then. In 1971 President Marcos declared that the national language would be known as Pilipino, and in 1986 the new constitution made Filipino the national language, with the intention to create a broader national language in the future, which would include borrowings from other major languages such as Ilocano, Cebuano, Pangasinan and so on. Meanwhile it would still be based on Tagalog, but Tagalog would eventually be just another regional language. We understand that the debate is ongoing.

In Thailand, where there is one main language, Thai, the process of modernization began early with the efforts of HRH Prince Wan Waithayakon Krommun Naradhip Bongspraband, an Oxford graduate and respected diplomat and scholar, who on his return from Europe in 1919 started coining words which were needed for a Thai version of the Civil and Commercial Code, and went on from there. He is said to have created around 300 words, which are now mostly in common use, making use of Pali and Sanskrit. His work in this area has been continued till the present by a Bureau of the Royal Institute, so that Thai has a complete range of terms needed for modern life.

The need for new terms grows by the day, and Indonesian keeps pace with this by either creating a new word or by adopting the English. Some examples from the field of information technology can serve to illustrate this.

ENGLISH	INDONESIAN
information technology	**téknologi informasi**
net(work)	**jaringan**
server	**penyedia jaringan**
operating system	**sistém operasi**
software	**perangkat lunak**
application	**aplikasi**
screen	**layar**
memory	**mémori**
access	**aksés**
patch	**perisai** ("shield")

The Spelling and Sounds of Indonesian

Indonesian has a distinctive sound, with lots of soft labial and nasal consonants, and with comparatively more syllables per word than English, so it flows smoothly like a babbling brook.

The writing system

Indonesian is written in the familiar roman script (although Malay was once written in the Arabic-Persian script), and this system was originally introduced by the Dutch during the colonial period, although it has been modified since then. The spelling system is regular and predictable, with very few odd cases. We will describe the sounds of Indonesian below, but first introduce the alphabet. This is important, if you have to spell out your name, for example, as the names of the letters are different from English.

The alphabet

First we give the letter, and then an approximation of the pronunciation of its name. Note that in a number of cases we have to use the letter é (e acute), as found in French, in order to avoid the English sound "ay".

A	*ah*, but short	**N**	*en*
B	*bé*	**O**	*oh*
C	*ché*	**P**	*pé*
D	*dé*	**Q**	*kee*, but short
E	*é*	**R**	*air*, with the "r" sounded
F	*ef*	**S**	*ess*
G	*gé*, like "gay", not "gee"!	**T**	*té*
H	*ha*	**U**	*oo*
I	*ee*, but short	**V**	*fé*
J	*jé*	**W**	*wé*
K	*kah*, but short	**X**	*iks*
L	*el*	**Y**	*yé*
M	*em*	**Z**	*zet*

These sounds are also important because they turn up frequently in the acronyms of various institutions and concepts in Indonesia. Some examples are:

RI (*air-ee*) **Republik Indonesia** the Republic of Indonesia
SD (*ess-dé*) **Sekolah Dasar** Primary/Elementary School
SMP (*ess-em-pé*) **Sekolah Menengah Pertama** Junior High School
SMU (*ess-em-oo*) **Sekolah Menengah Umum** Senior High School

One should be especially careful with **A** and **R**, as well as **C**, **G**, **H** and **K**, while **Q**, **V**, **X** and **Z** are very rare.

The sounds

In order to be understood, it is essential to pronounce words correctly. Below we offer a brief description of the sounds of Indonesian, with some examples, beginning with the vowels, and then looking at the consonants.

Letter	How to Pronounce It
A	• This is the sound of "a" in English "Ha!" It is never the "a" of English "cat". Examples: **apa?** What? **ada** there is **saya** I • In some derived forms of nouns we find two letters "a" alongside each other; in that case, they must be sounded separately, e.g. **pertanyaan**, not run together.
E	• There are two quite distinct sounds written with this letter. (a) The first is a "mute" or unstressed "e" sound (called schwa), as in English "ragged", "delight", or "burden", where we could insert an apostrophe: "ragg'd", "d'light", "burd'n". Examples: **cemar** dirty, polluted **pesan** order **resmi** official The "mute" "e" can never be stressed. On stress, see page xvii. (b) The second is less common, and like the familiar "e" of English "met". In normal Indonesian writing, the two kinds of "e" are not distinguished, but luckily the dictionaries help us by marking this second "e" with an acute accent (é). Examples: **bécak** pedicab **meréka** they **rém** brake
I	• This is pronounced as in English "in". Keep it short – not like English "ee". Examples: **sini** here, this place **hari** day **kecil** small
O	• There are two sounds here. (a) First, as in English "hot": **pohon** tree **roti** bread, cake **tonton** to watch (for entertainment) (b) And second, as in English "open", "only", e.g. **obat** medicine **toko** store, shop
U	• This is pronounced like the "u" in English "put", or the "oo" in "foot"; remember to keep it rounded, clear and clipped. Examples: **susu** milk, breast **tikus** rat, mouse **ungu** purple

LETTER	HOW TO PRONOUNCE IT
(Combined vowels)	• Apart from the above simple vowels, there are also combined vowels. Normally, when two vowels occur together, they are pronounced separately, giving us two syllables instead of one, e.g. **air** (*a-ir*) water **kain** (*ka-in*) cloth **lain** (*la-in*) other **laut** (*la-ut*) sea

However, we also have cases of genuine diphthongs, as follows:

AI	• This gives us a sound like the "i" in English "like", but it often changes to resemble "ay" as in "say". For example: **capai** tired **sampai** to arrive; up to

AU	• This sounds like the "ow" in "down", e.g. **kalau** if **mau** to want to **saudara** sibling, cousin

OI	• This sound is very rare. It is like the "oy" in English "boy", e.g. **hoi!** Hey! **boikot** boycott

As for the consonants, the majority are pronounced as in English. However, several of them need to be explained further.

C	• This letter always has the sound of English "ch", so never the "c" of "cat", or the "c" of "centre". A few examples are: **cantik** pretty **cinta** love **celana** pants, trousers

G	• This letter always has the sound of "g" in English "get" or "give", never as in "genes" or "giant", or "gym". Examples: **guru** teacher **pagi** morning

LETTER	HOW TO PRONOUNCE IT
H	• This sound can be found at the beginning, in the middle, or at the end of a word. In principle, it must always be heard. Examples of initial "h": **hari** day **hidup** to live, be alive **hujan** rain, to rain • Examples of final "h": **sudah** already **bersih** clean **mudah** easy • A medial "h" is sounded between like vowels: **paha** thigh **léhér** neck **pohon** tree • But it is elided between unlike vowels: **lihat** to see **tahun** year **tahu** to know • With the exceptions of: **tahu** bean curd ("h" heard), and **Tuhan** God ("h" heard)
K	• Like English, except that in final position it is "unreleased" (glottal stop), e.g. **tidak** no, not **nénék** grandmother **cétak** to print
KH	• This is a special case, as these two letters in combination represent a "guttural fricative", found only in loanwords borrowed from Arabic. The sound is that of the "ch" of Scottish "loch", e.g. **akhir** end **khusus** specific, special
NG	• As in English, but there are two points to note. (a) First, this sound can, in rare cases, be found in an initial position (something that does not happen in English), so one has be very careful to pronounce it correctly – not like "ny". Examples: **nganga** to gape **ngeri** horrifying (b) Second, it never sounds like the "ng" in English "finger". For this sound, we write "ngg", e.g. **tinggal** to live, dwell **tangga** steps, stairs **tunggu** to wait, watch over

LETTER	HOW TO PRONOUNCE IT
R	• This letter is always sounded, no matter where is occurs. It is the lightly rolled "r", not the American "r" or the guttural "r" of French or German, in any position. So if you see the letter-combination e plus r, as in **kerja** (to work), then both have to be heard; similarly with **ar**, as in **sukar** (hard, difficult), and **ur**, as in **syukur** (thank God). Practise saying: **perlu** necessary **harus** must, has to **bubur** porridge
SY	• This combination of letters has the same value as English "sh". It is found only in Arabic loanwords. Examples: **masyarakat** society **syahadat** the Profession of Faith **syukur** thank God

Stress

Indonesian does not have a heavy stress or syllable-accent. So in a multi-syllabic word such as **masyarakat** above, each part of the word receives an even stress. However, it is also true to say that in words of two syllables the first one gets slightly more stress than the second, except when this contains the mute "e", in which case the stress moves to the second syllable. But as a general rule we must avoid any tendency to stress the final syllable.

Aims

Basic Indonesian is intended for students who are beginning the study of the Indonesian language. We start from the assumption that the reader has never studied Indonesian before – and may never have studied *any* foreign language, or have much idea about English grammar for that matter.

The book is designed as a coursebook. Regarding level, it aims to bring the student from zero to a level equivalent to secondary Year 12, or tertiary First Year level (in the Australian system). This means that it covers a range of word-forms and sentence structures, and introduces a range of basic vocabulary, and in this way forms a foundation for higher levels and working with more advanced materials.

Expressed as objectives, we hope that our students will gain both passive and active skills in key areas, namely:

Listening comprehension (being able to understand what people say);

Speaking ability (being able to speak and be understood);

Reading comprehension (being able to interpret a simple written passage correctly); and

Writing ability (being able to write a simple message using correct language).

In the process of achieving this, someone using Indonesian will also need to absorb a certain amount of background information on social, cultural or other matters, bearing in mind that the language does not exist in a vacuum, but is used by people interacting in particular situations.

In this connection, we should be aware that with Indonesian, just as with any living language, there are significant variations in the way it is used for different purposes. One finds that the spoken and written languages differ, and both can be shaped to fit what is appropriate, depending on where or to whom we are speaking or writing.

Having said this, though, we feel that it is the best method to start out with teaching and learning "good and correct" Indonesian; slang or sub-standard forms should be avoided at this stage. This means that we aim to teach standard Indonesian, and not what is termed "Jakarta dialect", although a few examples of colloquial words will be used.

Method of study

The book consists of carefully graded materials organized in 28 lessons. Each lesson represents a step forward and introduces new topics and new vocabulary:

When studying a lesson, first read through the **Story**, then consult the **Wordlist** and **Language notes**, and then read it through again. **Cultural notes** are added when necessary.

Resist the temptation to look at the **Translations** (at the end of the book) until you have finished, then you can check. Bear in mind that sometimes other translations are also correct. It is a good method to read the story aloud, rather than just silently. The wordlists can be used for drills, by covering one column and testing yourself, going both ways.

We recommend making ample use of the dictionary to double-check meanings, to see what other meanings or forms a word may have, and in some cases to see where it is derived from. This will help in the process of remembering new words, which is, after all, a large part of the study.

The **Exercises** and drills can be used to reinforce and refresh your memory. Don't forget to consult the **boxes**. Reviews or tests can be inserted after each seven units if required.

Materials

This book is complete in itself, but for further reference we suggest:

Sneddon, James Niel: *Indonesian Reference Grammar* (Allen & Unwin, 1996, 2nd ed. 2010).
_____: *Understanding Indonesian Grammar* (Allen & Unwin, 2000).

It is a good idea to own at least one dictionary. The biggest and the best one is:

Stevens, Alan M. and A. Ed. Schmidgall-Tellings: *A Comprehensive Indonesian-English Dictionary* (Ohio U.P., 2004).

And a good two-way dictionary is:

Davidsen, Katherine: *Compact Indonesian Dictionary: Indonesian-English, English-Indonesian* (Tuttle, 2008), or

Davidsen, Katherine: *Concise Indonesian Dictionary: Indonesian-English, English-Indonesian* (Tuttle, 2006).

For further reading, see:

Robson, Stuart: *From Malay to Indonesian; The genesis of a national language* (Working Paper 118, Centre of Southeast Asian Studies, Monash University, 2002).

Robson, Stuart: *Welcome to Indonesian* (Tuttle, 2004).

Sneddon, James: *The Indonesian Language: Its history and role in modern society* (Sydney: UNW Press, 2003).

LESSON 1

Getting to Know Each Other
Berkenalan

SARI	Saya Sari. Saya mahasiswa.
	Saya mahasiswa di Universitas Indonesia. Ini rumah saya.
	Selamat datang! Ini ibu saya. Ini teman saya, Joel, dari Australia.
JOEL	Selamat pagi, Bu.
IBU SARI	Apa kabar, Joel?
JOEL	Kabar baik, Bu.
SARI	Dan itu bapak saya.
JOEL	Selamat pagi, Pak.
AYAH SARI	Silakan masuk, Joel.
JOEL	Terima kasih, Pak.
SARI	Bapak saya dosén, dan ibu saya dokter.
	Dan ini kakak saya.
KAKAK SARI	Nama saya Agus.
JOEL	Hi, Agus!
SARI	Dan ini adik saya.
ADIK SARI	Nama saya Ratih.
JOEL	Hi, Ratih!

WORDLIST

N.B. This wordlist contains only words not discussed in the cultural and language notes. See also the translation on p. 250.

apa kabar?	What's the news?; how are you?	**ibu**	mother
baik	good	**kabar**	news
berkenalan	to get to know each other	**masuk**	come in
dan	and	**nama**	name
dari	from	**selamat datang!**	welcome!
datang	to come	**silakan**	please!
di	at	**teman**	friend
dokter	doctor (medical)	**terima kasih**	thank-you
dosén	lecturer	**univérsitas**	university

CULTURAL NOTES

1. As a greeting, we can use **selamat** with the time of day: **pagi** for morning, **siang** for the middle of the day, **soré** for the late afternoon, and **malam** for night, thus "good morning" and so forth. It is best to add a term of address for the recipient, as then our greeting sounds less abrupt: **Bu** for an older lady, or **Pak** for an older man. Or else add somebody's name, if you know it.

2. The family (**keluarga**) is very important; it is the main part of our social context. We should pay attention to "who's who", especially someone's parents, and note the order of siblings — there are particular terms for them, **kakak** for elder sibling (regardless of gender), and **adik** for younger sibling (again regardless of gender).

3. We use the word **bapak** "father" for our own father, and **ayah** for someone else's father. The meaning is the same, but **ayah** is considered more refined.

LANGUAGE NOTES

The simplest kind of sentence is the "equational" sentence, in which we say "A = B".

The first part of this sentence is the topic or "subject", and the rest is what is being said about it, or the "predicate".

These slots (A and B) can be filled by a noun or pronoun, either a single word or a group of words. In its simplest form, there is no need to put in a word to indicate the equation (=), like the English "is", "are" and so on.

Examples:

Saya mahasiswa. I am a student.
  (A)   (B)

Here a pronoun, **saya**, occupies the A slot, and a noun, **mahasiswa**, occupies the B slot. So the sentence conveys a piece of information about "I", that I am something, namely a student. There is no word here for "am" – it would not be right to put one in, so an English-speaker should avoid the temptation to supply something in this position.

Itu dosén. That is a lecturer.
  (A)   (B)

In this case, the word **itu**, that, occupies the A slot; we can regard it as a pronoun, meaning "that thing, person". The rest of the sentence explains who that is. Similarly, we have the word **ini**, "this (thing, person)". There is no word for the English "is" in this sentence.

Before going any further, we should discuss possession. In Indonesian, this is expressed by means of word-order, and not with a word for "of" or "apostrophe's". The rule is that *the possessor follows the thing possessed*. So we can give a noun, and follow it by a pronoun, to say who the thing belongs to, e.g.

    rumah saya "the house of me", i.e. my house.

This is not yet a full sentence; but it could be, if we add a subject:

    <u>Ini</u> rumah saya. <u>This</u> is my house.

We will talk about personal pronouns again shortly, but can comment here that there are no changes equivalent to "I-me-my" in English.

Finally, you will have noticed that in Indonesian we don't use words like English "a, an" or "the". They are not part of Indonesian grammar, but you do need to supply them when translating from Indonesian to English.

Berkenalan
Getting to Know Each Other

A. Pertanyaan untuk bacaan | Questions for the reading

■ *Jawablah pertanyaan-pertanyaan di bawah ini sesuai dengan isi bacaan!*
(Answer the questions below in accordance with the content of the reading!)

1. P: Di mana Sari belajar?

   J: _____

2. P: Siapa Joel dan dari mana dia?

   J: _____

3. P: Apa pekerjaan bapak dan ibu Sari?

   J: _____

4. P: Berapa jumlah saudara Sari?

   J: _____

5. P: Siapa itu Agus dan Ratih?

   J: _____

NB. P = Pertanyaan (Question); J = Jawaban (Answer)

B. Menyimak | Listening comprehension

■ *Dengarkanlah dan perhatikanlah baik-baik Tape Latihan 1 untuk menjawab pertanyaan di bawah ini! (Listen carefully and pay attention to the Exercise Tape 1 to answer the questions below!)*

1. P: Apakah bapak dan ibu Sari lahir di Jakarta?

   J: _____

2. Siapa yang memilih nama untuk Sari ketika dia baru lahir?

   J: _____

3. P: Binatang piaraan apa yang dimiliki keluarga Sari?

   J: _____

4. P: Berapa umur binatang itu dan siapa namanya?

   J: _____

5. P: Apakah hobi Sari?

    J: _____

6. P: Apa yang biasanya dilakukan oléh ibu Sari pada hari Minggu?

    J: _____

7. P: Di mana Joel bertemu Sari?

    J: _____

8. P: Bahasa apa yang dipakai di rumah Sari selain bahasa Indonesia?

    J: _____

9. P: Sudah berapa tahun bapak Sari bekerja menjadi dosén?

    J: _____

10. P: Apakah rumah sakit di mana ibu Sari bekerja jauh dari rumah meréka?

    J: _____

C. Menulis | Writing

■ *Ceritakanlah tentang keluarga Sari dengan menulis kalimat-kalimat seperti contoh nomor 1!*
(Tell about Sari's family by writing sentences like example 1!)

Foto keluarga Sari

CONTOH (EXAMPLE) 1. (Sari): Sari mahasiswa dan dia berumur 22 tahun

2. (Agus): _____

3. (Bapak Sari): _____

4. (Ibu Sari): _____

5. (Ratih): _____

D. Teka-teki | Puzzle

■ *Carilah kata-kata yang menunjukkan pekerjaan dalam kolom-kolom di bawah ini!*
(Look for the words which refer to a profession in the columns below!)

T	U	K	A	N	G	K	A	Y	U
O	G		P	E	S	U	L	A	P
M	E	P	I	L	O	T	R		O
U	W	A	L	A	P	O	T	U	L
R	P	E	N	Y	I	A	R	P	I
I	P	E	N	A	R	I	H	U	S
D	O	S	E	N	A	L	U	R	I
I	G	I	G	R	E	T	K	O	D
P	O	L	I	T	I	K	U	S	A
S	T	P	E	R	A	W	A	T	U

■ *Tulislah kata yang dapat kamu temukan! (Write down the words you have found!)*

1. _____   8. _____

2. _____   9. _____

3. _____   10. _____

4. _____   11. _____

5. _____   12. _____

6. _____   13. _____

7. _____

E. Definisi profesi | Definition of a profession

■ *Tulislah définisi pekerjaan-pekerjaan di bawah ini menurut kamu! (Write the definitions of professions below as you see them!)*

1.

Dia mengajar di sekolah.

6.

_____

2.

_____

7.

_____

3.

_____

8.

_____

4.

_____

9.

_____

5.

_____

10.

_____

LESSON 2

At the Campus
Di Kampus

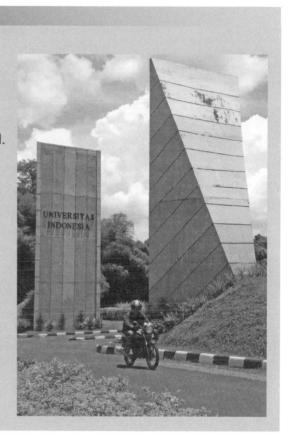

Sari lahir di Jakarta.
Keluarga Sari tinggal di Pasar Minggu.
Sari pergi ke kampus UI di Dépok.
Dia ikut ayahnya.
Ayah Sari punya mobil.
Di kampus Sari belajar Hubungan Internasional.
Soré dia pulang dari kampus.

Di kantin Sari minum Pepsi.
Di rumah dia minum téh.
Adiknya suka minum és jeruk.
Kakaknya suka minum Bir Bintang.
Meréka suka makan nasi goréng.

Sari makan siang di kampus.
Di kampus dia makan mi goréng.

WORDLIST

belajar	to study	**kantin**	canteen
bintang	star	**lahir**	to be born
bir	beer	**mi goréng**	fried noodles
és jeruk	cold orange juice	**mobil**	car
hubungan	relations	**nasi goréng**	fried rice
ikut	to go along, accompany	**pulang**	to go home
internasional	international	**téh**	tea
kampus	campus		

LANGUAGE NOTES

Personal pronouns

It will be useful to set out the personal pronouns of Indonesian by means of a table. The advantage of this is that we can reveal the system, and you can see what choices you have when you want to use a pronoun.

We have horizontal rows for the three persons: first person is the person speaking (I and we); second person is the person being addressed (you); and the third person is the one being spoken about (he, she, they). Then we have three columns, which list the pronouns as non-formal, neutral or formal. A number of notes follow below, to explain further.

		non-formal	neutral	formal
first person	I	aku	-	saya
	we (inclusive)	-	kita	-
	we (exclusive)	-	kami	-
second person	you	kamu	anda	saudara etc.
		engkau	-	-
	you (plural)	kalian	-	-
third person	he, she	-	dia, ia	beliau
	they	-	meréka	-

1. The best word to choose for "I" is **saya**, as **aku** is only suitable if you know somebody very well.
2. When you want to say "we", you do have to make a choice: do you mean "I and you" (inclusive), or "I/we and not you" (exclusive)? This can make a big difference.
3. When you want to say "you", it is best to use the neutral **anda**, or something formal, including a pronoun substitute (see Lesson 3); **kamu** should only be used to a good friend.
4. The pronoun **engkau** is obsolete except in the Christian scriptures ("thou").
5. For "he" or "she", choose **dia**; **beliau** is only suitable if you want to show high respect for someone.
6. In fact, you will find that pronouns tend to be omitted if the sentence is clear without them. In particular, avoid referring to yourself too much.
7. There is no special word for "it"; depending on the context, there are other ways of saying "it".
8. Indonesian has no separate forms according to gender: "he" and "she" are the same.
9. The word **meréka**, "they", refers only to people, not to things; if you want to talk about things, just repeat the relevant noun.

More about possession

We can now expand a little on what has already been said about possession. We have seen **rumah saya**, "my house". Similarly, we could also have **rumah kami**, "our house", or **rumah meréka**, "their house". But when the possessor is **aku**, **kamu** or **dia**, then an interesting change takes place: the pronoun takes another form, and is attached to the noun as a suffix, **-ku**, **-mu** and **-nya**, as in the following examples, using the word **adik**, "younger brother or sister":

adikku	my younger brother/sister
adikmu	your younger brother/sister
adiknya	his/her younger brother/sister

The suffix **-nya** is worth making a special note of, as it has various uses. It can be used as a possessive instead of **meréka**, so "of them, their" (but not people), and it can refer to a thing possessor, so "its". We will meet it again later.

Simple verbs

In order to create a predicate, we can have a noun (as we saw in Lesson 1), or we could have an adjective (to be mentioned later), or a verb. Verbs come in two categories: simple and derived. Simple verbs have no affixes, that is, elements attached to them, whereas derived verbs are produced by various processes of affixation that we will introduce step by step later.

Simple verbs come in two kinds, ones that have no object, and ones that do have an object. The difference is clear enough when you look at the meaning of the word. So here are a few examples of simple verbs without an object:

masuk	to go in
keluar	to go out
pergi	to go
datang	to come
tinggal	to live

Because they do not have objects they are called intransitive. The transitive/intransitive distinction will become relevant when we have to deal with the Indonesian passive. By the way, note also that in our translations of verbs we use the "infinitive" with "to…"; this is in order to make it absolutely clear that we are dealing with a verb and not a noun (in English this may not be evident without a context).

And now some examples of verbs that can have objects:

makan	to eat
minum	to drink
punya	to have, own

Obviously, you can eat, drink or have *something* – that something is the object, and it follows its verb directly, just where you would expect it.

The usual word-order in our sentence will be: subject–verb–object–expression of place. However, we could vary this, and have: expression of place–subject–verb–object. What is the difference? If the expression of place is put first, then it gets extra emphasis; it says, for example, specifically "at home", not somewhere else.

Three prepositions are introduced here: **di** "in, at", **ke** "to", and **dari** "from". These will help us to make expressions of place.

Di Kampus
At the Campus

A. Pertanyaan untuk bacaan | Questions for the reading

■ *Jawablah pertanyaan-pertanyaan di bawah ini sesuai dengan isi bacaan!*
(Answer the questions below in accordance with the content of the reading!)

1. P: Sebutkan nama kota di mana Sari lahir!

   J: _____

2. P: Di mana rumah keluarga Sari?

   J: _____

3. P: Di kampus mana Sari belajar?

   J: _____

4. P: Apa yang dipelajari Sari?

   J: _____

5. P: Bagaimana Sari pergi kuliah setiap hari?

   J: _____

6. P: Sebutkan minuman dan makanan kesukaan Ratih dan Agus!

   J: _____

B. Menyimak | Listening comprehension

■ *Simaklah dan dengarkan baik-baik Tape Latihan 2 lalu berilah tanda (√) untuk suka dan tanda (X) untuk tidak suka. (Pay attention and listen carefully to the Exercise Tape 2 and then place a sign (√) for like and a sign (X) for don't like.*

1. Nama (Name): Sari	Suka (√)	Tidak suka (X)
Minum kopi		
Minum téh		
Minum bir		
Makan pisang		
Belajar		
Membaca novel		

	Suka (√)	Tidak suka (X)
Menonton olahraga di télévisi		
Bermain game di komputer		
Memasak		
Bermain sépak bola		
Berenang		
Naik gunung		
Naik sepéda		
Mendengarkan musik pop		
Melihat berita di télévisi		
Membaca surat kabar		
Menari		
Mendayung		
Pergi ke gym		
Menyanyi		
Melukis		
Merokok		

2. Nama (Name): Ratih

	Suka (√)	Tidak suka (X)
Minum kopi		
Minum téh		
Minum bir		
Makan pisang		
Belajar		
Membaca novel		
Menonton olahraga di télévisi		
Bermain game di komputer		
Memasak		
Bermain sépak bola		
Berenang		
Naik gunung		
Naik sepéda		
Mendengarkan musik pop		
Melihat berita di télévisi		
Membaca surat kabar		
Menari		
Mendayung		
Pergi ke gym		

	Suka (√)	Tidak suka (X)
Menyanyi		
Melukis		
Merokok		

3. Nama (Name): Agus

	Suka (√)	Tidak suka (X)
Minum kopi		
Minum téh		
Minum bir		
Makan pisang		
Belajar		
Membaca novel		
Menonton olahraga di télévisi		
Bermain game di komputer		
Memasak		
Bermain sépak bola		
Berenang		
Naik gunung		
Naik sepéda		
Mendengarkan musik pop		
Melihat berita di télévisi		
Membaca surat kabar		
Menari		
Mendayung		
Pergi ke gym		
Menyanyi		
Melukis		
Merokok		

C. Teka-teki | Puzzle

■ *Carilah kata-kata yang ada dalam kotak sesuai dengan daftar kata-kata Inggris lalu lingkari-lah! (Look for Indonesian words in the box that match the English list. Circle these words!)*

1. Star
2. To study
3. Beer
4. To go along
5. To be born
6. Fried rice
7. To go home
8. Tea
9. You (formal)
10. You (informal)
11. To drink
12. Child
13. Day
14. To eat

B	E	L	A	J	A	R	N
I	F	A	N	D	A	I	A
N	G	H	A	R	I	B	S
T	M	I	N	U	M	O	I
A	A	R	K	C	G	I	G
N	K	A	M	U	V	X	O
G	A	I	K	U	T	W	R
A	N	A	K	E	M	L	E
C	T	E	H	T	A	P	N
D	J	P	U	L	A	N	G

D. Tata bahasa | Grammar

■ *Jawablah pertanyaan-pertanyaan yang berhubungan dengan tata bahasa di bawah ini! (Answer the questions connected with the grammar below!)*

1. P: Sebutkan nama orangtuamu!

   J: _____

2. P: Sebutkan di mana alamat rumahmu!

   J: _____

3. P: Apakah pekerjaan utamamu?

   J: _____

4. P: Carilah 5 kata kerja intransitif selain yang sudah disebutkan di Pelajaran 2 (masuk, keluar, pergi, datang dan tinggal)! (Look for 5 intransitive verbs besides the ones mentioned in Lesson 2.)

   J: a. _____   d. _____

       b. _____   e. _____

       c. _____

LESSON 3

Lectures
Kuliah

Sari sudah selesai makan pagi.
Sekarang dia sudah siap berangkat ke kampus.
Kemarin dia lupa payungnya.
Jadi hari ini Sari tidak akan lupa.
Sari sudah tiba di kampus.
Dia akan ikut kuliah.
Kuliah akan mulai.
Dia masuk ke ruangan, lalu dia balik lagi.
"Bodoh aku!" pikirnya.
"Ada apa, Sari?" temannya bertanya.
Hari ini tidak ada kuliah!
Dosénnya tidak ada.
Beliau sedang pergi.
Mahasiswa sedang mengobrol:
"Ayo, pulang saja!" katanya.
"Tidak ada gunanya tinggal di kampus."
Tapi Sari ingin ke Fakultas Hukum.
"Saya kira bisa ketemu Joel lagi", pikirnya.
Biasanya Joel akan keluar siang...

WORDLIST

ayo	come on!	lalu	then
balik	to go back	lupa	to forget
berangkat	to leave, set out	mengobrol	to chat
bertanya	to ask	mulai	to begin
bisa	to be able; can	payung	umbrella
bodoh	stupid, silly	pikirnya	she thought
guna	use	ruangan	room, hall
ingin	to want to	saja	only; just
jadi	so	selesai	finished
katanya	they said	siap	ready
ketemu	to meet	tapi	but
kuliah	lecture	tiba	to arrive
lagi	again	tidak	not; no

When talking to someone, or when referring to them, we should use the appropriate title in front of their name, and not just the name, so **Pak Hasan** or **Bu Yoto**. This means that a title will be found even where Mr or Mrs is not usual in English. A Western male is likely to be addressed with the title **Om** (from Dutch **oom** "uncle"), so **Om John** (using his first name, not his family name). If he is addressed as **Pak John**, this means that he is becoming integrated into the Indonesian social world.

Similarly, there are quasi-kinship titles for younger people as well, namely **Mas** "elder brother" or alternatively **Kang**; **Mbak** "elder sister"; and **Dik** "younger brother or sister". These can be followed by the person's name. In general, terms of address are much more frequent in Indonesian than in English, and to use just someone's name, without a title, would suggest a high degree of intimacy, a big age-gap or a superior-inferior relationship.

To say "Ladies and Gentlemen", as when beginning a speech, we say **Bapak-bapak dan Ibu-ibu** —note the doubling for the plural, and the order, men first! In a formal letter, we could use as pronouns **Bapak** or **Ibu**, both with a capital letter, to mean "you".

Pronoun substitutes

As well as the genuine pronouns set out in Lesson 2, in Indonesian we find the frequent use of other words (nouns) that take their place and function in exactly the same way as pronouns. It will make your Indonesian more idiomatic if you can use them in the right way.

The nouns concerned are terms for family relationships. The main ones are **bapak** "father" and **ibu** "mother". These can be used to mean "you", and would replace **anda** or **saudara**. They have quite a different "feel": on the one hand they express respect, because a parent is someone you look up to, and on the other hand they have a certain warmth, because they mean that we are entering a quasi-familial relationship. Obviously, **bapak** is used for addressing a mature male, and **ibu** for a mature female.

Abbreviated forms of **bapak** and **ibu** can be used for addressing or calling someone: **Pak! Bu!** There does not seem to be a real English equivalent for this (not Mr! or Mrs!). (See also the Cultural comments on page 18.)

Proper nouns, that is, people's names, can also serve as pronouns, not only second person (= you) instead of **kamu**, but also first (= I) instead of **aku**, especially when children are speaking, e.g.

> **Rini lapar**, I am hungry. (Rini speaking)

Tense

We have already seen a number of examples of simple verbs. In Indonesian, the verb does not change its form to indicate tense, as English does (e.g. *to gain*: *gains*, *gained*, and so on). As a result, when translating from Indonesian into English the appropriate tense markers have to be supplied. You can use present, past or future tense depending on what is needed.

However, all this does not mean that Indonesian is lacking in precision. We have ways of indicating the tense when it is necessary to be explicit, by using special words which are placed directly in front of the verb concerned, as follows:

The Past

The word which indicates the past, that is, that something happened or has been done, is

> **sudah**

Note that this expresses both the English "simple past" (-ed) and the "perfect" tense (has –ed). And sometimes the translation "already" fits well too. These words can also be used in front of certain adjectives, meaning that the condition indicated has been reached, even if an English present is used in translation, e.g. **Sudah tua** he is old (i.e. is already old or has reached this state). Another word that can be used in the same way here is **telah**.

The Present

This is like the "default" setting of the verb, referring to something happening now or something that happens regularly. However, we do have a word that can be inserted to suggest that we are "in the midst of" or "in the process of" doing something, namely

> **sedang**

So we can contrast **makan** "eats" with **sedang makan** "is in the process of eating". But **sedang** will only be put in when it really is necessary to stress this "continuous" meaning. Another word that can be used in the same way here is **tengah**.

The Future

To express the future, "will" or "is going to", we have the word

akan

This is placed in front of its verb, just like the cases above.

Another word with a similar meaning **mau**, "going to, on the point of"; this has another common meaning, "want to".

Finally, please note that these words cannot be combined with each other to make other tenses, such as the English future perfect ("will have"), and there is no special form for the conditional ("would").

Use of *ada*

As will be seen in the story, this important word has a range of meanings: "to be there; exist"; "to be there, to be present"; "to be there, to have". An idiomatic use is **Ada apa?** meaning "What's up?" (What's wrong, what's the matter?).

Another use of *-nya*

Apart from the possessive use already noted, this suffix also has a "demonstrative" use, best translated with "the", that is, making a noun definite. It can also be found idiomatically, attached to an adjective forming a word with adverbial meaning, as in e.g.:

Biasanya   usually
Sayangnya   unfortunately

Verbs with *ber-*

As well as simple verbs, we will meet some verbs that feature a prefix **ber-**; examples above are **berangkat** "to set out", and **bertanya** "to ask". Verbs of this type are always intransitive. We will have more to say about them in Lesson 13.

LATIHAN 3 EXERCISE 3

Kuliah
Lectures

A. Pertanyaan untuk bacaan

■ *Jawablah pertanyaan-pertanyaan di bawah ini sesuai dengan isi bacaan!*
(Answer the questions below according to the story.)

1. P: Apa yang akan dilakukan Sari sesudah makan pagi?

    J: _____

2. P: Menurut kamu mengapa Sari perlu membawa payung ke kampus?

    J: _____

3. P: Apa yang terjadi kemudian ketika Sari tiba di kampus?

    J: _____

4. P: Mengapa kuliah ditiadakan hari ini?

    J: _____

5. P: Apa yang dilakukan oleh teman-teman kuliah Sari?

    J: _____

6. P: Apa yang ingin dilakukan Sari?

    J: _____

B. Menyimak

■ *Dengarkanlah baik-baik dan simaklah isi Tape Latihan 3 lalu jawablah pertanyaan di bawah ini! (Listen carefully to the tape for Lesson 3 and then answer the questions below.)*

1. P: Ada berapa mahasiswa yang belajar di kelas Sari hari ini?

    J: _____

2. P: Apa cita-cita Sari di masa depan?

    J: _____

3. P: Dari mana teman-teman kuliah Sari berasal?

    J: _____

4. P: Kemampuan apa yang paling penting yang harus dikuasai oleh mahasiswa seperti Sari?

    J: _____

5. P: Di mana biasanya Sari dan Joel bertemu di kampus?

    J: _____

6. P: Untuk apa Sari dan Joel bertemu setiap minggu?

    J: _____

7. P: Mengapa Joel harus menguasai bahasa Indonesia?

    J: _____

C. Tata bahasa

1. Tulislah tiga kegiatan yang sudah kamu lakukan minggu kemarin dengan memakai kata keterangan waktu (sudah) (Write down three activities which you have carried out last week using the tense word sudah.)

a. _____

b. _____

c. _____

2. Tulislah tiga kegiatan yang sedang kamu lakukan minggu ini dengan memakai kata keterangan waktu (sedang) (Write down three activities which you are carrying out this week using the tense word sedang.)

a. _____

b. _____

c. _____

3. Tulislah three kegiatan yang akan kamu lakukan minggu depan dengan memakai kata keterangan waktu (akan) (Write down three activities which you will carry out next week using the tense word akan.)

a. _____

b. _____

c. _____

D. Mencocokkan | Matching

■ *Cocokkan kata-kata di bagian A yang berhubungan dengan jenis fakultas di bagian B, lalu tariklah garis penghubung (Match words from A with words from B and then draw a line connecting them.)*

A	B
1. Politik	a. Fakultas Ekonomi
2. Obat-obatan	b. Fakultas Kehutanan
3. Pengadilan	c. Fakultas Kedokteran Gigi
4. Penyakit	d. Fakultas Perikanan
5. Kucing	e. Fakultas Psikologi
6. Bangunan	f. Fakultas Sosial-Politik
7. Jual-beli	g. Fakultas Sastra
8. Puisi	h. Fakultas Farmasi
9. Reboiasi	i. Fakultas Hukum
10. Udang	j. Fakultas Kedokteran
11. Gusi	k. Fakultas Kedokteran Héwan
12. Keséhatan méntal	l. Fakultas Arsitéktur

E. Teka-teki

- *Carilah kata-kata yang berhubungan dengan tema 'Universitas' di dalam kotak, lingkarilah lalu tulislah di bagian yang tersedia. (Look for words connected with 'university' theme in the boxes. Circle these and then write the words in the blanks provided.)*

C	S	E	M	I	N	A	R	M
A	P	P	E	N	S	I	L	A
T	Q	S	T	A	U	V	R	H
A	R	W	Y	I	X	E	L	A
T	M	M	O	J	T	L	I	S
A	B	U	K	U	J	K	B	I
N	O	R	P	E	R	P	U	S
K	A	M	U	S	F	G	R	W
D	O	S	E	N	H	I	B	A
K	U	L	I	A	H	T	E	S

1. _____   6. _____

2. _____   7. _____

3. _____   8. _____

4. _____   9. _____

5. _____

LESSON 4

At the Mall
Di Mall

SARI	Apakah Joel mau jalan-jalan ke Mangga Mall?
JOEL	Ya, mau. Saya suka jalan-jalan di toko macam itu.
SARI	Baiklah, mari kita pergi sekarang.
JOEL	Boléh tanya, ya, Sari. Orang itu sedang apa?
SARI	Orang itu minta uang. Namanya "pengemis".
JOEL	Ini toko apa?
SARI	Itu toko sepéda motor / sepatu / bunga…
JOEL	Bau apa itu?
SARI	Itu bau kacang goréng. Joel suka kacang goréng?
JOEL	Suka! Sari suka?
SARI	Mari kita terus saja, ya.
JOEL	Apakah ada minuman di kafé ini?
SARI	Saya kira ada. Mau minum apa?
JOEL	Itu apa?
SARI	Itu és jeruk. Coba, ya!
JOEL	Terima kasih, Sari. Sari mau apa?
SARI	Saya sama saja.
JOEL	Nah, apakah ada uang kecil…?

WORDLIST

baiklah	okay! good!	**minuman**	drink
bau	smell	**nah**	well, …
boléh	may (allowed)	**pengemis**	beggar
bunga	flower	**sama**	same
coba	to try	**sepatu**	shoe(s)
jalan-jalan	to go out, on a trip	**sepéda motor**	motorcycle
kacang	peanuts	**suka**	to like
kafé	café	**terus**	straight on
kira	to think, guess	**toko**	shop, store
macam	sort, kind	**uang**	money
mari	come! (inviting)	**uang kecil**	small change
minta	to ask for	**ya**	yes; right?

LANGUAGE NOTES

Demonstrative words

In Lesson 1 we already mentioned the words **ini** (this) and **itu** (that), and showed how they can be used as the subject of a sentence. In that position they could be interpreted as "this thing" and "that thing".

But there is a different way to use them (and this also applies to English): they can function as qualifying words. This means that they stand alongside another word (a noun), and tell us something about it: they point, "this... here", or "that... there".

In this function, **ini** and **itu** always follow the word they are working with; this is the place that qualifying words occupy in Indonesian (in contrast to English, where they come in front). For example:

Orang ini...	this person
Mobil itu...	that car

This is of course not a complete sentence, merely the beginning of one; to finish the sentence, we would have to say something about it. We could add one of our simple verbs, e.g.

Orang ini tidur.	This person is asleep.
Mobil itu keluar.	That car is going out.

Asking questions

A simple way to make a question is to use a rising intonation at the end of the sentence, without any other change, providing the sense is clear, e.g. **Suka makan nasi?** Do you like eating rice?

Further, in order to turn a statement into a question, we use the word **apakah**, which is placed at the head of the sentence (nowhere else). We do not use inversion (reversing the order of subject and verb), or an auxiliary verb "do", as in English. For example:

Apakah orang itu tidur?	Is that person asleep?
Apakah mobil itu keluar?	Is that car going out?

(There is only one exception to what was said above: we seem to find inversion in the question **Boléh saya...** May I...?)

As well as using question sentences, we also have a range of interrogative words, such as How? When? Who? and so on. These will be introduced in following lessons, but here we can make a start with **apa?** "What (thing)?" Using this, we can produce very useful questions, such as:

Ini apa?	What is this?
Itu apa?	What is that?
Bahasa Inggrisnya apa?	What is the English for it?

This is the normal word-order; note that it is the opposite of English. Indonesian prefers to place the question-word last, although this can sometimes be varied. As a general principle, the word that comes first in the sentence gets most prominence. In **Ini apa?** we are focusing on **ini** "this", and want to know what it is (**apa?**). If **apa** comes first, there is extra stress on the questioning force of the sentence: **Apa itu?** What on earth is that?

Di Mall
At the Mall

A. Pertanyaan untuk bacaan | Questions for the reading

■ *Jawablah pertanyaan-pertanyaan di bawah ini sesuai dengan isi bacaan! (Answer the questions below in accordance with the content of the reading.)*

1. P: Ke mana Sari mengajak pergi Joel hari ini?

    J: _____

2. P: Apa itu Mangga Mall?

    J: _____

3. P: Apa yang dilihat Joel ketika berjalan menuju Mangga Mall?

    J: _____

4. P: Menurut kamu mengapa banyak pengemis di Jakarta?

    J: _____

5. P: Apa saja yang dijual di Mangga Mall?

    J: _____

6. P: Ada bau yang menyenangkan dari kafé dekat Mangga Mall, bau apa itu?

    J: _____

7. P: Apakah Joel dan Sari memutuskan untuk berhenti di kafé?

    J: _____

B. Menyimak | Listening Comprehension

■ *Simaklah baik-baik Tape Latihan 4 lalu cobalah menjawab pertanyaan-pertanyaan di bawah ini! (Listen to the tape for Lesson 4 carefully and then try to answer the questions below.)*

1. P: Berapakah jumlah pusat pertokoan (Mall) yang ada di Jakarta?

    J: _____

2. P: Dari mana konsép bisnis Mall berasal?

    J: _____

3. P: Apakah masih ada orang yang pergi berbelanja di pasar tradisional?

    J: _____

4. P: Di negara seperti Indonesia, biasanya siapa yang suka berbelanja di pasar tradisional?

    J: _____

5. P: Apa yang biasanya dilakukan bapak Sari di Mangga Mall?

    J: _____

6. P: Apa yang tidak disukai Ratih tentang Mangga Mall?

    J: _____

7. P: Toko macam apakah yang ada di pusat pertokoan seperti Mangga Mall?

    J: _____

C. Tata bahasa | Grammar

■ *Jawablah pertanyaan-pertanyaan sesuai dengan contoh 1 di bawah ini! (Answer the questions in accordance with example 1 below.)*

1.

CONTOH (EXAMPLE)

Q: Ini toko apa?

A: Ini toko sepatu. _____

2.

Q: Ini toko apa?

A: _____

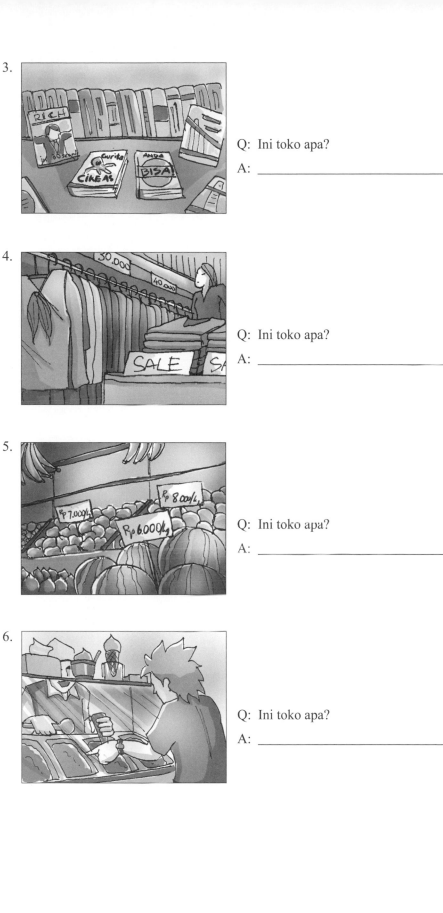

3.

Q: Ini toko apa?

A: _____

4.

Q: Ini toko apa?

A: _____

5.

Q: Ini toko apa?

A: _____

6.

Q: Ini toko apa?

A: _____

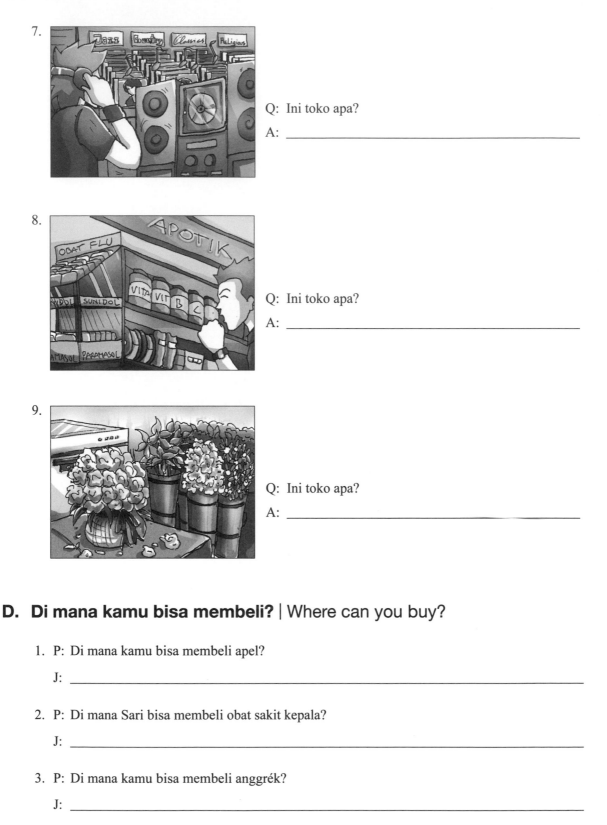

7.

Q: Ini toko apa?

A: _____

8.

Q: Ini toko apa?

A: _____

9.

Q: Ini toko apa?

A: _____

D. **Di mana kamu bisa membeli?** | Where can you buy?

1. P: Di mana kamu bisa membeli apel?

   J: _____

2. P: Di mana Sari bisa membeli obat sakit kepala?

   J: _____

3. P: Di mana kamu bisa membeli anggrék?

   J: _____

4. P: Di mana Joel bisa membeli kamus?

   J: _____

5. P: Di mana Mas Agus bisa membeli CD gamelan Jawa?

   J: _____

6. P: Di mana Pak Kusmanto bisa membeli roda sepéda?

   J: _____

7. P: Di mana Ratih bisa membeli celana panjang?

   J: _____

8. P: Di mana biasanya kamu bisa membeli penggaris?

   J: _____

9. P: Di mana biasanya ibu membeli mangga?

   J: _____

10. P: Di mana Hanif membeli kasét lagu pop?

    J: _____

LESSON 5

Prices
Harga

Joel perlu pergi ke toko buku.
Dia naik taksi ke Toko Buku Gramedia.
Berapa ongkosnya?
Ongkos naik taksi ke toko buku itu kira-kira Rp 50.000.
Joel beli penggaris. Harganya Rp 1.500.
Dia beli buku tulis. Harganya Rp 25.000.
Joel cari kamus istilah hukum. Harganya Rp 450.000.
Dia beli surat kabar. Harganya Rp 2.000.
Juga ada majalah berbahasa Inggris. Harganya Rp 350.000.
Akhirnya Joel beli tiga komik Tin-Tin dan roman Bahasa Indonesia. Harganya Rp 40.000.
Semuanya harga pas. Berapa jumlahnya?

WORDLIST

akhirnya	finally, in the end	**kamus**	dictionary
berbahasa...	in the ... language	**komik**	comic
beli	to buy	**majalah**	magazine
buku	book	**naik**	to go by (mode of transport)
buku tulis	notebook	**ongkos**	fare
harga	price	**penggaris**	ruler
harga pas	fixed price	**perlu**	to need to
hukum	law; legal	**roman**	novel
Inggris	English	**semuanya**	all of them, altogether
istilah	term	**surat kabar**	newspaper
jumlah	total, amount	**taksi**	taxi

LANGUAGE NOTES

Numbers

Something that one should learn early is the number system. This is useful when you have to deal with money and negotiating prices, for example, and we find lots of statistical data in newspapers and magazines as well.

We begin with the cardinal numbers. (The ordinals, fractions and decimals will be dealt with later.) The Indonesian numeral system is very simple and regular. Having memorized the words for one to ten, there is a special term for the "teens" **belas**, and then we can build up the multiples of ten using **puluh**, multiples of a hundred using **ratus**, multiples of a thousand using **ribu**, and multiples of a million using **juta**. In a big number, the items are strung together without the use of "and". Note that **satu**, "one", takes the form of the prefix **se-** when linked with **puluh**, **ratus** and so on. The numbers are as follows:

1	**satu**	11	**sebelas**	30	**tiga puluh**
2	**dua**	12	**dua belas**	40	**empat puluh**
3	**tiga**	13	**tiga belas**	50	**lima puluh**
4	**empat**	14	**empat belas**	60	**enam puluh**
5	**lima**	15	**lima belas**	70	**tujuh puluh**
6	**enam**	16	**enam belas**	80	**delapan puluh**
7	**tujuh**	17	**tujuh belas**	90	**sembilan puluh**
8	**delapan**	18	**delapan belas**	100	**seratus**
9	**sembilan**	19	**sembilan belas**	200	**dua ratus**
10	**sepuluh**	20	**dua puluh**	300	**tiga ratus**

And then we can go on to

1.000 **seribu**
2.000 **dua ribu**,

and so on, up to

1.000.000 **sejuta**
2.000.000 **dua juta**

Here are some examples of big numbers:

1945 **seribu sembilan ratus empat puluh lima**
    (Note that we do not say "nineteen forty-five", but "one thousand, nine hundred, forty-five".)
2009 **dua ribu sembilan**
1.500.230 **sejuta lima ratus ribu dua ratus tiga puluh.**

Note that in Indonesian a full-stop [**titik**] separates the thousands (e.g. 56.000 **lima-puluh enam ribu**), whereas a comma [**koma**] is used in decimals (e.g. 5,6 **lima koma enam**).

We will now need another question word: **berapa**, "how much?"

Harga
Prices

A. Pertanyaan untuk bacaan | Questions for the reading

■ *Jawablah pertanyaan-pertanyaan di bawah ini sesuai dengan isi bacaan!*
(Answer the questions below in accordance with the content of the reading!)

1. P: Apa yang harus dilakukan Joel hari ini?

    J: _____

2. P: Apa nama toko buku yang akan dikunjungi Joel dan bagaimana dia pergi ke sana?

    J: _____

3. P: Apakah menurut kamu ongkos taksi ke toko buku itu mahal?

    J: _____

4. P: Sebutkan alat-alat tulis apa yang dibeli Joel!

    J: _____

5. P: Kamus jenis apa yang dibeli Joel dan mengapa dia membeli itu?

    J: _____

6. P: Mengapa harga majalah berbahasa Inggris mahal menurut kamu?

    J: _____

7. P: Bacaan ringan apa yang dibeli Joel?

    J: _____

8. P: Berapa jumlah uang yang dihabiskan Joel di toko buku hari ini?

    J: _____

9. P: Jika Joel pergi ke toko buku Gramedia setiap minggunya, berapa ongkos taksi yang dia habiskan selama satu bulan?

    J: _____

B. **Menyimak** | Listening comprehension

■ *Simaklah baik-baik Tape Latihan 5 dan cobalah jawab pertanyaan-pertanyaan di bawah ini! (Listen carefully to Exercise Tape 5 and try to answer the questions below.)*

1. P: Joel ingin membelikan sesuatu dari toko buku Gramedia untuk Sari, apakah itu?

    J: _____

2. P: Buku-buku dan majalah apa yang disukai oléh ibu Sari?

    J: _____

3. P: Agus biasanya pergi ke toko buku dengan siapa dan mengapa?

    J: _____

4. P: Berapa buah komik Tin-Tin yang dibeli Ratih selama satu tahun dan berapa harga totalnya?

    J: _____

5. P: Mengapa Joel suka sekali pergi ke toko buku yang terletak di Mangga Mall?

    J: _____

6. P: Siapa nama pegawai toko buku yang sudah menjadi teman baru Joel?

    J: _____

7. P: Hari apa biasanya Sari dan Ratih pergi ke toko buku dan dengan siapa?

    J: _____

8. P: Berapa orang yang bekerja di toko buku itu?

    J: _____

9. P: Mengapa Agus suka pergi ke toko buku itu pada hari Senin?

    J: _____

C. **Tata bahasa** | Grammar

■ *Selesaikanlah kalimat-kalimat di bawah ini lalu terjemahkanlah ke dalam Bahasa Inggris yang baik! (Complete the sentences below and then translate them into good English!)*

1. Dua puluh ditambah lima sama dengan _____

    _____

2. Enam belas dikurangi delapan sama dengan _____

    _____

3. Tujuh puluh tujuh dikurangi dua ditambah sepuluh sama dengan _____

_____

4. Delapan dibagi empat dikalikan sembilan sama dengan _____

_____

5. Tiga ratus dua puluh lima dikalikan tiga sama dengan _____

_____

6. Dua ribu enam belas dikalikan tiga belas dikurangi dua ribu sama dengan _____

_____

7. Lima belas dikurangi tujuh dibagi tiga sama dengan _____

_____

8. Lima juta dikurangi tiga setengah juta dikalikan sebelas sama dengan _____

_____

D. Menulis | Writing

■ *Tuliskan nomor-nomor berikut ini ke dalam bahasa Indonesia (Write the following numbers in Indonesian.)*

1. 456.000 : _____

2. 1.900.450 : _____

3. 333.333.333 : _____

4. 56.768 : _____

5. 7.000.000.750 : _____

6. 886.725.945 : _____

7. 919.999 : _____

8. 100.000.650 : _____

LESSON 6

What Time?
Jam Berapa?

JOEL	Kapan ada waktu, Sari? Saya ingin bertemu lagi.
SARI	Bésok ada waktu. Jam 10?
JOEL	Maaf, saya punya janji dengan dosén jam 10. Jam 11 bisa?
SARI	Baiklah. Saya tunggu di pojok gedung Fakultas Hukum, ya?
JOEL	Hari ulang tahun Sari tanggal berapa?
SARI	Tanggal 10 April. Saya lahir tahun 1987.
JOEL	Jadi nanti berumur 22.
SARI	Ya. Dan Joel?
JOEL	Hari ulang tahun saya tanggal 11 Séptémber. Saya lahir tahun 1986.
SARI	Jadi sekarang berumur 23. Hampir sama!
JOEL	Jam berapa sekarang?
SARI	Sudah hampir jam 12. Hari ini hari Jumat. Orang Islam akan ke mesjid untuk salat Jumat. Selesai jam 1 siang. Lalu meréka pulang.

WORDLIST

bertemu	to meet	**maaf**	sorry! excuse me
berumur	to be aged…, … years old	**orang Islam**	Muslim(s)
bésok	tomorrow	**pojok**	corner
hampir	almost	**salat**	ritual prayer (five times daily)
hari ulang tahun	birthday	**tunggu**	to wait
janji	appointment, date, promise	**waktu**	time

CULTURAL NOTE

For those who wish to observe them, there are five times (**waktu**) for ritual prayer (**salat**) for Muslims. These times are calculated precisely, and as a result the call to prayer will be broadcast from the mosque loudspeakers at almost the same moment, all over the city. The times vary slightly according to the time of year. On Thursday 22 January 2009 in Jakarta, for example, they were:

Isya	7.27 p.m.
Subuh	4.38 a.m.
Lohor	12.05 p.m.
Asar	3.28 p.m.
Maghrib	6.17 p.m.

Here's a way to remember the five times:
I S L A M.

You can perform the ritual at home or at the local mosque. But Friday midday prayer, as mentioned in the Story, is a communal time, and there will be a sermon (**khotbah**) as well, given by the leader (**imam**).

LANGUAGE NOTES

Talking about time

In answer to the question "**Kapan?** When?" we can provide information of various kinds, as follows:

Telling the time

Jam berapa? What time is it? **Jam** means "o'clock", and **berapa** means "how much?" To give an answer, we repeat **jam** and add a number:

Jam satu	one o'clock
Jam dua	two o'clock
Jam tiga	three o'clock, and so on

Then to indicate time past the hour, we use the word **léwat** "past", followed by the number of minutes (**menit**), thus:

Jam dua léwat sepuluh	ten past two
Jam enam léwat dua puluh	twenty past six

A quarter past is expressed with **léwat seperempat**, e.g.

Jam lima léwat seperempat	a quarter past five

Half past the hour needs special attention, as it is different from English (but like Dutch). We do not say "half past" but "half to the next hour", thus:

Jam setengah delapan	half past seven

For a quarter to the hour, we say the hour "less a quarter", e.g.

Jam tujuh kurang seperempat	a quarter to seven

For extra clarity, we can add words to indicate what period of the day it is:

pagi	morning
siang	the middle of the day
soré	the late afternoon
malam	night, e.g.
jam sebelas malam	eleven o'clock at night

Note that in a formal context, for example on radio or TV, we will hear **pukul** instead of **jam**. And in airline and other timetables we will also find the twenty-four hour clock being used, e.g.

pukul delapan belas tiga puluh	18.30

The days of the week

Hari apa? What day of the week is it? Answer:

hari Minggu	Sunday (or, more formally, **hari Ahad**; not to be confused with **minggu** "week")
hari Senin	Monday
hari Selasa	Tuesday
hari Rabu	Wednesday
hari Kamis	Thursday
hari Jumat	Friday
hari Sabtu	Saturday

Note that it is usual to repeat the word **hari** (day) here, as also in special days, such as **Hari Ibu** (Mother's Day, 22 December), or **Hari Ulang Tahun (HUT)** the birthday or anniversary of something.

The months of the year

Bulan apa? What month is it? Answer:

bulan Januari	January
bulan Fébruari	February
bulan Maret	March
bulan April	April
bulan Mei	May (N.B. pronounce like "May")
bulan Juni	June
bulan Juli	July
bulan Agustus	August (Note the spelling)
bulan Séptémber	September
bulan Oktober	October
bulan Novémber	November
bulan Désémber	December

Dates

Tanggal berapa? What date is it? Answer:

Hari ini tanggal sepuluh Mei	Today is 10 May ("the tenth of May")
Tanggal tujuh belas Agustus	17 August ("the seventeenth of August")

Note that we use the cardinal, not the ordinal ("-th") numeral in dates, and must include the word **tanggal**.

Years

Tahun berapa? What year? Answer:

Tahun seribu tiga ratus enam puluh lima   The year 1365

Finally, some useful adverbs that relate to time:

selalu	always
sering	often
kadang-kadang	sometimes
sekarang	now
hari ini	today

LATIHAN 6 EXERCISE 6

Jam Berapa?
What Time?

A. Pertanyaan untuk bacaan

■ *Jawablah pertanyaan-pertanyaan di bawah ini sesuai dengan isi bacaan!*

1. P: Apa yang akan dilakukan Joel bésok pagi?

   J: _____

2. P: Jam berapa dan di mana Joel berjanji untuk bertemu dengan Sari?

   J: _____

3. P: Mengapa Joel tidak bisa bertemu Sari pada jam 10?

   J: _____

4. P: Di mana Sari akan menunggu Joel bésok pagi?

   J: _____

5. P: Siapa yang lebih tua, Sari atau Joel? Berapa bulan selisihnya?

   J: _____

6. P: Berapa umur Sari dan berapa umur Joel?

   J: _____

7. P: Apa artinya hari Jumat untuk umat Islam?

   J: _____

8. P: Jam berapa biasanya solat Jumat di Masjid dimulai?

   J: _____

B. Menyimak

■ *Dengarkanlah dan simaklah baik-baik isi Tape Latihan 6 dan cobalah jawab pertanyaan-pertanyaan di bawah ini!*

1. P: Sari dan Joel sudah berjanji untuk saling membantu dalam hal apa?

   J: _____

2. P: Apa yang biasanya dilakukan Joel untuk membantu bahasa Inggris Sari?

   J: _____

3. P: Sebaliknya apa yang biasa dilakukan Sari untuk membantu pengetahuan Joel tentang Indonesia?

   J: _____

4. P: Berapa orang dalam keluarga Sari yang lahir di bulan April?

   J: _____

5. P: Apa yang biasanya dilakukan keluarga Sari jika ada yang berulang tahun?

   J: _____

6. P: Makanan apa yang biasa disajikan pada hari ulang tahun di keluarga Sari?

   J: _____

C. Jam berapa?

■ *Lihatlah gambar di bawah ini dan tulislah jam berapa.*

1.

P: Jam berapa?

J: _____

3.

P: Jam berapa?

J: _____

5.

P: Jam berapa?

J: _____

2.
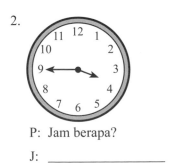

P: Jam berapa?

J: _____

4.
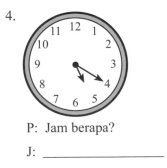

P: Jam berapa?

J: _____

6.
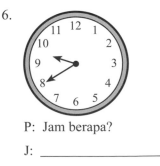

P: Jam berapa?

J: _____

D. Menggambar jam

■ *Bacalah kalimat-kalimat di bawah dengan hati-hati, lalu gambarlah!*

1.

Jam lima tepat

5.

Jam enam kurang seperempat

2.
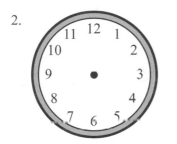
Jam sepuluh léwat lima menit

6.

Jam satu léwat dua puluh

3.
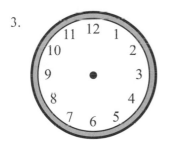
Jam setengah sembilan

7.
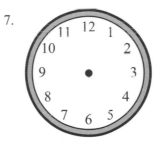
Jam tujuh léwat dua puluh lima

4.
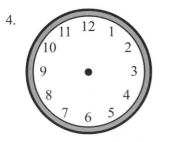
Jam tujuh léwat seperempat

8.
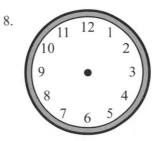
Jam dua belas kurang dua puluh

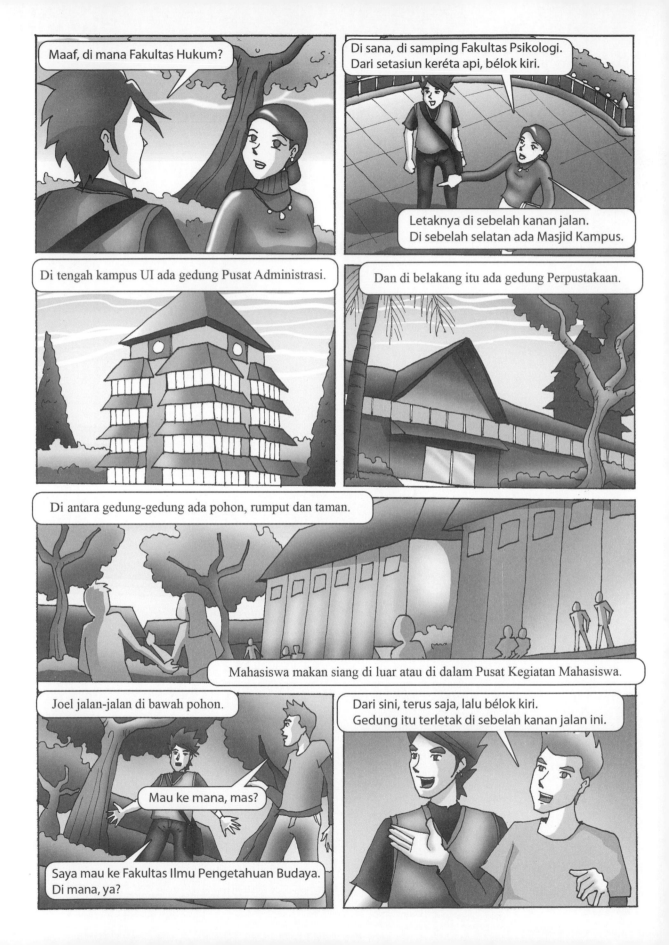

Where?
Di Mana?

"Maaf, di mana Fakultas Hukum?"
"Di sana, di samping Fakultas Psikologi. Dari setasiun keréta api, bélok kiri. Letaknya di sebelah kanan jalan. Di sebelah selatan ada Mesjid Kampus."

Di tengah kampus UI ada gedung Pusat Administrasi.
Dan di belakang itu ada gedung Perpustakaan.
Di antara gedung-gedung ada pohon, rumput dan taman.
Mahasiswa makan siang di luar atau di dalam Pusat Kegiatan Mahasiswa.

Joel jalan-jalan di bawah pohon.
"Mau ke mana, mas?"
"Saya mau ke Fakultas Ilmu Pengetahuan Budaya. Di mana, ya?"
"Dari sini, terus saja, lalu bélok kiri. Gedung itu terletak di sebelah kanan jalan ini."

WORDLIST

administrasi	administration	**perpustakaan**	library
bélok	to turn	**pohon**	tree
gedung	building	**psikologi**	psychology
gedung-gedung	buildings	**pusat**	centre; central
humaniora	humanities	**rumput**	grass
jalan	road, street	**setasiun**	station
kegiatan	activities	**taman**	garden
keréta api	train	**tengah**	centre, middle
letak	location	**terletak**	located

LANGUAGE NOTES

Talking about place

Di mana? Where? (or: "in what place"). Answer:

Di sini.	Here ("in this place")
Di situ.	There ("in that place")
Di sana.	There ("in that place, out of sight")

In each of these phrases, we can see the word **di**, placed in front of a word indicating place. So **di** is a preposition, and means "in, at". In contrast to English "here" and "there", we do need the preposition in Indonesian. There are two more words that have the function of indicating direction—**ke** "to" and **dari** "from"—and can be combined in the same way as above, e.g.

Ke mana?	Where to? (lit. "to where?")
Dari mana?	Where from? (lit. "from where?")

So the pattern is becoming clearer now: preposition + place-word = indication of place. These three prepositions can be put in front of any noun that we might need, e.g.

Di rumah.	At home
Ke pasar.	To the market
Dari masjid.	From the mosque

There is also a set of position words that are useful to know:

dalam	inside
luar	outside
depan	front
belakang	back
atas	top
bawah	bottom
samping	side
antara	the space between

Each of these can have, indeed must have, one of the three prepositions mentioned, **di**, **ke** or **dari**, in order to make good sense. So we get:

Di dalam	inside (lit. "on the inside"), within
Di luar	outside (lit. "on the outside")
Di depan	in front
Di belakang	behind, at the back
Di atas	above, on top, at the top
Di bawah	below, under, at the bottom
Di samping	at the side, beside
Di antara	between

And so on. But then we can add more information, by using another noun in a possessive relation: on the inside/outside etc. of what? For example:

Di atas méja	on the table (lit. "on the top of the table")
Di bawah kursi	under the chair (lit. "on the underside of the chair"). And so on.

Directions

In Indonesia it is quite common to give directions using the points of the compass:

utara	north
timur	east
selatan	south
barat	west

and of course also

kanan	right
kiri	left

These are generally accompanied by the word **sebelah** "side", as in e.g. **di sebelah kanan**, "on the right, on the right-hand side". When turning, we can say **bélok ke kanan**, or just **bélok kanan**, "turn right".

More interrogative words

We have already seen **kapan**? when?.

mana	what place?

Here are some more words for asking questions:

Bagaimana?	How? In what way? Like what?
Mengapa?	Why? For what reason?
Berapa?	How many?

For the sake of completeness, we should add a second use of **mana**, alongside the one mentioned above; this is "which?", when we are making a choice among several alternatives. In this case it follows the word it applies to, e.g.

Jalan mana?	Which street? (We have several possibilities, and want to know which one to take.)

Etiquette and Body Language

Communication isn't exclusively a matter of language. It includes the whole body and what we do with it.

Let's start with the top: the head. In Indonesian thinking, this is sacred. That means you should never touch someone else's head. (Lovers might do it, but that probably doesn't apply to you yet…) So you may find that the hairdresser asks permission before setting to work on your hair. Even ruffling a pal's hair for fun is a no-no. Don't pat little children on the head either, even if they're very cute.

But there's more. This relates to the level of the head. We can't invade the space above a person's head, so this means keeping our own head down to their level – and this applies in particular to old people. So if they're sitting down and you have to pass close by, then you should "duck", just to show respect and not tower over them. If you have to pass food, or reach for something on a shelf above someone's head, for example, then you must ask permission first: **Permisi**, **ya**, **Pak/Bu**. And they will answer, **Ya, mari**, or **silahkan** "Go ahead".

And no revealing neck-line, please. Otherwise the local lads will look into it and draw certain conclusions. Arms and legs should be well covered when going out, both out of politeness and to protect them from the sun.

Hands are important. We normally have two, and have to make a choice: only the right hand may be used for passing and receiving things, not the left. Why? Because the left is considered unclean. But to use both hands at once is fine. If it's unavoidable to use your left hand, just say **Maaf!** "Excuse me!" If you have to beckon, use the right hand, but with the fingers pointing down, not up! Don't point directly at people. And it's better not to hold hands in public, even if you see others doing it.

Standing with hands on hips is seen as a challenging or aggressive posture in Indonesian body language. Waving the hands about or gesticulating wildly shows a lack of self-control and is considered to be the conduct of demons. It's better just to keep your hands clasped in front.

As a greeting, people shake hands (**salaman**). Ladies are less likely to do this. Only shake a lady's hand if she offers it. Some ladies, who know each other well, may kiss each other on the cheek. The Indonesian kiss, just for your information, is a sniff on the cheek…

Which brings us to feet. Obviously, they are the lowest part, geographically and ritually. So you must never touch anyone with your feet, with or without footwear, and this includes pointing with the foot. It's best to keep the foot turned down, so as not to show the dirty sole to someone opposite.

If people are seated on the floor, you'll notice they sit on mats or carpets. And they always take their shoes off first. Never step on a mat or carpet with your shoes on; leave them outside. And as we're sure you already know, shoes are always removed before entering a mosque.

As a general guide on what to do, we suggest you first observe what others do, and then follow them. Leave the questions for later. There's a time and place for everything.

Di Mana?
Where?

A. Pertanyaan untuk bacaan

■ *Jawablah pertanyaan-pertanyaan di bawah ini sesuai dengan isi bacaan!*

1. P: Di mana letak Fakultas Hukum?

   J: _____

2. P: Apakah di kampus ada Mesjid? Di sebelah mana?

   J: _____

3. P: Letak gedung Administrasi di mana?

   J: _____

4. P: Di mana biasanya para mahasiswa makan?

   J: _____

5. P: Ke mana Joel ingin pergi hari ini?

   J: _____

6. P: Apakah kampus Depok UI termasuk kampus yang 'hijau' menurut kamu? Apa buktinya?

   J: _____

B. Menyimak

■ *Simaklah baik-baik isi Tape Latihan 7 lalu jawablah pertanyaannya!*

1. P: Apa nama kampus UI yang paling besar?

   J: _____

2. P: Mengapa Kantor Pusat Administrasi dibangun di tengah-tengah kampus Depok?

   J: _____

3. P: Fakultas apa saja yang biasa dikunjungi Joel untuk belajar?

   J: _____

4. P: Bangunan apa yang ada di kampus UI yang menurut Joel sangat menarik?

   J: _____

5. P: Siapa saja yang pergi bersembahyang di Masjid Kampus?

   J: _____

6. P: Apakah banyak mahasiswa asing yang belajar di kampus itu?

   J: _____

7. P: Darimana saja mahasiswa asing yang balajar di kampus UI?

   J: _____

8. P: Di universitas mana Sari ingin belajar untuk mengambil gelar Master?

   J: _____

C. Préposisi

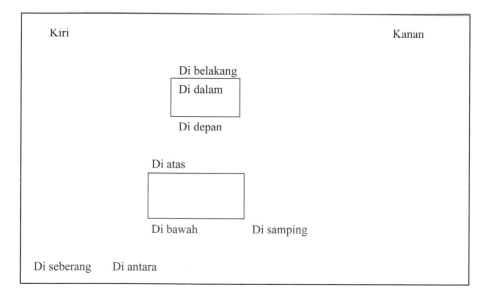

■ *Lihatlah keterangan préposisi di atas, lalu jawablah pertanyaan-pertanyaan di bawah ini!*

1.

   P: Di mana Biru di gambar ini?

   J: _____

2.

   P: Di mana Biru di gambar ini?

   J: _____

3.

P: Di mana Biru di gambar ini?

J: _____

7.

P: Di mana kantor pos di gambar ini?

J: _____

4.

P: Di mana Joel di gambar ini?

J: _____

8.

P: Di mana burung berada di gambar ini?

J: _____

5.

P: Di mana Ratih di gambar ini?

J: _____

9.

P: Di mana ikan emas di gambar ini?

J: _____

6.

P: Di mana Agus di gambar ini?

J: _____

D. Terjemahan

■ *Terjemahkanlah kalimat-kalimat di bawah ini ke dalam bahasa Inggris yang baku!*

1. Gedung Fakultas Hukum terletak di belakang Perpustakaan.

2. Rumah Sari di seberang toko bunga.

   _____

3. Di depan rumah kos Joel ada warung kopi yang bernama 'Batavia'.

   _____

4. Di bawah jembatan-jembatan di Jakarta banyak pengemis.

   _____

5. Di dalam Masjid Istiqlal banyak orang yang sedang bersembahyang.

   _____

6. Di luar bandara Sukarno-Hatta banyak orang menunggu taksi.

   _____

In the Street
Di Jalan

JOEL	Maaf, Pak, apakah di sini ada kantor pos?
ORANG LÉWAT	Ya, ada. Di sana. Di seberang jalan.
JOEL	Terima kasih, Pak.
O.L.	Wah, sudah lancar bahasa Indonesia...
JOEL	Ya, sedikit bisa, Pak.
O.L.	Bagus kok! Sudah berapa kali ke Indonesia?
JOEL	Ini baru pertama kalinya.
O.L.	Senang di Indonesia?
JOEL	Senang, Pak. Menarik sekali. Tapi panas!
O.L.	Siapa namanya?
JOEL	Joel, Pak.
O.L.	Joel sudah punya keluarga?
JOEL	Maaf?
O.L.	Anu, apakah sudah kawin?
JOEL	O, tidak.
O.L.	Maksudnya, "belum", ya.
JOEL	O ya, salah saya.
O.L.	Joel dari Amerika, kan?
JOEL	Bukan, Pak. Saya orang Australia.
O.L.	Dari negeri kangguru! Mau cari pacar di sini?
JOEL	Ya, mau. Tapi cukup sulit.
O.L.	Mengapa?
JOEL	Cantik-cantik semua! Mari, Pak. (Joel mau menyeberang jalan.)
O.L.	Hati-hati, ya. Sampai jumpa!

WORDLIST

anu	er, um	**malah**	even
bagus	excellent	**menarik**	interesting
baru	(adv.) just, only	**mengapa**	why?
cantik	pretty	**menyeberang**	to cross (over)
cari	to look for	**negeri**	land, country
cukup	quite	**pacar**	girlfriend
hati-hati	careful	**panas**	hot
kali	time, occasion (cf. **waktu**, p. 40)	**pertama kali**	the first time
kangguru	kangaroo	**salah**	to be wrong, make a mistake
kantor pos	post office	**sampai jumpa**	see you later ("till meet")
kawin	married	**seberang**	the other side
kok	(no separate translation; a particle used in speech, in this position expressing mild disagreement)	**sedikit**	a little bit
		sekali	very
		semua	all (of them)
lancar	fluent	**senang**	happy
léwat	to pass by	**sulit**	difficult
maksudnya	you mean	**wah**	wow!

CULTURAL NOTE

It can sometimes happen that we strike up a conversation with a perfect stranger, in the train, on the bus and so on, and they start asking questions that may seem intrusive and personal, such as "Are you married?" And if you say "Yes", then they'll ask how many children you have, and you say "None", then they ask "Why?" and so on. Don't succumb to the temptation to say "Mind your own business!" Just smile and give a non-committal answer, or question them in return. It's only out of interest in social matters and meant to establish contact, nothing more.

LANGUAGE NOTES

Saying "yes" and "no"

For conversation, we need to be able to say "yes" and "no". In fact, these form a one-word sentence, meaning "I agree" or "That's right", and "I don't agree" or "That's not right" respectively. The words are: **ya** and **tidak**.

> **Ya.**   Yes.

This could be the answer to a question. In that case, seeing that **ya** is such a short (and abrupt-sounding) word, our sentence should contain the verb being questioned, like this:

Apakah ada roti?	Do you have any bread?
Ya, ada.	Yes, we do.

Suka makan nasi?	Do you like eating rice?
Ya, suka.	Yes, I do.

While on the subject, we should mention another usage of **ya**, at the end of a sentence. In this position it either emphasizes an order, or seeks confirmation: "you have heard, haven't you?", or "you do agree, don't you?". This is very common in conversation; a translation with "yes" does not seem to fit.

Tidak.   No.

In the same way as **ya**, this could also be the answer to a question, and could also be followed by a verb:

Apakah suka makan durian?   Do you like eating durian?
Tidak suka.   No, I don't.

Two colloquial forms of **tidak** are often heard: **ndak** or **nggak**. These are only appropriate in an informal context, and are not normally written.

Further, **tidak** is the normal word for negating any verb or adjective: "not…"; "is not…, does not…" and so forth. As in the example above, **Tidak suka**, it comes in front of the word it applies to.

However, there is a second word for negating, **bukan**. This is found in front of a noun or pronoun. It also means "not", e.g.

Bukan saya.   Not me.

Bukan can form a one-word sentence: "No." It has the sense of "No, not that", or "No, it's different".

And **bukan** can also be found at the end of a sentence, or even in the middle of a sentence, often abbreviated to **kan**, with the meaning of "That's right, isn't it", asking for confirmation, so it can be translated in a variety of ways, e.g. "isn't it", "doesn't it" and so on.

Finally, there is another negative word, **belum**, which stands for two English words, "not yet" (even if these are separated in an English sentence). This word occupies the same place as **tidak**, but is used in different circumstances. Where we answer "no" in English, if there is still a possibility that something might happen, then in Indonesian we have to use **belum**, "not yet". For example:

Sudah sembuh?   Have you recovered?
Belum.   No (but in time I will).

More about numbers

We have already seen a complete set of cardinal numbers (see Lesson 5), so now we can deal with the ordinals. These are formed by prefixing **ke-** to the numeral. The only exception is **pertama**, "first". So we get:

pertama   first
kedua   second
ketiga   third, and so on

Fractions are formed with the prefix **per-** prefixed to the numeral. The only exception is half. Thus:

setengah		half
pertiga:	**sepertiga**	one third;
	dua pertiga	two thirds
perempat:	**seperempat**	one quarter/fourth
	tiga perempat	three quarters/fourths; and so on

seperempat

Similarly,

Lima setengah   five and a half (Note: no word used for "and").

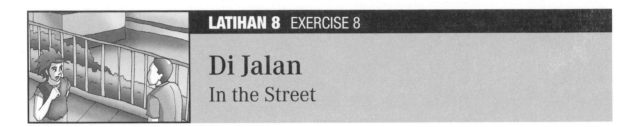

LATIHAN 8 EXERCISE 8

Di Jalan
In the Street

A. Pertanyaan untuk bacaan

■ *Jawablah pertanyaan-pertanyaan di bawah ini sesuai dengan isi bacaan!*

1. P: Ke mana Joel ingin pergi hari ini?

    J: _____

2. P: Apakah bahasa Indonesia Joel bagus menurut kamu? Apa buktinya?

    J: _____

3. P: Apa yang kurang disukai Joel tentang tinggal di Indonesia?

    J: _____

4. P: Apa yang ditanyakan orang lain yang membuat Joel merasa héran?

    J: _____

5. P: Negeri asal Joel juga sering disebut sebagai negeri apa dan mengapa?

    J: _____

B. Menyimak

■ *Dengarkanlah isi Tape Latihan 8 dengan baik dan cobalah menjawab pertanyaan-pertan-yaannya!*

1. P: Mengapa Joel ingin mencari kantor pos?

    J: _____

2. P: Bagaimana Joel berkomunikasi dengan kakaknya di Australia?

   J: _____

3. P: Selain ibu Joel yang masih suka menerima surat dari anaknya, siapa lagi yang selalu menunggu surat darinya?

   J: _____

4. P: Siapa yang lebih senang menerima kabar dari Joel léwat email?

   J: _____

5. P: Mengapa semakin banyak anak muda yang jarang memakai jasa pos untuk berkomunikasi?

   J: _____

6. P: Apa yang biasa dibeli Joel di kantor pos?

   J: _____

C. Tata bahasa (bukan)

■ *Jawablah pertanyaan-pertanyaan, dengan memakai kata negatif yang tepat.*

P: Apakah Joel dari Amérika?

J: Bukan, dia dari Australia.

1.

   P: Apakah Joel dari Amérika?

   J: <u>Bukan, dia dari Australia.</u>

3.

   P: Apakah Témbok Cina ada ini Hong Kong?

   J: _____

2.

   P: Apakah Sari dari Singapura?

   J: _____

4.

   P: Apakah menara Eiffel ada di Italia?

   J: _____

5.

P: Apakah loncéng Big Ben ada di Skotlandia?

J: _____

7.

P: Apakah Mahatma Gandhi dari Mongolia?

J: _____

6.

P: Apakah Jembatan Golden Gate ada di

Texas?

J: _____

8.

P: Apakah Nelson Mandela dari Kenya?

J: _____

D. Menulis

■ *Data pribadi*

1. Joel lahir di Geelong, Melbourne, pada tanggal 4 Januari dua puluh dua tahun yang lalu. Joel, yang bernama lengkap Joel Robinson, belajar hukum dan kajian Indonesia di sebuah universitas ternama di Melbourne. Dia ingin menjadi ahli hukum dengan spésialisasi hukum Indonesia. Joel mempunyai satu kakak perempuan dan satu adik laki-laki. Joel anak kedua dalam keluarganya. Seperti ibunya, Joel suka sekali membaca novel, bermain tenis méja, dan menonton filem kung-fu. Warna kesukaan Joel adalah hijau. Joel tidak suka minum bir, karena menurut dia terasa pahit. Joel sangat menyukai lumpia.

Isilah daftar pribadi Joel dengan memakai informasi dari tulisan di atas!

Nama lengkap	
Jenis kelamin	
Tempat, tanggal lahir	
Pekerjaan	
Jumlah saudara	
Hobi	
Cita-cita	
Warna kesukaan	

2. Sari adalah anak kedua dari tiga bersaudara. Seperti kedua saudaranya, Sari lahir di Jakarta. Hari ulang tahun Sari adalah 1 Mei. Sari sekarang berusia dua puluh tahun. Selama dua tahun ini Sari belajar di Jurusan Hubungan Internasional di UI. Sari ingin sekali bekerja menjadi diplomat. Selain memasak, Sari juga suka menulis puisi dan cerita péndék. Sejak tiga tahun yang lalu Sari menekuni bulu tangkis. Mérah dan ungu adalah warna yang paling disukainya.

Nama lengkap	
Jenis kelamin	
Tempat, tanggal lahir	
Pekerjaan	
Jumlah saudara	
Hobi	
Cita-cita	
Warna kesukaan	

3. Tulislah satu paragraph tentang kamu, lalu isilah kolom-kolom yang tersedia di bawah ini!

Nama lengkap	
Jenis kelamin	
Tempat, tanggal lahir	
Pekerjaan	
Jumlah saudara	
Hobi	
Cita-cita	
Warna kesukaan	

LESSON 9

Buying a Fan
Beli Kipas Angin

Joel sedih.
Dia merasa capai.
Tapi bukan karena belajar terlalu keras.
Di luar hawanya panas dan lembab.
Lalu lintas bising sekali.
Akibatnya, sulit tidur.
Joel berpikir, "Lebih baik pulang saja. Bagaimana bisa belajar di Jakarta?"

Ketok, ketok! (suara pintu)
"Siapa?"
Sari masuk, dengan senyum manis.
Katanya, "Saya tadi pikir-pikir. Saya kira Joel perlu beli kipas angin kecil. Mari kita cari di toko alat listrik!"

Mereka dapat kipas bagus. Warnanya biru. Nah, sekarang rasanya lebih sejuk.
"Scjuk, Sari!"
"Segar, ya, Joel."
Sekarang Joel sudah merasa kuat lagi. Dia penuh tenaga baru.
"Terima kasih, Sari. Kamu sangat baik hati!"
"Sama-sama," kata Sari.

WORDLIST

akibatnya	as a result	**karena**	because
alat	apparatus, appliance	**kecil**	small
angin	wind	**keras**	hard
bagus	very good, fine	**ketok**	knock
baik hati	kind (character)	**kipas**	fan
baru	(adj.) new	**kuat**	strong
biru	blue	**lalu lintas**	traffic
bising	noisy	**lembab**	humid, moist
capai	tired	**listrik**	electricity; electric
hawa	air, atmosphere	**manis**	sweet

merasa	to feel	**sejuk**	cool
penuh	full (of)	**senyum**	smile
pikir-pikir	to be thinking things over	**suara**	sound
pintu	door	**sulit**	difficult
rasanya	it feels	**tadi**	just now
sama-sama	you're welcome!	**tenaga**	strength
sedih	sad	**tidur**	to sleep
segar	fresh	**warna**	colour

LANGUAGE NOTES

Nouns and adjectives

Beginning in Lesson 1, we have met simple nouns, and have seen how they can be a subject, the object of a verb, or in a possessive relation with another noun or a pronoun. As well as simple nouns, there are also derived forms (as with verbs too), which will be discussed in detail later.

Nouns are described (or "qualified") by adjectives. Adjectives always follow the nouns they describe, in contrast to English, where they come in front. Some examples:

> **cuaca baik**   good weather ("weather" "good": noun + adjective)
> **gaji tinggi**   a high salary
> **istana lama**   the old palace

Note how the words "a" and "the" have to be supplied in translation, depending on the context.

As well as this function, adjectives also form a predicate, that is, can form a complete sentence together with a subject. They do this without any joining word like English "is", "are" and so on, and in this way are similar to (but not the same as) verbs. The following two words could form a complete sentence, or could just be a noun with adjective:

> **Sawah hijau.**   The rice field is green; *or* The green rice field….

So in order to make the situation clearer, in the former case we could include another little word, describing **sawah**, e.g.

> **Sawah ini hijau.**   This rice field is green.

Here the word-group **sawah ini** is the subject, and **hijau** is the predicate. This is a complete sentence.

Further, adjectives themselves can be modified, for example by saying "very", "too" and so on, e.g.

> **besar sekali**   very big
> **terlalu mahal**   too expensive

Here word-order needs special attention, as **sekali**, "very", always comes after its adjective, and **terlalu**, "too", always in front. There is another word meaning "very", **sangat**, which comes in front, e.g.

> **sangat panas**   very hot

Sometimes, when they follow a verb, adjectives could be said to have an adverbial function, e.g.

> **bekerja keras**   to work hard
> **pulang cepat**   to return home quickly

There will be more on adverbs in the next lesson.

In order to form the comparative ("more, -er"), we use the word **lebih**, placed in front of the adjective. And in order to form the superlative ("most, -est"), we use the word **paling**, also put in front of the adjective.

Finally, adjectives can serve as base-word in certain derived forms, for example forming an abstract noun, referring to a quality ("-ness"). This will be dealt with later.

LATIHAN 9 EXERCISE 9

Beli Kipas Angin
Buying a Fan

A. Pertanyaan untuk bacaan

■ *Jawablah pertanyaan-pertanyaan di bawah ini sesuai dengan isi bacaan!*

1. P: Perasaan apa yang dialami Joel sekarang ini?

   J: _____

2. P: Selain cuaca apa yang menyebabkan Joel merasa lelah?

   J: _____

3. P: Kesulitan besar apa yang dihadapi Joel tinggal di Jakarta?

   J: _____

4. P: Apa gagasan Sari untuk membantu Joel mengatasi panasnya Jakarta?

   J: _____

5. P: Mengapa banyak orang membeli kipas angin di Indonesia?

   J: _____

6. P: Mengapa orang-orang tidak memasang AC di Indonesia menurut kamu?

   J: _____

B. Menyimak

■ *Dengarkanlah baik-baik isi Tape Latihan 9 lalu cobalah menjawab pertanyaan-pertanyaan di bawah ini!*

1. P: Ada berapa musim di Indonesia?

    J: _____

2. P: Mengapa ibu Sari lebih suka musim hujan?

    J: _____

3. P: Resiko apa yang dihadapi jika di Jakarta terlalu banyak hujan?

    J: _____

4. P: Mengapa keluarga Sari merasa beruntung pada musim banjir di Jakarta?

    J: _____

5. P: Apa yang biasanya terjadi jika Joel kurang tidur?

    J: _____

6. P: Menurut Joel, di Australia bagaimana cuaca pada musim panas?

    J: _____

7. P: Masalah besar dan berbahaya apa yang dihadapi oleh masyarakat Australia pada musim panas?

    J: _____

8. P: Mengapa bapak Sari tidak suka memasang AC di rumahnya?

    J: _____

C. Tata bahasa

1. Carilah 5 kata kerja di dalam bacaan!

    a. _____   d. _____

    b. _____   e. _____

    c. _____

2. Carilah 10 kata sifat di dalam bacaan!

    a. _____   f. _____

    b. _____   g. _____

    c. _____   h. _____

    d. _____   i. _____

    e. _____   j. _____

D. Mencocokkan

■ *Cocokkan kata-kata di sebelah kiri dengan kata-kata yang ada di sebelah kanan yang mempunyai hubungan!*

1.	Basah	a.	Api
2.	Salju	b.	Gula
3.	Panas	c.	Senyum
4.	Langit	d.	Pintu
5.	Capai	e.	Hujan
6.	Buka	f.	Putih
7.	Senang	g.	Tinggi
8.	Manis	h.	Lelah

E. Pertanyaan umum (kuis)

■ *Jawablah pertanyaan-pertanyaan di bawah ini sesuai dengan keadaan kamu!*

1. P: Ada berapa musim di negerimu? Sebutkan!
   J: _____

2. P: Musim apa yang paling kamu sukai? Mengapa?
   J: _____

3. P: Olahraga apa yang biasa dimainkan orang di musim dingin?
   J: _____

4. P: Olahraga apa yang biasa dimainkan orang di musim panas?
   J: _____

5. P: Mengapa sebuah musim disebut 'musim gugur'? Jelaskan!
   J: _____

6. P: Jelaskan apa yang dimaksud dengan 'musim semi'!
   J: _____

F. Lawan kata

■ *Isilah lawan kata di bawah ini dengan memakai daftar kosa kata yang ada*

a.	Panas	f.	Kering	k.	Bawah	p.	Sakit
b.	Tinggi	g.	Mahal	l.	Basah	q.	Séhat
c.	Buka	h.	Dingin	m.	Murah	r.	Besar
d.	Depan	i.	Tutup	n.	Sedih	s.	Kecil
e.	Atas	j.	Belakang	o.	Senang	t.	Péndék

1. Panas vs _____ 2. Tinggi vs _____
3. Buka vs _____ 4. Depan vs _____
5. Atas vs _____ 6. Kering vs _____
7. Mahal vs _____ 8. Sedih vs _____
9. Sakit vs _____ 10. Besar vs _____

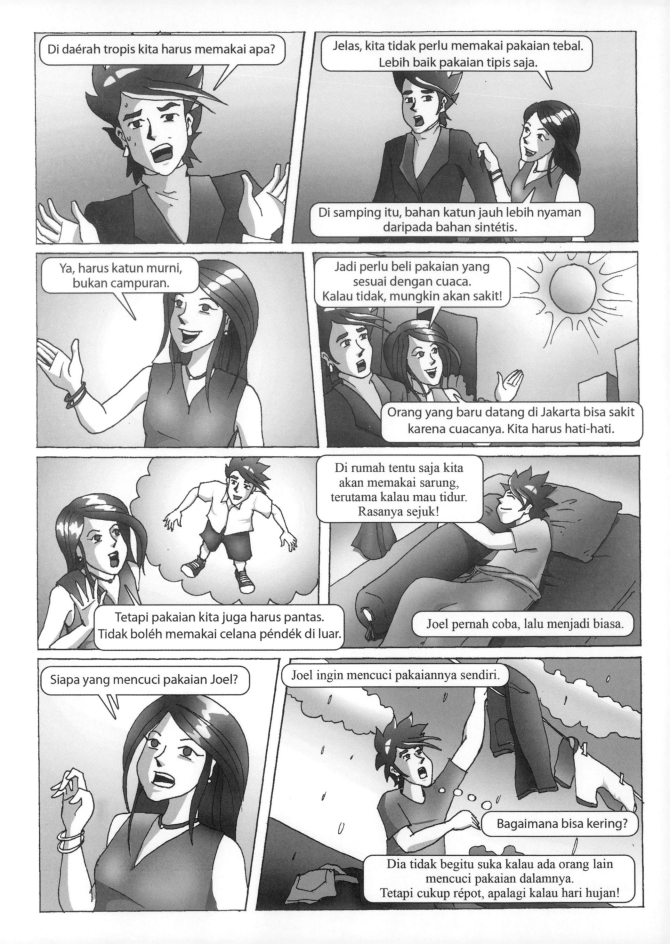

LESSON 10

Clothes
Pakaian

Di daérah tropis kita harus memakai apa?
Jelas, kita tidak perlu memakai pakaian tebal.
Lebih baik pakaian tipis saja.
Di samping itu, bahan katun jauh lebih nyaman daripadi bahan sintétis.
Ya, harus katun murni, bukan campuran.
Jadi perlu beli pakaian yang sesuai dengan cuaca.
Kalau tidak, mungkin akan sakit!
Orang yang baru datang di Jakarta bisa sakit karena cuacanya.
Kita harus hati-hati.

Tetapi pakaian kita juga harus pantas.
Tidak boléh memakai celana péndék di luar.
Di rumah tentu saja kita akan memakai sarung, terutama kalau mau tidur.
Rasanya sejuk!
Joel pernah coba, lalu menjadi biasa.

Siapa yang mencuci pakaian Joel?
Joel ingin mencuci pakaiannya sendiri.
Dia tidak begitu suka kalau ada orang lain mencuci pakaian dalamnya.
Tetapi cukup répot, apalagi kalau hari hujan!
Bagaimana bisa kering?

WORDLIST

apalagi	especially, above all, all the more	**mungkin**	possible, possibly
bahan	material	**murni**	pure
biasa	usual; used, accustomed to	**nyaman**	comfortable
begitu	like that	**pakaian**	clothes
campuran	mixture	**pakaian dalam**	underclothes
celana	pants	**pantas**	fitting, proper
cuaca	weather	**péndék**	short
daérah	area	**répot**	troublesome, a lot of bother

daripada	than		sakit	sick
dengan	with		sarung	sarong
hari hujan	rainy day		sendiri	own; self
jauh	far; much		sesuai	appropriate, in keeping with
jelas	clear		sintétis	synthetic
kalau	if		tebal	thick
katun	cotton		tentu saja	of course, certainly
kering	dry		terutama	especially, in particular
lain	other		tipis	thin
memakai	to wear (second meaning "to use"). On **me-** see Lesson 15.		tropis	tropical
			yang	who; which (on the uses of **yang**, see Lessons 12 and 26).
mencuci	to wash			
menjadi	to become			

LANGUAGE NOTES

Modal words

This term refers to a group of very useful words (sometimes called "auxiliary verbs"), which can be found directly in front of verbs. A complete list is as follows:

bisa	can; to be able, be capable of, know how to
dapat	can; to be able; to be within the range of one's ability
boléh	may; to be allowed to
harus	should; to have to; ought to
mesti	must; to have to
perlu	must; to need to
mampu	able; to have the capacity; to be able to afford
sanggup	prepared to; willing
sempat	to have the opportunity
mau	to want to
ingin	to want, wish, desire to

We have already seen a number of these.

Of course there are other words that come in front of verbs too, such as negatives and tense markers, so the question of order arises. The principle is that the one placed first modifies the meaning of the ones that follow. Normally we would expect the negative, **tidak**, to come first, e.g.

tidak mau	does not want to
tidak akan	will not
tidak perlu	does not need to

Adverbs

With this term we are referring to words or phrases which tell us when or how an action takes place. Some useful words saying "when" are:

sekarang	now
sebentar	(for) a moment
kadang-kadang	sometimes
sering	often
jarang	rarely, seldom
selalu	always
tadi	just now, a moment ago
nanti	shortly, soon

The last two have another interesting use with nouns indicating times of day, when they show past and future times, within a 24-hour period, e.g.

tadi malam	last night (said in the morning, about the night just past)
tadi pagi	this morning (said in the afternoon, about the morning just past)
nanti soré	this afternoon/evening (said in the morning, about the afternoon coming)
nanti malam	tonight (said in the afternoon, about the night coming)

Adverbs that say "how" are sometimes the same as adjectives, e.g.

bekerja keras	to work hard
turun cepat	to go down fast

while others are formed by using the preposition **dengan** ("with"), e.g.

dengan teliti	accurately
dengan rajin	diligently

and there are yet others formed with the word **secara** ("in a ... manner") preceding a verb, e.g.

secara teratur	regularly ("in a regular manner")
secara terbuka	openly ("in an open manner")

More uses of this prefix **se-** will be mentioned later.

We have already seen the word **lebih** meaning "more" before an adjective. A word with an opposite meaning is **kurang**, which when placed before an adjective can mean "not very", e.g.

kurang énak	not very nice (of food)

This is similar to **tidak begitu**, "not particularly", e.g.

tidak begitu jelas	not particularly clear

On the positive side, we have **cukup**, which alongside its usual meaning of "enough" also means "quite", e.g.

cukup ramai	quite busy (pretty busy, but not very)

Finally, we have the idioms for "ever" and "never", **pernah** and **tidak/belum pernah** respectively. For example, you might hear the question:

Sudah pernah ke Surabaya? Have you ever been to Surabaya?

The answer could be:

Pernah.   Yes, I have (or: "Once", but not "Ever"!).

Or you might answer:

Belum pernah.   No, I haven't. *Or*: Never. (This means that you haven't been yet, but you might still.)

(The answer **Tidak pernah** would apply to someone who has died, as there is no longer a possibility of going.)

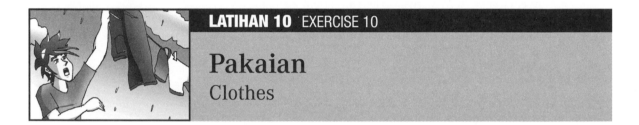

LATIHAN 10 EXERCISE 10

Pakaian
Clothes

A. Pertanyaan untuk bacaan

■ *Jawablah pertanyaan-pertanyaan di bawah ini sesuai dengan isi bacaan!*

1. P: Pakaian apa yang cocok untuk daérah tropis? Jelaskan!

    J: _____

2. P: Mengapa bahan sintétis tidak baik untuk daérah tropis?

    J: _____

3. P: Apa yang terjadi kalau kita memakai pakaian yang tidak sesuai dengan cuaca di mana kita tinggal?

    J: _____

4. P: Apa yang perlu kita ketahui dalam hal berpakaian ketika kita tinggal di sesuatu tempat, selain cuaca?

    J: _____

5. P: Menurut kamu apa resikonya kalau kita tidak mematuhi aturan atau budaya setempat dalam berpakaian?

   J: _____

6. P: Ceritakan bagaimana laki-laki déwasa berpakaian di Jawa!

   J: _____

7. P: Apa yang dicoba Joel ketika dia tinggal di Indonesia?

   J: _____

8. P: Apakah kamu tahu sarung biasanya dibuat dari bahan apa?

   J: _____

B. Menyimak

■ *Simaklah baik-baik isi Tape Latihan 10 dan cobalah jawab pertanyaan-pertanyaan di bawah ini!*

1. P: Apakah Joel lebih menyukai musim dingin atau panas?

   J: _____

2. P: Apa yang biasanya dilakukan Joel pada musim panas di Australia?

   J: _____

3. P: Banyaknya kendaraan bermotor di Indonesia memberi resiko apa terhadap lingkungan?

   J: _____

4. P: Jelaskan tentang pengaruh penebangan hutan di wilayah Indonesia terhadap lingkungan?

   J: _____

5. P: Lembaga semacam apa di Indonesia yang sekarang aktif membicarakan masalah lingkungan?

   J: _____

6. P: Ada satu mata kuliah baru yang dipelajari Agus di kampus, apakah itu?

   J: _____

7. P: Apa yang dilakukan keluarga Sari di rumah untuk berpartisipasi dalam memelihara lingkungan?

   J: _____

8. P: Apa yang dilakukan ibu Sari untuk menjaga keséhatan dan lingkungan di sekelilingnya?

J: _____

C. Menulis (tata bahasa)

■ *Tulislah 5 kalimat yang menerangkan masing-masing musim di bawah ini!*

1. Musim dingin

   a. _____
   _____

   b. _____
   _____

   c. _____
   _____

   d. _____
   _____

   e. _____
   _____

2. Musim panas

   a. _____
   _____

   b. _____
   _____

   c. _____
   _____

   d. _____
   _____

   e. _____
   _____

3. Musim semi

   a. _____
   _____

b. _____

_____

c. _____

_____

d. _____

_____

e. _____

4. Musim gugur

a. _____

_____

b. _____

_____

c. _____

_____

d. _____

_____

e. _____

LESSON 11

In the Kampong
Di Kampung

Dari jalan besar ada gang-gang yang menuju ke kampung di belakang toko-toko. Gang itu sempit-sempit. Mobil hampir tidak bisa léwat. Di sana anak-anak sedang main layangan. Sekarang ini musim angin laut. Ada layangan tinggi di udara, dan ada layangan yang turun cepat, lalu tersangkut di pohon-pohon di halaman orang, atau tiang-tiang listrik. Dari jendéla Joel melihat ada anak nakal naik ke atas atap mesjid dengan layangan di tangannya…

Sekarang sudah soré. Ada suara "Allahu akbar…Allahu akbar" berkali-kali keluar dari mesjid-mesjid. Lalu anak-anak masuk ke rumahnya, karena sebentar lagi akan gelap. Matahari cepat hilang ke dalam kabut kelabu di sebelah barat, dan lampu-lampu nyala di jalan-jalan. Joel rindu. Pikirnya, "Bagaimana keluargaku di rumah di Australia? Mudah-mudahan meréka séhat-séhat saja!"

WORDLIST

Allahu akbar	(Arabic) "God is great"	**melihat**	to see
atap	roof	**menuju**	to head for, go in the direction of
atau	or		
berkali-kali	repeatedly	**mudah-mudahan**	I hope
besar	big, main (road)	**musim**	season
gang	alleyway	**naik**	to climb up
gelap	dark	**nakal**	naughty
halaman	yard	**nyala**	to shine
hampir	almost	**orang**	person; people
hilang	to disappear	**rindu**	to feel longing, be homesick
jendéla	window	**sebentar lagi**	in a moment
kabut	haze, gloom	**séhat**	well, healthy
kampung	residential area	**suara**	sound; voice
kelabu	grey	**tangan**	hand
lampu	lamp	**tersangkut**	caught
laut	sea	**tiang**	post, pole
layangan	kite	**tinggi**	high
matahari	sun	**udara**	air

Doubling of nouns and adjectives

The process of doubling (also called "reduplication") is quite common in Indonesian. It is indicated with a hyphen (and in older texts with the digit 2). Strictly speaking, the doubled form is not in fact two words joined, but a new word formed on the basis of the non-doubled one. We find doubling with nouns, adjectives, verbs, a few adverbs, and even numerals and others.

Nouns

1. The simple form of the noun is neutral with regard to plurality. In other words, it does not contain a mark, comparable to English –s, to tell us whether one or more objects are involved: we can translate with a singular or a plural in English, depending on what is implied in the context. This is not normally a problem, but there is the possibility of using doubling.

    Doubling always involves the idea of plurality. This is often combined with the idea of variety or generality as well.

    Any noun, whether simple or derived, can be doubled. But this is not usually done unless it is unclear that more than one object is being referred to, or if it is important to make it explicit that plurality or generality is intended. In general, one should resist the temptation to always double an Indonesian noun merely to indicate an English plural – that would become rather cumbersome.

    A noun is never doubled if it is associated with a numeral, because the number already makes it clear that the noun is plural. Similarly, if the noun refers to a class of things, there is no need for doubling. It is also not found when we use the word **para** to indicate a group or collectivity, e.g. **para petani**, "farmers" (as a group).

2. We should also mention that there are a few nouns that have a doubled form which is not the result of a process of doubling, because they have no "non-doubled" form in contrast to them. Some examples are:

gado-gado	a dish of mixed vegetables with a tasty sauce
oléh-oléh	a present brought back from a trip for those at home

    In a case like this, a doubled form, such as **gado-gado-gado-gado**, would obviously be out of the question!

3. When we have a concept made up of a combination of two nouns, e.g. **pohon mangga**, "mango-tree", when doubling occurs this only applies to the first part: **pohon-pohon mangga**, "mango-trees"; **surat kabar** "newspaper": **surat-surat kabar**, "newspapers".

Adjectives

Doubling of an adjective occurs when the noun it describes is plural. Doubling suggests that the quality indicated by the adjective applies to all the objects. Doubling is found in either the noun or the adjective, never both. An example:

Anaknya kurus-kurus. His children are (all) thin.

Contrast:

Anak-anaknya kurus. His (various) children are thin.

LATIHAN 11 EXERCISE 11

Di Kampung
In the Kampong

A. Pertanyaan untuk bacaan

■ *Bacalah baik-baik isi bacaan lalu cobalah menjawab pertanyaan-pertanyaan di bawah ini!*

1. P: Jelaskan gang-gang yang ada di kampung di belakang toko-toko.

   J: _____

2. P: Siapa saja yang biasa terlihat di gang-gang itu?

   J: _____

3. P: Menurut kamu, kendaraan apa yang bisa meléwati gang-gang itu?

   J: _____

4. P: Pada musim angin laut anak-anak biasanya bermain apa?

   J: _____

5. P: Mengapa bermain layangan di gang-gang itu berbahaya? Jelaskan!

   J: _____

6. P: Apa yang dilihat Joel dari jendéla kamarnya?

   J: _____

7. P: Suara apa yang didengar oléh Joel dan dari mana asalnya?

   J: _____

8. P: Apa artinya kata 'Allahu akbar' dan dari bahasa apakah itu?

   J: _____

B. Menyimak

■ *Perhatikan dan dengarkan baik-baik isi Tape Latihan 11 lalu jawablah pertanyaan-pertanyaan di bawah ini!*

1. P: Apakah définisi 'kampung' berbéda dengan 'désa'?

    J: _____

2. P: Siapa yang biasanya tinggal di kampung-kampung di kota?

    J: _____

3. P: Suasana khas yang bagaimana yang kita temui di kampung-kampung?

    J: _____

4. P: Mengapa banyak sekali mesjid di Indonesia?

    J: _____

5. P: Siapa yang biasanya pergi bersembahyang ke masjid?

    J: _____

6. P: Apakah Joel awalnya terkejut mendengar suara-suara dari masjid?

    J: _____

7. P: Berapa kali satu hari suara panggilan 'Adzan' dari masjid terdengar?

    J: _____

8. P: Di mana keluarga Joel tinggal?

    J: _____

9. P: Apakah meréka pernah pergi ke Indonesia?

    J: _____

C. Tata bahasa

1. Carilah empat kata sifat (adjectiva) yang ada dalam bacaan!

    a. _____   c. _____

    b. _____   d. _____

2. Carilah empat kata benda (nomina) yang ada dalam bacaan!

    a. _____   c. _____

    b. _____   d. _____

D. Pertanyaan umum (kuis)

■ *Jawablah pertanyaan-pertanyaan umum di bawah ini!*

1. Apa nama tempat bersembahyang umat Kristen?

   _____

2. Apa nama tempat bersembahyang umat Islam?

   _____

3. Apa nama tempat bersembahyang umat Buddha?

   _____

4. Apa nama tempat bersembahyang umat Yahudi?

   _____

5. Di Bali kebanyakan orang memeluk agama apa?

   _____

6. Di mana tempat kepala Geréja Katolik tinggal?

   _____

7. Apa nama agama yang berasal dari Jepang?

   _____

8. Kitab suci agama Islam ditulis dalam bahasa apa?

   _____

9. Kelahiran Yésus disebut sebagai hari apa?

   _____

10. Apa nama agama yang berasal dari Cina?

   _____

E. Menerangkan

■ *Tulislah keterangan masing-masing tokoh atau kata di bawah ini menurut kamu!*

1. Paus Paulus: _____

2. Dalai Lama: _____

3. Muhammad: _____

4. Siddharta Gautama: _____

5. Desmond Tutu: _____

Law Lectures
Kuliah Hukum

Menurut rencana, Joel akan tinggal di Jakarta selama enam bulan. Dia mengikuti kuliah di Fakultas Hukum dengan rajin, semuanya dalam bahasa Indonesia. Tidak apa-apa, karena bahasa Indonesianya sudah lumayan, sejak belajar di Melbourne. Hanya istilah-istilah hukum yang masih sulit. Dosén-dosénnya yang membantu Joel.

Menurut Joel, tatahukum di Indonesia sangat menarik, karena berbéda dengan Australia. Sistém hukum sipil dan pidana berasal dari hukum jaman kolonial Belanda. Di Indonesia juga ada hukum syariat dan hukum adat

Beberapa rekan kuliah sering minta Joel melatih bahasa Inggris meréka. Ada yang sudah lancar, ada yang hanya iseng. Pada awalnya, Joel senang mengobrol dengan meréka dalam bahasa Inggris, tetapi kadang-kadang menjadi bosan juga, menjawab pertanyaan yang selalu sama saja. Katanya, "Kapan-kapan saja, ya."

WORDLIST

awal	beginning; early	**membantu**	to assist
Belanda	Dutch	**menarik**	interesting
berasal	to originate	**mengikuti**	to follow
berbéda dengan	to differ from	**mengobrol**	to chat
bosan	sick of it, fed up, bored	**menjawab**	to answer
hanya	only (in front, cf. **saja** after the word concerned)	**menurut**	according to
		pada	in, at
hukum adat	customary law	**pertanyaan**	question
hukum pidana	criminal law	**rajin**	diligent
hukum sipil	civil law	**rencana**	plan
hukum syariah	Islamic law	**sejak**	since (time)
iseng	for fun, not serious	**selama**	for (a period of time)
jaman	era	**sérius**	serious
kolonial	colonial	**sistém**	system
lumayan	not bad, fairly good	**tatahukum**	legal structure
melatih	to practise		

The relative pronoun

Indonesian has an all-purpose relative pronoun: **yang**. This is a word which has several important uses.

The first is to introduce a relative clause, that is, a clause that adds extra information about a noun and contains a verb or adjective. This clause begins with **yang**. This is translated with "who" (for people), or "that" or "which" for things. It is important not to confuse these with the question-words "who?" and "which?" Here are some examples, showing the noun, and the added information introduced by **yang**.

> **… ibu, yang selalu sibuk di dapur**
> mother, who is always busy in the kitchen

> **… jalan, yang kadang-kadang macet**
> the road, which is sometimes blocked

> **… murid-murid, yang senang belajar di gedung baru**
> the pupils, who enjoy studying in the new building.

A second use of **yang** can be found between a noun and its adjective. In this case we do not translate it as a relative pronoun ("who, that, which"); in fact we do not give it a separate translation at all. But it does have a special meaning: it tells us that we have a variety of objects, and we are selecting only the one(s) with the quality indicated by the adjective. Note the difference between the following phrases:

> **pakaian bersih**   clean clothes
> **pakaian yang bersih** (the) clean clothes (among the many)

In the second case, we have a choice out of a range of possibilities: we are selecting only the clean items.

> **jalan sepi**   a quiet street
> **jalan yang sepi** a quiet street (among the many)

We could live anywhere, but I don't want a noisy street. I want a quiet one.

There are two more interesting uses of **yang**, which will be mentioned in again in Lesson 26, but one needs to be noted here: when our sentence begins with a noun, followed by **yang**, this serves to highlight that noun, as in the story above: **Dosén-dosénnya yang membantu**, which should be translated with "It is his lecturers who assist". Clearly, there are no separate words in the Indonesian sentence for "it" or "is" here.

Finally, the idiom **Ada yang…, ada yang** should be translated with "Some…, (and) others…"

Indefinite words

Here are some words which have an indefinite meaning and will prove useful in conversation. Note how they are formed: by full or partial duplication.

> **apa-apa**   anything (with a negative: not anything, = nothing)
> **Tidak apa-apa** it's nothing; it doesn't matter; I don't mind

kapan-kapan	some time (an undefined time in the future), e.g.

Kapan-kapan saya mau ke Bali lagi.   Some time I want to go to Bali again.

sesuatu   something (note the link with **satu** "one"), e.g.

Ada sesuatu yang tidak bérés di sini.   There's something not in order here.

seseorang   someone, e.g.

Ada seseorang mengetok pintu.   There's someone knocking at the door.

beberapa   some, several, a few (not to be confused with **berapa** "how many?"), e.g.

Beberapa minggu (yang) lalu …   A few weeks ago …

A note on *pada*

The word **pada** is a preposition which can be translated with "in", "on" or "at" (depending on the context), sometimes relating to time, e.g.

Pada jam sebelas …	at eleven o'clock
Pada bulan April …	in the month of April, or, as in the story,
Pada awalnya, …	in the beginning,
Pada waktu itu …	at that time,

but also more generally, e.g.

Pada pendapat saya,…   In my opinion…

and following certain words expressing feelings, e.g.

cinta pada …	to be loving toward
benci pada …	to hate

So it is quite different from the words **di** "in, at, on", normally used for location only, and **dalam** "in, within".

A. Pertanyaan untuk bacaan

■ *Bacalah baik-baik isi bacaan lalu cobalah menjawab pertanyaan-pertanyaan di bawah ini!*

1. P: Berapa semester Joel akan belajar di Indonesia?

    J: _____

2. P: Bidang apa yang akan Joel pelajari selama di Jakarta?

    J: _____

3. P: Bahasa apa yang dipakai sebagai bahasa pengantar dalam kuliah Joel?

    J: _____

4. P: Di mana Joel mulai belajar bahasa Indonesia?

    J: _____

5. P: Bagaimana tatahukum Indonesia dibandingkan dengan tatahukum Australia?

    J: _____

6. P: Pengaruh besar dari mana yang ditemukan dalam sistém hukum Indonesia?

    J: _____

7. P: Sebutkan beberapa aspék hukum Indonesia yang tidak ditemukan di sistém hukum dunia Barat.

    J: _____

8. P: Menurut kamu mengapa teman-teman kuliah Joel sering meminta dia untuk berbicara bahasa Inggris kepada meréka?

    J: _____

B. Menyimak

■ *Dengarkan baik-baik isi Tape Latihan 12 lalu jawablah pertanyaan-pertanyaan berikut!*

1. P: Apa alasan Joel untuk belajar hukum di Indonesia selama enam bulan?

    J: _____

2. P: Sejak kapan Joel belajar bahasa Indonesia?

    J: _____

3. P: Siapa yang mendorong Joel untuk meneruskan belajar bahasa Indonesia di universitas?

    J: _____

4. P: Apa yang dia ikuti ketika Joel masih di SMA?

    J: _____

5. P: Mengapa waktu itu sangat berkesan bagi Joel?

    J: _____

6. P: Apakah Joel masih sering berkomunikasi dengan keluarga angkatnya?

    J: _____

7. P: Di mana kota Bandung terletak?

    J: _____

8. P: Kota Bandung juga disebut sebagai apa?

    J: _____

C. Tata bahasa

■ *Menterjemahkan kata 'Yang'*
Terjemahkanlah kalimat-kalimat di bawah ini ke dalam bahasa Inggris yang baik!

1. Nénék, yang selalu sibuk di kebun

    _____

2. Agus, yang kadang-kadang tidak makan di rumah

    _____

3. Ratih, yang senang belajar bahasa asing

    _____

4. Cuaca di Jakarta, yang selalu panas

    _____

5. Bapak Sari, yang selalu pulang malam

    _____

6. Bu Tuti, yang senang menonton sinétron

_____

7. Bu Mar, yang pandai memijat

_____

8. Joel, yang suka sekali bepergian

_____

D. Menulis

■ *Pada jam . . . . (jadwal kegiatan Joel)*

Jadwal kegiatan Joel

Pada jam	Kegiatan
6.00 pagi	Bangun lalu mandi
6.30 pagi	Makan pagi
7.00 pagi	Naik bis ke kampus UI
8.00 pagi – 12.0 siang	Kuliah di Fakultas Hukum
12.30 siang	Makan siang di kantin kampus
1.30 – 2.30 siang	Ke internet kafé
3.00 – 5.00 soré	Berolahraga di kampus

■ *Tulislah satu paragraf tentang kegiatan Joel dengan memakai informasi di atas! (Write down a paragraph about Joel's activities based on the information above!)*

Jadwal kegiatan Joel

Joel bangun pagi pada jam enam. _____

_____

_____

_____

_____

_____

_____

_____

■ *Isilah jadwal kegiatan anda! (Complete your activity!)*

Jadwal kegiatan saya

Pada jam	Kegiatan

■ *Tulislah satu paragraf tentang jadwal kegiatan anda! (Write down a paragraph about your own activity!)*

Jadwal kegiatan saya

Saya bangun pada jam _____

_____

_____

_____

_____

_____

_____

_____

The Poor
Orang Miskin

Sambil berkeliling-keliling di kota, naik taksi atau naik bis, Joel melihat ada banyak gedung yang tinggi dan méwah di pusat kota Jakarta, seperti Menara BCA di Jalan MH Thamrin 1, di sebelah barat Bundaran HI. Dia berpendapat bahwa Indonesia adalah negara berkembang, karena ada banyak perusahaan yang besar-besar.

Tetapi tidak jauh dari situ juga ada daérah kotor dengan sampah bertimbun-timbun, misalnya di tebing sungai Ciliwung. Sampah itu berbau busuk. Rakyat miskin bermukim di bawah jembatan dan di samping rél keréta api, atau bernaung di bawah pohon-pohon besar.

Setelah tiba di kampus, lalu Joel bertanya kepada teman-temannya: "Mengapa pemerintah tidak berbuat apa-apa untuk orang miskin itu?" Jawab meréka: "Ya, mungkin pemerintah menganggap masalah orang jalanan itu terlalu berat. Begitulah nasibnya! Lalu bagaimana di Melbourne? Kami kira, orangnya kaya-kaya semua."

Joel menjawab: "Sebenarnya, di sana juga ada yang tidur di luar, di serambi toko-toko atau berbaring di atas bangku di taman umum, juga pada musim dingin…"

"Ah, masa!"

adalah	is, was	**masa!**	you must be kidding!
bahwa	(conjunction) that	**masalah**	problem, matter
bangku	bench	**mémang**	of course
banyak	many	**menganggap**	to consider, think, regard as
berat	serious; heavy	**méwah**	luxurious
berbaring	to lie	**misalnya**	for example
berbuat	to do	**miskin**	poor
berkeliling-keliling	to keep going around	**musim dingin**	winter
berkembang	developing	**nasib**	fate
berkumpul	to gather, come together	**negara**	country, state
bermukim	to dwell	**orang jalanan**	street people
bernaung	to shelter	**pemerintah**	government
berpendapat	to have the opinion	**perusahaan**	company, business
bertimbun-timbun	to pile up	**pusat**	centre
berusaha	to make an effort	**rakyat**	common people
bis	bus	**rél**	rail, track
busuk	bad, rotten	**sampah**	rubbish, garbage
diri sendiri	themselves	**sambil**	while
jembatan	bridge	**serambi**	porch
kaya	rich	**sungai**	river
kota	city, town	**tebing**	bank (of river)
kotor	dirty	**umum**	public

The prefix *ber-*

This is the first of the verbal prefixes to be described. We have already included several examples. Whenever we come across a word with the prefix **ber-**, we know that the word is a verb, and we also know that it will be intransitive. That is, it does not have an object. This is an important point, because the ability to have an object is related to the question of active and passive forms (which will be dealt with in Lesson 18).

Regarding formation, the prefix **ber-** is found attached to the front of a base-word. The only real complication is when the base-word begins with the letter **r-**; in that case only one r is written, e.g. **rambut** → **berambut** "to have hair". Another point is that when the base-word contains an **r** (in the middle or at the end), we can sometimes see the prefix take the form of **bel-**, e.g.

> **ajar** → **belajar**   to study

As for meaning, it might be useful to observe the kind of base-word involved in the formation of a **ber-**verb: is it a noun, or a verb, or perhaps an adjective? If it is a noun, then we see a meaning of "to have" (whatever the base-word means) — sometimes quite clearly, otherwise only in a very general sense, e.g.

> **bernama** to have a name, to be called; *or* **berumur** to have an age, to be aged

With both of these words, we would expect the meaning of the verb to be completed in some way: a noun following is not an object, but can be termed a complement, thus:

> **Anaknya bernama Freddy.**
> His/her son is named (called) Freddy.
>
> **Dia berumur lima-belas tahun.**
> He is aged fifteen years. (*Or*: He is fifteen years old.)

In other cases, the verb has to be interpreted according to the meaning of the base-word, e.g.

baju (shirt)	→	**berbaju**	to wear a shirt, to have a shirt on
hasil (yield)	›	**berhasil**	to have a (good) result, to succeed
teman (friend)	→	**berteman**	to be friends (with someone, use **dengan**…)

There are some very common **ber-** verbs which have "verbal" base-words. It cannot be said that the prefix has a special meaning — it just has to be there in order to make an acceptable form. Such words are:

berjalan	to go, travel
berangkat	to set out, depart, leave
berbuat	to do, act
bekerja	to work
bertemu	to meet (with, use **dengan**…)
berpikir	to think
berdiri	to stand

Alongside these, there are a few examples where a verb with the prefix **ber-** is found alongside one without, in almost the same meaning: the difference is that the one with **ber-** is more formal. And it is worth noting that the prefix **ber-** is often omitted in colloquial Indonesian.

There are more kinds of verb which have the prefix **ber-**, but then in combination with a suffix. These have particular meanings, and are all intransitive. They will be discussed in Lesson 24.

A note on *adalah* and *ialah*

In Lesson 1 we said that there is no separate word for "is" ("are", etc.) in Indonesian between subject and predicate ("this is that"). And now the exceptions. Especially in longer sentences, it is sometimes felt necessary to insert a word showing clearly the link. This word is **adalah** ("is", "was"), as we see in the story above. The word **ialah** is the same, except that it is found only after third-person subjects.

LATIHAN 13 EXERCISE 13

Orang Miskin
The Poor

A. Pertanyaan untuk bacaan

■ *Jawablah pertanyaan-pertanyaan di bawah ini berdasarkan isi bacaan!*

1. P: Joel naik apa ketika dia berkeliling kota Jakarta?

   J: _____

2. P: Apa saja yang dilihatnya?

   J: _____

3. P: Apa pendapat Joel tentang Negara Indonesia?

   J: _____

4. P: Apa yang dilihat Joel di sekitar sungai Ciliwung?

   J: _____

5. P: Siapa yang tinggal dan hidup di daérah yang kotor itu?

   J: _____

6. P: Menurut kamu bagaimana perasaan Joel ketika dia melihat kondisi orang-orang miskin tersebut?

   J: _____

7. P: Apakah menurut bacaan ini pemerintah Indonesia sudah berbuat sesuatu untuk membantu orang-orang miskin itu?

   J: _____

8. P: Apakah ada orang miskin di negera seperti Australia?

   J: _____

B. Menyimak

■ *Simaklah baik-baik isi Tape Latihan 13 lalu cobalah menjawab pertanyaan-pertanyaan di bawah ini!*

1. P: Mengapa banyak orang yang kurang suka berjalan kaki di kota Jakarta?

   J: _____

2. P: Apakah pemerintah lokal Jakarta sudah mencoba mengatasi masalah polusi udara?

   J: _____

3. P: Apa penyebab utama polusi udara di kota Jakarta?

   J: _____

4. P: Bcrapa kira-kira jumlah penduduk Jakarta?

   J: _____

5. P: Mengapa banyak orang ingin pergi dan hidup di Jakarta?

   J: _____

6. P: Mengapa banyak orang yang pergi ke Jakarta kemudian mengalami kesulitan hidup secara ekonomi enggan untuk pulang ke tempat asalnya?

   J: _____

7. P: Apakah kota-kota besar di dunia menghadapi persoalan yang sama seperti Jakarta?

   J: _____

C. Tata bahasa

■ *Awalan **Ber-** (prefix **Ber-**)*
   *Tulislah kata dasar dari kata yang berawalan **Ber-** di bawah ini!*

No	Kata	Kata dasar
1. (CONTOH/EXAMPLE)	Berjalan	Jalan
2.	Berbaring	
3.	Berkembang	
4.	Berkumpul	
5.	Bermukim	
6.	Berpendapat	
7.	Berusaha	
8.	Bernaung	
9.	Berkeliling	
10.	Bertanya	
11.	Berlari	
12.	Bernama	

No	Kata	Kata dasar
13.	Berteman	
14.	Berbaju	
15.	Berdiri	
16.	Bertemu	
17.	Berpikir	
18.	Berumur	
19.	Berenang	
20.	Bersepeda	
21.	Beruang	
22.	Berbau	
23.	Berbaring	
24.	Bersepatu	

D. Menterjemahkan

■ *Terjemahkanlah kalimat-kalimat di bawah ini ke dalam bahasa Inggris!*

1. In: Joel suka berenang di hari Minggu.

   Eng: _____

2. In: Sampah-sampah yang banyak di sekitar Jakarta berbau menyengat.

   Eng: _____

3. In: Bersepéda adalah olahraga yang baik untuk keséhatan jantung.

   Eng: _____

4. In: Sari bercita-cita untuk berkeliling dunia sesudah lulus univérsitas.

   Eng: _____

5. In: Banyak orang miskin yang berbaring di halte bis di malam hari.

   Eng: _____

E. Mencocokkan

■ *Cocokkan kata bagian (A) dengan kata atau konsep yang berhubungan di bagian (B)!*

A.	B.
1. berbaring	a. olahraga
2. berlari	b. tidur
3. berbau	c. kaya
4. berpikir	d. tinggal
5. berbelanja	e. otak
6. bermukim	f. diskusi
7. berenang	g. telanjang
8. berbaju	h. sahabat
9. bertanya	i. pandai
10. berumur	j. jawab
11. belajar	k. pergi
12. berpendapat	l. sedap
13. berteman	m. putar
14. bersepatu	n. tua
15. beruang	o. beli
16. berkeliling	p. air
17. berangkat	q. tumbuh
18. berambut	r. kepala
19. berkembang	s. kaki

F. Negara dan Nama ibu kota

■ *Cocokkan negara (A) dan nama ibu kota (B) dengan menarik garis panjang!*

A. Negara	**B. Nama ibu kota**
1. Malaysia	a. Madrid
2. Turki	b. Moskow
3. Cina	c. Tokyo
4. Amerika Serikat	d. Oslo
5. Australia	e. Beijing
6. Perancis	f. Pretoria
7. Italia	g. Manila
8. Spanyol	h. Jakarta
9. Afrika Selatan	i. Angkara
10. Denmark	j. Washington DC
11. Polandia	k. Kairo
12. Rusia	l. Canberra
13. Norwegia	m. London
14. Pilipina	n. Paris
15. Indonesia	o. Kuala Lumpur
16. Mesir	p. Roma
17. Jepang	q. Warsawa
18. Korea Selatan	r. Seoul
19. Inggris	s. Dublin
20. Irlandia	t. Kopenhagen
21. Kenya	u. Nairobi

LESSON 14

Smoking
Merokok

Di perempatan jalan sering ada orang yang menjual rokok. Kalau lampu mérah menyala dan lalu lintas berhenti, meréka lari-lari lalu menawarkan barangnya. Méreknya bermacam-macam. Misalnya, ada Gudang Garam Mérah. Isinya 12 batang sebungkus. Harga sebung-kus kira-kira Rp 7.500. Ada juga Gudang Garam Internasional Mérah, dengan mottonya "Priya Punya Seléra". Dalam satu slof ada 10 bungkus. Rokok filter dan rokok luar negeri pasti lebih mahal.

Di Indonesia masih banyak orang yang merokok. Suatu hari Joel dan temannya, Hanafi, duduk-duduk di luar. Hanafi menyulut sebatang rokok. Lalu Joel berkata, "Di tempat saya, ada larangan merokok di dalam gedung univérsitas dan di sekitarnya. Katanya, kurang séhat." Hanafi adalah perokok berat. Dia sering batuk-batuk. Hanafi menjawab: "Sebe-narnya saya sependapat dengan kamu. Tetapi habis belajar ingin menikmati harumnya, ka-lau asap tembakau mengepul di udara soré seperti ini…" Dan Hanafi masih batuk-batuk.

WORDLIST

asap	smoke	**menikmati**	to enjoy (on the suffix **-i**, see Lesson 17)
barang	wares, goods		
batuk-batuk	to keep on coughing	**menjual**	to sell
berhenti	to stop	**menyala**	to shine, be on (light)
berkata	to say	**menyulut**	to light up
bermacam-macam	of various sorts	**mérek**	brand, make
		perempatan	crossroads, intersection
bungkus	packet	**perokok**	smoker
habis	after finishing	**priya**	man
harum	aroma, fragrance	**priya punya**	men's (N.B. colloquial or sub-standard)
isi	contents		
katanya	they say	**rokok**	cigarette
lampu mérah	traffic lights	**seléra**	taste
larangan	ban, prohibition	**slof**	carton (of cigarettes)
lari-lari	to come running	**suatu**	a certain, one
menawarkan	to offer (for sale)	**tembakau**	tobacco
mengepul	to rise in clouds	**tempat**	place

CULTURAL NOTE

While smoking may be in decline in some other parts of the world, it still thrives in Indonesia. We think of the famous **kréték** cigarette, for example those made at the Gudang Garam factory in Kediri, East Java, set up by Tjoa Ing Hwie in 1958 and employing many thousands of workers. These cigarettes produce the characteristic aroma of cloves (**cengkéh**) and spices mixed in the tobacco. This is much appreciated and is quite different from Western cigarettes. Smoking can be said to have a social function, for example when men sit down to relax and have a chat, and it is the custom to provide cigarettes for guests as part of one's hospitality.

LANGUAGE NOTES

Classifiers

Indonesian uses a small number of words termed "classifiers" to indicate the number of certain objects; they are common for one or low numbers. As the term suggests, they "classify" or group the noun concerned. The classifier is preceded by the number and followed by the noun. The commonest classifiers are:

orang "human being" for people, e.g.

seorang guru a teacher (lit. "one human being of teachers")

ékor "tail" for animals, e.g.

dua ékor kambing two goats (lit. "two tail of goats", cf. English "head of cattle")

buah "fruit" for largish, inanimate objects, e.g.

dua buah rumah two houses

biji "seed" for small, round objects, e.g.

tiga biji telur three eggs

batang "cylinder" for long, round objects, e.g.

sepuluh batang rokok ten cigarettes

helai "sheet" for thin objects, e.g.

sehelai sapu tangan a handkerchief

You should look out for more such words when you start reading Indonesian prose.

The prefix se-

In some of the examples above we see the prefix **se-**. It also occurs in the numerals **sepuluh** ten, **seratus** one hundred, and **seribu** one thousand. So it means "one" or "a". It is found in this meaning with other words that measure quantities, e.g.

sekilo a kilo: **sekilo beras** or **beras sekilo** a kilo of rice
seliter a liter: **seliter bénsin** or **bénsin seliter** a liter of petrol/gas

Seeing that **se-** means "one", we could also say **satu** kilo or **satu** liter to stress "one", not two or some other number.

Other words indicating quantities or numbers refer to containers (e.g. **bungkus** "packet"); to time (e.g. **jam** "hour"); distance (e.g. **méter** "metres"); natural groups (e.g. **kawan** "herd"), and so on. A very useful one is **semacam** "a kind of", e.g. **semacam séndok besar** "a kind of big spoon".

The prefix **se-** has several other important functions that can be mentioned here:

"-ly" with expressions of time, e.g. **tiga kali seminggu** three time a week/weekly; **dua kali sebulan** twice monthly

"whole", e.g. **seisi** the whole contents; **seAsia** pan-Asia; **sekitar** around, surrounding

"of the same", e.g. **serupa** similar, of the same appearance; **semasa** contemporary, of the same time; **seumur** of the same age; **setempat** local, from the same place; **sekelas** in the same class; **sependapat** of the same opinion

"as... as", with an adjective, in comparisons, e.g. **sebesar gunung** as big as a mountain; **setinggi langit** as high as the sky

"to the amount of", e.g. **cék sebesar 1000 dolar** a cheque to the amount of (for) $1,000; **selama seminggu** for a week

"as far as", with a verb, e.g. **setahu saya** as far as I know; **seingat saya** as far as I remember

"in accordance with", in particular with the word **secara** in a ... manner, e.g. **secara resmi** officially (lit. "in an official way"); **secara tertulis** written (not oral) (lit. "in a written way")

"after, upon", with certain verbs, e.g. **setibanya di Semarang** when she arrived in Semarang...; **sepulangnya dari luar negeri** when he got back from overseas...

The prefix se- with suffix -nya

The following forms can be regarded as adverbs. They are all useful for conversation.

sebenarnya	in fact, actually
sebaiknya	ought to, better, preferably
seharusnya	should have (but didn't)
semaunya	at will, as one likes, randomly, arbitrarily

But with doubling of an adjective base-word we find the meaning of "at the …-est", e.g.

kurang	→	**sekurang-kurangnya**	at the least
banyak	→	**sebanyak-banyaknya**	at the most
cepat	→	**secepat-cepatnya**	at the quickest, as quickly as possible

At the Table

Seeing that one is very likely to be invited to a home for a meal, or perhaps to eat together at a restaurant, there are a few things to bear in mind.

Rice is normally the main part of the meal. This will be served first. It is good manners to invite others to take some first; then take a spoonful and put it in the middle of your plate. The other dishes are termed "side dishes", because they accompany the rice. We take a little from the big dish or bowl and put it next to the rice, and then pass it on.

Indonesians use a spoon and fork. One's own spoon never goes in the common dish. It's okay to use fingers for something difficult like a chicken wing!

For passing and receiving we use the right hand; we never touch our food with the left hand.

If you're not used to hot food, be careful of the chilis. There will probably be some chili sauce on a separate little dish, but any food with a red colour is likely to be hot. But paradoxically the tiny green chilis are the hottest of all. If you get into trouble, the heat can be soothed with plain rice, or banana, or cucumber.

As for meats, you may find beef, chicken, or even goat, but never pork in Muslim areas. The food is termed **halal** if it is permitted, that is, contains nothing not allowed by Islamic custom.

When you've finished eating, place your spoon and fork together on the plate; if the spoon is turned down, it means you don't want any more.

And as for drinks with the meal, tea is a safe bet, as it has been boiled. This will be served in a glass, with a coaster and lid; it may have sugar in it, but never milk. Never drink water straight from the tap, or you may have a problem.

Javanese or Balinese coffee is excellent, with a snack in the afternoon, for instance.

Merokok
Smoking

A. Pertanyaan untuk bacaan

■ *Jawablah pertanyaan-pertanyaan berikut ini sesuai dengan isi bacaan!*

1. P: Siapa yang sering kita jumpai di jalan-jalan besar di Indonesia?

    J: _____

2. P: Di mana dan kapan orang-orang itu sibuk mencoba menjual dagangannya?

    J: _____

3. P: Sebutkan contoh mérek rokok yang banyak dijual di Indonesia.

    J: _____

4. P: Apa artinya ungkapan 'Pria Punya Selera'?

    J: _____

5. P: Siapa kebanyakan yang merokok di Indonesia?

    J: _____

6. P: Siapa itu teman Indonesia Joel yang senang merokok?

    J: _____

7. P: Apakah menurut kamu dia seharusnya berhenti merokok? Mengapa?

    J: _____

8. P: Apa alasan teman Joel masih merokok? Jelaskan!

    J: _____

B. Menyimak

■ *Simaklah isi Tape Latihan 14 dengan baik dan jawablah pertanyaan-pertanyaan di bawah ini!*

1. P: Di mana saja kita bisa menjumpai iklan rokok di Indonesia?

    J: _____

2. P: Siapa yang menjadi targét utama iklan rokok?

    J: _____

3. P: Apa alasan merokok menurut teman-teman mahasiswa Joel dari universitas?

    J: _____

4. P Penyakit apa saja yang bisa menjadi risiko merokok? Sebutkan!

    J: _____

5. P: Apa yang dimaksud dengan 'perokok pasif"?

    J: _____

6. P: Apa yang dianggap kurang dilakukan di Indonesia yang berkaitan dengan kebiasaan merokok?

    J: _____

7. P: Siapa yang bertanggung jawab untuk mendidik masyarakat tentang bahaya merokok?

    J: _____

C. Mencocokkan

■ *Cocokkan slogan di bagian B dengan produk iklan di bagian A!*

A.

a. Rokok
b. Sampo
c. Obat sakit kepala
d. Pasta gigi
e. Kamus
f. Sepéda motor

g. Tusuk Jarum
h. Tablét pelangsing tubuh
i. Es Krim
j. Internet café
k. Toko bunga
l. Réstoran India

B.

1. _____

    Ingin rambut yang berkilau dan selembut sutra?

2. _____

    Rasa pening hilang seketika!

3. _____

    Menyejukkan dan menyegarkan mulut anda!

4. _____

    Menawarkan seléra oténtik India

5. _____

    Edisi terbaru dengan lebih dari 200 ribu kata dan dilengkapi gambar!

6. _____

Tanpa diet! Tanpa olahraga berat! Hanya dalam waktu 6 bulan Anda akan mendapatkan tubuh idéal!

7. _____

Alternatif pengobatan yang aman dengan jarum

8. _____

Rasa kelapa, coklat, vanili, mangga……semua rasa ada!

9. _____

Ungkapkan rasa dengan bunga

10. _____

Hanya Rp.4000 per jam dengan fasilitas komputer terbaru

D. Tata bahasa

■ *Carilah kata benda (nomina) sebanyak mungkin di dalam kotak-kotak di bawah ini dan tulis-lah di tempat yang disediakan beserta terjemahannya dalam bahasa Inggris.*

F	I	L	E	M	N	A	R	O	K
K	I	M	O	K		I	P	O	K
A	S	E	P	A	T	U	K	C	E
R	M	S	Y	I	P	O	T	O	R
T	O	K	E	U	R	O	P	K	A
U	B	R	L	P	A	L	U	L	N
J	I	I	G	E	A	S	A	A	J
A	L	M	N	N	U	T	K	T	A
B	A	B	A	A	A	N	U	I	N
J	P	M	U	S	I	K	E	W	G

Indonesian		English
1. _____	=	_____
2. _____	=	_____
3. _____	=	_____
4. _____	=	_____
5. _____	=	_____
6. _____	=	_____
7. _____	=	_____
8. _____	=	_____
9. _____	=	_____
10. _____	=	_____
11. _____	=	_____
12. _____	=	_____

LESSON 15

The "Taman Mini"
Taman Mini

Sari sudah tahu[1] bahwa Joel akan merayakan hari ulang tahunnya. Menjelang harinya, Sari bertanya kepada ayahnya: "Bagaimana kalau kita mengajaknya main-main ke Taman Mini, Pak? Setahu saya, Joel belum pernah ke sana."

Ayah Sari: "Ya, mémang banyak turis suka ke sana. Tapi si Joel sebenarnya bukan turis…"

Sari: "Namun pasti menarik untuk dia juga, Pak!"

Tepat pada waktunya, meréka menjemput Joel naik mobil ke TMII, lengkapnya Taman Mini Indonesia Indah. Dalam perjalanan ke Jakarta Timur, sambil bergelut dengan lalu lintas, ayah Sari bercerita:

"Pada tahun 1970 Bu Tien[2] Suharto mendapat idé membangun taman itu, sebagai semacam paméran, terutama untuk arsitéktur, kesenian dan kehidupan sehari-hari dari semua propinsi Indonesia. Lalu Taman Mini dibuka tahun 1973. Pada jaman itu ada 26 propinsi – sekarang jumlahnya sudah bertambah!"

Setiba meréka di Taman Mini, tempat parkir sudah hampir penuh. Ongkos parkir untuk mobil sebesar Rp 10.000. Joel terhéran-héran melihat bangunan yang tepat serupa dengan rumah-rumah asli, masing-masing dengan papan nama dalam bahasa Indonesia dan Inggris, misalnya "Sumatera Barat, West Sumatera" di depan rumah adat Minangkabau. Pikir Joel pasti mahal membangun TMII.

Ayah Sari menerangkan: "Istilah bahasa Indonesia untuk bangunan macam ini ialah anjungan. Inggrisnya 'pavilion', bukan?"

Joel: "Ya benar, Pak, saya mengerti."

Meréka naik keréta gantung, lalu menonton tari-tarian dari daerah Riau. Haus sekali! Nah, di mana mencari minuman yang tidak terlalu mahal?

---

1   Note on pronunciation: in the word **tahu** "to know" the *h* is silent; if it is sounded, we get the meaning "bean curd" (with the same spelling).

2   Pronounced like "teen", not "ti-en".

WORDLIST

ajak: mengajak	to invite	**lengkap**	complete, in full
arsitéktur	architecture	**main-main**	to go out and have fun
asli	original	**masing-masing**	each one
bangun:	to build, set up	**maka**	and so
membangun		**namun**	even so
bangunan	building	**paméran**	exhibition
begitu	so	**papan nama**	sign, board
benar	right	**parkir**	parking
bertambah	to increase, grow in number	**propinsi**	province
bergelut	to wrestle, struggle	**raya: merayakan**	to celebrate
cari: mencari	to find, look for	**rumah adat**	traditional house
dalam perjalanan	on the way	**sebagai**	as (in the capacity of)
dapat: mendapat	to get	**sehari-hari**	daily
dari	from; (also sometimes) of	**si**	"our", "old" (familiar particle before a name)
dibuka	opened (N.B. a passive verb with prefix **di-**)	**tari-tarian**	dances
erti: mengerti	to understand	**tempat parkir**	parking area
haus	thirsty	**tepat**	exact, exactly
idé	idea	**terang:**	to explain, clarify (N.B. suffix **-kan**, see Lesson 16)
indah	beautiful	**menerangkan**	
jelang: menjelang	to approach (time)	**tonton: menonton**	to watch
jemput:	to fetch, go and get	**turis**	tourist
menjemput			
kagum	amazed, astonished		
kebudayaan	culture		
kehidupan	life		
kepada	to		
keréta gantung	cable car		
kesenian	art		

LANGUAGE NOTES

Verbs with the prefix *meN-*

We have already seen a number of verbs of this type. This is a very common form for Indonesian verbs to take: the prefix **me-** combined with a nasal sound (**N**). This sound (**ng, m, n, ny**) either comes in front of the base-word, or replaces its initial consonant according to certain rules, as will be shown in the table next page. It is essential to be able to "deconstruct" **meN-** verbs to find their base-word, so that one can use a dictionary, as good dictionaries list derived forms under the base-word. This system has the advantage that you can see all existing derived forms listed together, rather than spread over different pages. From here on, our Wordlists will use this method.

Verbs formed this way are normally transitive and active. In other words, they are verbs which can have an object, and are found in the sentence pattern:

subject–**meN**-verb–object

This means that they are active verbs, not passive. With the passive (which will be discussed in Lesson 18), we find a different form of the verb, and a different sentence pattern. Having said this, it is true that there exist a small number of **meN-** verbs which are intransitive, that is, cannot have an object, and therefore have no passive. There are also a great number of **meN-** verbs which feature a suffix **-kan** or **-i**. These will be treated separately, in Lessons 16 and 17.

The following table shows how verbs are formed from their base-word:

Initial letter of the base-word	Form of the prefix meN-
any vowel, h, g, kh	**meng-**
r, l, y, w	**me-**
m, n, ny, ng	**me-**
k	**me-, ng** replaces **k**
p	**me-, m** replaces **p**
s	**me-, ny** replaces **s**
t	**me-, n** replaces **t**
d, c, j, z	**men-**
b, f, v	**mem-**

Here are some examples of how this works.

Base-words beginning with:

Any vowel	**ambil**	→	**mengambil**	to take
h	**hambat**	→	**menghambat**	to delay, obstruct
g	**ganggu**	→	**mengganggu**	to annoy, bother
r	**rasa**	→	**merasa**	to feel
l	**langgar**	→	**melanggar**	to transgress
m	**mérah**	→	**memérah**	to become red
n	**nikah**	→	**menikah**	to marry
k	**kenal**	→	**mengenal**	to know, recognize, be familiar with
p	**pilih**	→	**memilih**	to choose
s	**suruh**	→	**menyuruh**	to order, command
t	**tulis**	→	**menulis**	to write
d	**dapat**	→	**mendapat**	to get, obtain
c	**cari**	→	**mencari**	to look for
j	**jadi**	→	**menjadi**	to become
b	**bawa**	→	**membawa**	to carry, take

In the above list, **memérah** and **menjadi** are intransitive verbs (cannot have an object).

There are a few ambiguous cases, where you may have to look in two places in the dictionary to find a word. For example, if you come across the word **mengurus**, is the base-word **urus** or **kurus**? (In the first case, it would mean "to arrange", and in the second "to become thinner", so which one fits your context?)

Unfortunately, there are a few exceptions and unusual cases that should be noted:

a) With loanwords adopted from English or Dutch the rules may not apply, e.g.

prakték	→	**memprakténkan**	to put into practice
sistématik	→	**mensistématikkan**	to systematize

b) Other words where the same can be seen are:

punya	→	**mempunyai**	to possess
pengaruh	→	**mempengaruhi**	to influence

(The prefix **memper-** will be mentioned in Lesson 16.)

c) Monosyllabic base-words may cause problems:

sah → **mengesahkan** or **mensahkan**   to legalize, authorize

d) Some more odd cases:

tahu	→	**mengetahui**	to find out
terjemah	→	**menerjemahkan** or **menterjemahkan** to translate

With **makan** "to eat" and **minum** "to drink" a prefix **me-** is not normally found. And in Jakarta dialect, the rules of nasalization are different: **me-** is not used.

Pronoun objects

When a **meN-** verb (with or without a suffix) has an object which is a personal pronoun, this can be expressed in the form of a suffix, that is, be attached to the verb, with forms for each person, thus:

1st person pronoun **aku** "I": object **-ku** "me"
2nd person pronoun **kamu** "you": object **-mu** "you"
3rd person pronoun **dia** "he, she": object **-nya** "him, her". Also "it", e.g.:

mempelajari "to study" (transitive) → **mempelajarinya** to study it

Note that these suffixes, despite the fact that they may look the same, are not to be confused with the possessive suffixes **-ku**, **-mu** and **-nya**. These pronoun objects can only occur when the verb has the **meN-** prefix, and only refer to the pronouns mentioned.

LATIHAN 15 EXERCISE 15

Taman Mini
The "Taman Mini"

A. Pertanyaan untuk bacaan

■ *Bacalah baik-baik isi bacaan lalu cobalah menjawab pertanyaan-pertanyaan di bawah ini!*

1. P: Siapa yang akan berulang tahun dan ada apa?

   J: _____

2. P: Apa singkatan TMII? Di mana letak TMII?

   J: _____

3. P: Siapa yang mempelopori dibangunnya TMII?

   J: _____

4. P: Apa sebenarnya tujuan TMII?

   J: _____

5. P: Berapa jumlah propinsi Indonesia pada tahun 70an?

   J: _____

6. P: Berapa jumlah propinsi di Indonesia sekarang?

   J: _____

7. P: Bagaimana perasaan Joel ketika dia tiba di TMII?

   J: _____

8. P: Apa artinya 'anjungan' dan kata itu dipakai untuk apa di TMII menurut kamu?

   J: _____

9. P: Apa saja yang bisa kita temui di TMII?

   J: _____

10. P: Menurut pendapatmu mengapa ada keréta gantung di TMII?

    J: _____

B. Menyimak

■ *Simaklah baik-baik Tape Latihan 15 dan jawablah pertanyaan-pertanyaan berikut!*

1. P: Mengapa Sari ingin sekali mengajak Joel untuk melihat Taman Mini?

   J: _____

2. P: Menurut bapak Sari siapa yang suka mengunjungi Taman Mini?

   J: _____

3. P: Apa artinya ungkapan 'Bhinneka Tunggal Ika'?

   J: _____

4. P: Apa yang bisa dilihat dari keréta gantung di Taman Mini?

   J: _____

5. P: Di zaman pemerintahan Suharto siapa yang sering mengunjungi Taman Mini?

   J: _____

6. P: Ceritakan apa yang dikatakan oléh para pengritik keberadaan Taman Mini?

   J: _____

7. P: Bagaimana Taman Mini sekarang ini?

   J: _____

8. P: Aspék apa yang dianggap menarik oléh Joel dari idé pembangunan Taman Mini?

   J: _____

C. Mencocokkan

■ *Cocokkan nama tempat wisata terkenal (A) dengan negara (B).*

A.	B.
1. Air terjun Niagara	a. Yunani
2. Témbok Besar	b. Kanada
3. Candi Borobudur	c. Indonesia
4. Menara Pisa	d. Perancis
5. Makam Taj Mahal	e. Cina
6. Piramida Spink	f. India
7. Parthenon	g. Tanzania
8. Disney World	h. Amerika
9. Menara Eifel	i. Italia
10. Opera House	j. Inggris
11. Gunung Kilimanjaro	k. Indonesia
12. Danau Toba	l. Mesir
13. Loncéng Big Ben	m. Australia

D. Pertanyaan umum (Kuis)

■ *Jawablah pertanyaan-pertanyaan di bawah ini dengan singkat!*

1. P: Apa nama ibu kota Rusia?

   J: _____

2. P: Di mana kota Sao Paolo berada?

   J: _____

3. P: Siapa nama présidén Amerika sekarang ini?

   J: _____

4. P: Di negara mana féstival melémpar tomat diadakan?

   J: _____

5. P: Apa nama mata uang Singapura?

   J: _____

6. P: Di mana Hollywood berada?

   J: _____

7. P: Di mana Bollywood berada?

   J: _____

8. P: Dari mana beruang Panda berasal?

   J: _____

9. P: Apa makanan beruang Panda?

   J: _____

10. P: Sebutkan paling tidak tiga binatang asli Australia

    J: _____

11. P: Di mana Alaska terletak?

    J: _____

12. P: Di negara mana kota Berlin berada?

    J: _____

13. P: Apa bahasa nasional negara Selandia Baru?

    J: _____

14. P: Di mana bahasa Tagalog dipakai?

   J: _____

15. P: Di mana bahasa Jawa digunakan?

   J: _____

16. P: Tanaman apa yang terkenal dan berasal dari Meksiko?

   J: _____

17. P: Di mana negara Kenya berada?

   J: _____

18. P: Apa makanan pokok orang Indonesia?

   J: _____

19. P: Dari mana agama Shinto berasal?

   J: _____

20. P: Apa nama ibu kota Amerika?

   J: _____

21. P: Di mana kota Manila berada?

   J: _____

22. P: Kelompok musik Beatles berasal dari?

   J: _____

23. P: Kembang api berasal dari negara mana?

   J: _____

24. P: Apa nama negara yang berpenduduk paling besar di dunia?

   J: _____

25. P: Berapa kira-kira jumlah penduduk di Indonesia?

   J: _____

26. P: Berapa kira-kira jumlah penduduk di negara Anda?

   J: _____

E. Menulis

■ *Tulislah satu alinea (paragraf) untuk menjelaskan tempat-tempat wisata terkenal di bawah ini!*

1. Disney World

   _____

   _____

   _____

   _____

   _____

2. Haw Par Villa

   _____

   _____

   _____

   _____

   _____

3. Mount Fuji

   _____

   _____

   _____

   _____

   _____

4. Taj Mahal

   _____

   _____

   _____

   _____

   _____

TV Dramas
Sinétron

Pada saat Joel tiba di rumah, sudah léwat jam 9. Kebetulan ibu kosnya, Bu Tuti, sedang asyik menonton sinétron kesayangannya, *Cinta Fitri*, yang ditayangkan oleh SCTV setiap hari pada jam 21.00 WIB. Fitri adalah gadis berusia 19 tahun, berasal dari désa Wonogiri. Firman, calon suaminya, telah meninggal dunia. Lalu Fitri tinggal di Jakarta dan mengalami peristiwa-peristiwa yang menyedihkan.

Bu Tuti mengajak Joel ikut menonton, karena dia yakin Joel akan tertarik pada cerita tentang orang-orang kaya di Indonesia. Tokoh wanita sering menangis, lalu ada tokoh pria yang pandai menenangkannya. Alur cerita bergerak pelan-pelan, tetapi Joel tetap kurang mengerti jalannya. Masing-masing adegan terus-menerus diiringi musik yang mengharukan. Selalu ada masalah yang rumit.

Yang paling menarik bagi Joel, sebagai orang yang pernah mempelajari bahasa, ialah cara tokoh-tokoh berbicara: penuh émosi, berbicara cepat-cepat, dan memakai kata-kata dari bahasa percakapan sehari-hari, misalnya, "Aku pasti bantuin kamu", dan "Aku nggak apa-apa kok". Jelas ada gaya bahasa khusus untuk drama macam ini. Joel ingin menanyakan kepada Bu Tuti mengapa tokoh-tokoh selalu memakai kata "aku", bukan "saya", tetapi Joel tidak mau mengganggunya. "Lain kali saja", pikirnya.

WORDLIST

adegan	scene (of story)	**émosi**	emotion, feeling
alam: mengalami	to experience	**gadis**	girl
alur cerita	plot (of story)	**ganggu: mengganggu**	to disturb, bother
bagi	for	**gaya**	style
bantuin = membantu	to help	**haru: mengharukan**	touching, moving
berbicara	to speak	**ibu kos**	landlady
bergerak	to move	**jalan**	course, where it is going
berusia	aged	**kebetulan**	as it happened
calon	prospective	**khusus**	specific, particular
cara	manner	**lain kali**	some other time
diiringi	accompanied by	**musik**	music
ditayangkan	presented, shown	**nggak = tidak**	not

oléh	by	**suami**	husband
pakai: memakai	to use	**tangis: menangis**	to cry
pandai	clever	**tanya: menanyakan**	to ask about
pasti	certainly	**tenang: menenang-**	to calm, soothe
pelajar: mempelajari	to study	**kan**	
pelan-pelan	slowly	**tentang**	about, concerning
percakapan	conversation	**tertarik**	interested
peristiwa	event, incident	**terus-menerus**	continually
pria	male	**tiba**	to arrive
rumit	complicated	**tinggal: meninggal**	to pass away
saat	moment	**dunia**	
sedih: menyedihkan	saddening	**tokoh**	character
setiap	every	**wanita**	female
sewaktu-waktu	from time to time	**yakin**	sure, convinced
sinétron	TV series, soap opera		

LANGUAGE NOTES

Verbs with the suffix -*kan*

As mentioned earlier, verbs with the prefix **meN-** can also have a suffix, either **-kan** or **-i**. We will deal with the first in this lesson. We should stress that the purpose of the discussion is to help identifying the meaning of a given verb and getting an accurate feeling for its place in relation to the other words in a sentence. This is why we analyze words in terms of their base-word and affixes—we are not inviting anybody to make up forms for themselves!

When we see the suffix **-kan** we know for sure that we are dealing with a transitive verb, even if the object is not expressed. (There is one case which looks like an exception, see below.) For the sake of clarity, we can group the **-kan** verbs under several paragraphs.

1. In this group we can place a large number of verbs which have the suffix **-kan** merely in order to be complete and correct; in this sense, the suffix cannot be said to have a special "meaning". Examples:

		CONTRAST	
mengerjakan	to work on (something)	**bekerja**	to work
(base-word: **kerja**)			
membutuhkan	to need		
membicarakan	to discuss (something)	**berbicara**	to discuss [INTRANSITIVE]
memikirkan	to think about (something)	**berpikir**	to think
(base-word: **pikir**)			

2. In this group we can place verbs where a form with suffix **-kan** and one without can be contrasted with each other, each with a different translation, the form with **-kan** showing a more "transitive" effect on the object. Sometimes there is very little difference in practice. Examples:

		CONTRAST	
mengirimkan	to send off, dispatch	**mengirim**	to send
(base-word: **kirim**)			

			CONTRAST	
mendengarkan	to listen to		**mendengar**	to hear
membacakan	to read aloud, recite		**membaca**	to read
mendapatkan	to obtain, procure		**mendapat**	to get
menekankan	stress		**menekan**	to press down,
(base-word: **tekan**)				to hold back

3. One of the major areas of meaning associated with certain **-kan** verbs is "causative", that is, to bring about the action indicated by the base-word. Examples:

		CONTRAST	
mengadakan	to organize, create, make	**ada**	to be, to be there
meninggalkan	to leave behind	**tinggal**	to stay, stay behind
menjatuhkan	to drop, let somcthing fall	**jatuh**	to fall
mengembalikan	to return, send back	**kembali**	to go back
menaikkan	to raise	**naik**	to go up
menurunkan	to lower, reduce	**turun**	to go down
mendirikan	to set up, establish	**berdiri**	to stand
menghentikan	to stop (something)	**berhcnti**	to stop

4. The same causative meaning, but this time with an adjective as base-word, so "to bring about the quality indicated by the base-word". Examples:

membersihkan	to clean (cf. **bersih** clean)
mengeringkan	to dry (something) (cf. **kering** dry)
mematikan	to turn off, extinguish (e.g. a light) (cf. **mati** dead; out)

The above must have an object, but there are some interesting forms with adjectives as base-words that do not have objects; in fact they themselves behave like adjectives, in that they can be modified by adverbs, e.g. **sekali** "very". Examples:

menghérankan	amazing (cf. **héran** amazed)
membosankan	boring (cf. **bosan** bored)
menjijikkan	nauseating (cf. **jijik** nauseated)
menakutkan	frightening (cf. **takut** frightened)
memalukan	embarrassing (cf. **malu** embarrassed, ashamed)
menyenangkan	pleasing (cf. **senang** pleased, happy)

5. Another kind of "causative" meaning is "to have someone do something". These **-kan** verbs contrast with a simple transitive verb. Examples:

		CONTRAST	
mencucikan	to have (something) washed	**mencuci**	to wash
mencétakkan	to have (something) printed	**mencétak**	to print
meminjamkan	to lend (= have borrow)	**meminjam**	to borrow
(base-word: **pinjam**)			

memeriksakan to have examined, i.e. take to the doctor   **memeriksa** to examine
(base-word: **periksa**)

6. Another major area of meaning sometimes associated with **-kan** verbs is the "benefactive", that is, to do something for the benefit of someone else. Verbs of this kind have two objects, the first being the person for whom the action is done, and the second the thing to which it applies. (This has important consequences for a passive form.) An English example may help: "Bring me a glass of water". Here the idea is "for me". It is sometimes possible to omit the beneficiary, and still keep the benefactive meaning. Further, such a benefactive meaning is only found when the verb is not normally required to have **-kan**, either to be correct or to give a causative meaning; in that case the idea of "for" has to be expressed with the preposition **untuk** "for, on behalf of". Examples:

		CONTRAST	
mencarikan	to look for (something) for somebody	**mencari**	to look for
membukakan	to open (something) for somebody	**membuka**	to open

Finally, please note that verbs with the suffix **-kan** can sometimes be contrasted with ones featuring the suffix **-i**. This suffix will be discussed in Lesson 17.

The prefix *memper-*

While talking about causative meanings, it is convenient to mention the prefix **memper-**. Sometimes this is combined with a suffix **-kan** or **-i**. It occurs with an adjective as base-word, and means "to raise the degree of whatever the base-word indicates". It is not interchangeable with causative verbs with the suffix **-kan**; one or the other is preferred, or there is a distinction in meaning. Examples:

memperpanjang   to extend (e.g. a visa), from **panjang** long
(cf. **memanjangkan** to lengthen (an object))
memperdalam   to deepen (e.g. knowledge), from **dalam** deep
(cf. **mendalamkan** to make deeper (e.g. a well))
memperkaya   to enrich, from **kaya** rich (a form **mengayakan** does not exist)
memperindah   to beautify, from **indah** beautiful (but **mengindahkan** means to pay attention, and is not connected)
memperkenalkan   to introduce (one person to another), from **kenal** acquainted
(cf. **mengenalkan** to make known (a thing, when it was not known before))
memperbaiki   to repair, correct, from **baik** good
(cf. **membaikkan** to improve something, treat well)

This is not a complete account of all the possibilities. Remember that "hard-and-fast" rules are rare. If in doubt, please do some research in your dictionary, to see what actually occurs and what does not.

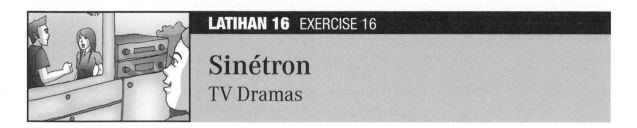
A. Pertanyaan untuk bacaan

■ *Jawablah pertanyaan-pertanyaan di bawah ini sesuai dengan isi bacaan!*

1. P: Siapa pemilik rumah yang ditinggali Joel di Jakarta?

   J: _____

2. P: Sebutkan acara televisi yang digemari Bu Tuti!

   J: _____

3. P: Ceritakan sedikit tentang sinétron Cinta Fitri!

   J: _____

4. P: Di mana désa Wonogiri terletak?

   J: _____

5. P: Apa alasannya Bu Tuti mengajak Joel untuk melihat sinétron Indonesia?

   J: _____

6. P: Bagaimana tokoh perempuan digambarkan dalam sinétron Indonesia?

   J: _____

7. P: Bagaimana pula penggambaran tokoh laki-laki dalam sinétron Indonesia?

   J: _____

8. P: Jelaskan bahasa yang dipakai dalam sinétron itu!

   J: _____

B. Menyimak

■ *Simaklah baik-baik isi Tape Latihan 16 dan jawablah pertanyaan-pertanyaan di bawah ini!*

1. P: Kira-kira jam berapa setiap harinya Joel pulang ke rumah kosnya?

   J: _____

2. P: Seberapa seringnya Joel pergi ke kampus?

   J: _____

3. P: Mengapa Joel selalu berusaha pulang ketika hari sudah mulai gelap?

    J: _____

4. P: Apa artinya 'sinétron'? Jelaskan!

    J: _____

5. P: Siapa yang menjadi penggemar berat sinétron?

    J: _____

6. P: Mengapa banyak orang menggemari sinétron di Indonesia?

    J: _____

7. P: Bahasa apa yang dipakai dalam sinétron Indonesia?

    J: _____

8. P: Jelaskan apa kata pengritik sinétron Indonesia!

    J: _____

C. Tata bahasa

■ *Tulislah kata dasarnya kemudian terjemahkanlah ke dalam bahasa Inggris!*

Kata	Kata dasar	Bahasa Inggris
mengerjakan		
membutuhkan		
membicarakan		
memikirkan		
membacakan		
mengharukan		
menyedihkan		
mempelajari		
memakai		
menanyakan		
ditayangkan		
menangis		

D. Menulis koméntar

■ *Tulislah sebuah koméntar tentang masing-masing acara télévisi berikut ini!*

1. Judul: 'Sex in the City'

   Koméntar: _____

2. J: 'Doctor Who'

   K: _____

3. J: 'The Simpsons'

   K: _____

4. J: NCIS

   K: _____

5. J: 'Sesame Street'

   K: _____

6. J: 'Big Brother'

   K: _____

E. Menulis

■ *Pilihlah sebuah drama télévisi yang kamu sukai lalu tulislah sebuah ringkasan tentang drama tersebut!*

Nama drama télévisi: _____

Ringkasan: _____

_____

_____

_____

_____

_____

_____

_____

_____

_____

_____

_____

LESSON 17

Visit to an Expat Family
Kunjungan Ke Keluarga Ékspat

Melalui jaringan mahasiswa Fakultas Hukum, Joel menghubungi keluarga orang asing Amerika yang tinggal di Tebet, Jakarta Selatan. Joel ingin mengetahui apa yang mempengaruhi keputusan meréka untuk bekerja di Indonesia.

Joel mencari rumahnya. Tetapi supir taksinya tersesat. Atau dengan sengaja menyesatkan diri? Atau alamatnya yang kurang jelas? Ada Jalan Tebet Dalam, Jalan Tebet Timur Dalam, Tebet Timur 1, Tebet Timur 2, Tebet Timur 3, dan seterusnya. Tentu saja membingungkan, sehingga Joel terpaksa menélepon meréka. Akhirnya tetangga dimintai petunjuk: "Di mana rumah keluarga Amerika Schroeder?"

Rumah yang meréka diami bukan milik meréka sendiri. Rumah itu dikontrak oléh perusahaan besar. Ada dua tingkat, ada AC di semua kamar tidur, ada dua orang pembantu, bahkan ada kolam renang... Airnya bening, sejuk, menggodai untuk langsung terjun.

Tetapi lantai tégel licin sekali kalau basah. Joel jatuh, melukai kakinya. Dia mulai menyesali rencananya ini. Baru setelah mencicipi sambal pecel dan bir dingin yang disediakan pembantu yang bermuka ramah, perasaannya pulih. Ah, énak juga!

WORDLIST

AC (pron. "ah-sé", not "ah-ché")	air-conditioning	**dimintai**	to be asked for something
		diri	himself
air	water	**disediakan**	provided, prepared
bahkan	even	**énak**	delicious, tasty
basah	wet	**ekspat**	expatriate
bening	clear (water)	**goda: menggodai**	to tempt
bermuka ria	with a cheerful face	**hubung: menghu-bungi**	to contact
bingung: mem-bingungkan	confusing		
		jaringan	network
cicip: mencicipi	to taste, sample	**jatuh**	to fall over
dan seterusnya	and so forth	**juga**	quite (not "also" here)
dengan sengaja	deliberately	**kaki**	foot
dikontrak	rented	**kamar tidur**	bedroom

keputusan	decision	**pulih**	recovered, better
kolam renang	swimming pool	**sambal pecel**	spicy peanut sauce
lalu: melalui	via; to go through	**sehingga**	till, to the extent that
langsung	straight, directly	**semua**	all, every
lantai	floor	**sesal: menyesali**	to regret
licin	slippery	**sesat**	lost
luka: melukai	to hurt, injure	**sesat: menyesatkan**	to lead astray
meréka diami	occupied by them (N.B. passive, see Lesson 18)	**setelah**	after
		supir	driver
milik	property, possession	**tahu: mengetahui**	to find out about
mulai	to begin	**tégel**	tile
orang asing	foreigner, expat	**télepon: menélepon**	to phone, call
pengaruh: mem-	to influence (N.B. irregular	**terjun**	to dive in
pengaruhi	formation)	**terpaksa**	forced (on **ter-**, see Lesson 22)
perasaan	feelings		
perusahaan	business, enterprise	**tetangga**	neighbour
petunjuk	directions	**tingkat**	level, storey

LANGUAGE NOTES

Verbs with the suffix *-i*

Verbs are also found with this suffix attached. Some transitive verbs have **-kan**, and others **-i**. There are also some cases where a base-word can be found with one or the other—mostly with a significant difference in meaning, of course.

Regarding meaning, there are two quite different functions to be distinguished, the first being much more important than the second.

Firstly, verbs with the suffix **-i** often have what can be called a "locative" meaning, that is, one in which the action of the verb is directed to or something is applied to a "place". In translation into English, in some cases a preposition has to be added to express this sense. Within this, rather vague, area several different groups of words can be listed, as follows:

1. Based on an intransitive verb:

duduk	to sit	→	**menduduki**	to sit on; to occupy
hadir	to be present	→	**menghadiri**	to be present at; to attend
percaya	to believe	→	**mempercayai**	to believe in, rely on
melangkah	to step	→	**melangkahi**	to step over; to disregard
menangis	to weep	→	**menangisi**	to weep over, bemoan

2. Intransitive verbs that occur with a following preposition have an alternative transitive form with this suffix:

cinta akan	to love	→	**mencintai**	to love
benci akan	to hate	→	**membenci**	(N.B. a form **membencii** is impossible)
gemar akan	to be fond of	→	**menggemari**	to be fond of, be a fan of

sadar akan	to be aware of	→	**menyadari**	to be aware of
tahu akan	to know about	→	**mengetahui**	to know about, find out about

3. With a noun as base-word, the meaning is to apply that object to something:

air	water	→	**mengairi**	to supply with water; to irrigate
obat	medicine	→	**mengobati**	to supply with medicine; to treat
minyak	oil	→	**meminyaki**	to apply oil to; to grease

Amusingly, we also find an example where the meaning is not to supply, but to remove something!

kulit	skin	→	**menguliti**	to skin, peel

4. Again with a noun as base-word, there are several verbs that mean to occupy a position with regard to something:

ketua	chairperson	→	**mengetuai**	to chair (e.g. a meeting)
kepala	head	→	**mengepalai**	to head (e.g. a committee)
wakil	deputy	→	**mewakili**	to stand in for; represent (somebody)

5. With base-words that indicate relative position, the verb with **–i** means to be or move at that distance:

lalu	past	→	**melalui**	to go past/through (some place)
dekat	near	→	**mendekati**	to go near (something, someone); to approach
jauh	far	→	**menjauhi**	to keep away from, avoid (something)

6. There are several adjectival base-words which form **-i** verbs that contrast with ones with **-kan**, showing an interesting difference in meaning:

panas	hot	→	**memanasi**	to warm up (by applying heat)
			(cf. **memanaskan** to heat, cause/allow to become hot)	

malu	ashamed	→	**memalui**	to bring shame on
			(cf. **memalukan** to make ashamed, disgrace (*also* disgraceful))	

kering	dry	→	**mengeringi**	to drain (a place)
			(cf. **mengeringkan** to dry, allow something to dry out)	

7. There are several more important verbs of this type, where the form with **-i** is the main one, and the one with **-kan** is less common, without a clear difference in meaning. Only the first need to be mentioned here:

lengkap complete	→	**melengkapi** to complete, supplement

kurang less   →   **mengurangi** to lessen, reduce
dalam deep   →   **mendalami** to deepen; to go more deeply into (something)

8. The following verbs have contrasting meanings, depending on the suffix:

masuk to go in   →   **memasuki** to enter (a place)
          (cf. **memasukkan** to put in (cause something to enter))
naik   to go up   →   **menaiki**   to climb up/onto (something)
              (cf. **menaikkan** to lift, raise (cause to go up))
turun to go down →   **menuruni** to descend (a place)
          (cf. **menurunkan** to lower, reduce (cause to go down))

9. While on the subject of contrasting forms, we have a small but very important group of words where the form with the suffix **-i** has the person as first object and the thing as second object, whereas the form with **-kan** has the thing as object. (This difference has consequences for the passive, see below.)

pinjam →   **meminjami** to lend (someone something)
              (cf. **meminjamkan** to lend (something to someone))
kirim →   **mengirimi**   to send (someone something)
              (cf. **mengirimkan** to send (something to someone))
beri   →   **memberi**   to give (someone something) (N.B. a form **memberii** does not exist)
              (cf. **memberikan** to give (something to someone))
tawar →   **menawari**   to offer (someone something)
              (cf. **menawarkan** to offer (something to someone))

In the case of these **-kan** verbs, the person is introduced with **kepada** "to".

Another example of a verb with the two suffixes is:

bertanya to ask a question; **menanyai** to ask, question, interrogate (someone)
    (cf. **menanyakan** "to ask about" (something))

For the sake of completeness, we should mention the second major usage of the suffix **-i,** which is quite different from the first. Here the basic sense seems to be repetition, which may lie in repeating the action, or in applying the action to a number of objects. Verbs that already have a suffix **-i** or **-kan** as discussed above cannot have the "repetitive" **-i**. In translation one should be aware of the possibility that this function may be present. Examples:

			CONTRAST	
bungkus →	**membungkus**	to wrap	**membungkusi**	to wrap (many things)
pindah →	**memindahkan**	to move (something from one place to another)	**memindahi**	to move (various things)
angkat →	**mengangkat**	to lift up; carry away	**mengangkati**	to carry away (many things)

In some cases this usage can be also interpreted as expressing intensity or thoroughness, as in:

			CONTRAST	
bakar	→ membakar	to burn	membakari	to burn (either plural objects, or completely)
lihat	→ melihat	to see	melihati	to look at closely, scrutinize
pegang	→ memegang	to hold	memegangi	to hold (either plural objects, or tightly)

(It is possible that the form **menanyai** mentioned on page 130 also shares a meaning of repetition or intensity, as expressed in the translation "to interrogate", suggesting asking repeatedly or thoroughly.)

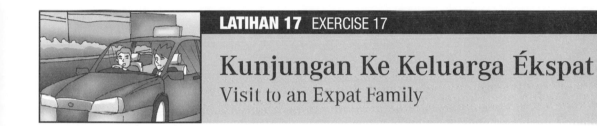

LATIHAN 17 EXERCISE 17

Kunjungan Ke Keluarga Ékspat
Visit to an Expat Family

A. Pertanyaan untuk bacaan

■ *Jawablah pertanyaan-pertanyaan di bawah ini berdasarkan isi bacaan!*

1. P: Bagaimana Joel mendapat informasi tentang keluarga ékspat yang tinggal di Jakarta?

   J: _____

2. P: Dari mana asal keluarga ékspat tersebut dan di mana meréka tinggal di Jakarta?

   J: _____

3. P: Mengapa Joel ingin bertemu dengan keluarga Schroeder?

   J: _____

4. P: Apakah Joel bisa menemukan rumah keluarga Schroeder dengan mudah?

   J: _____

5. P: Siapa akhirnya yang membantu Joel menemukan rumah Schroeder?

   J: _____

6. P: Bagaimana rumah séwaan keluarga Schroeder?

   J: _____

7. P: Apa yang terjadi dengan Joel di rumah itu?

   J: _____

8. P: Apa yang membantu dia merasa senang lagi setelah kecelakaan kecil yang dialaminya?

    J: _____

B. Menyimak

■ *Dengarkan baik-baik isi Tape Latihan 17 dan jawablah pertanyaan-pertanyaan berikut!*

1. P: Seberapa banyak ékspat yang bekerja dan tinggal di Jakarta?

    J: _____

2. P: Meréka bekerja di bidang apa saja?

    J: _____

3. P: Dari mana saja para ékspat itu berasal?

    J: _____

4. P: Apakah Joel tertarik untuk bertemu dengan ékspat yang tinggal di Jakarta? Jelaskan!

    J: _____

5. P: Aspék apa yang disukai para ékspat itu bekerja dan tinggal di Indonesia?

    J: _____

6. P: Apa keuntungan penting bagi para ékspat yang tinggal lama di Indonesia?

    J: _____

7. P: Apa naséhat penting Eric Schoeder yang diberikan kepada Joel?

    J: _____

8. P: Apakah Joel tertarik untuk bekerja di Indonesia setelah dia lulus univérsitas?

    J: _____

C. Tata bahasa

■ *Lengkapilah kalimat-kalimat di bawah ini dengan kata duduk, penduduk, pendudukan, menduduki, diduduki atau kedudukan.*

1. Cina adalah negara dengan jumlah _____ paling besar di dunia.

2. _____ penjajah Belanda di Indonesia berlangsung selama 300 tahun lebih.

3. Setiap soré hari, Eric Schroeder suka _____ di beranda rumahnya mendengarkan suara burung di pepohonan sambil minum téh yang dihidangkan pembantu.

4. Semakin lama semakin banyak politisi perempuan yang _____ jabatan sebagai kepala negara.

5. Jepang mengenalkan budaya militerisme ketika meréka _____ Indonesia di tahun 1940an.

6. Hasil PEMILU 2009 di Indonesia menunjukkan bahwa tampuk kepemimpinan negara Indonesia akan _____ oléh SBY untuk yang kedua kalinya.

7. _____ Singapura sebagai negara yang paling tertib dan bersih tidak tergoyahkan.

8. Diperkirakan jumlah _____ asli Australia yang biasa disebut Aborijin semakin berkurang setiap tahunnya.

9. _____ di depan komputer terlalu lama setiap harinya bisa menyebabkan kegemukan.

10. Joel _____ sebagai wakil présidén perhimpunan mahasiswa hukum di universitasnya di Australia.

D. Rumah séwa keluarga Schroeder di Jakarta

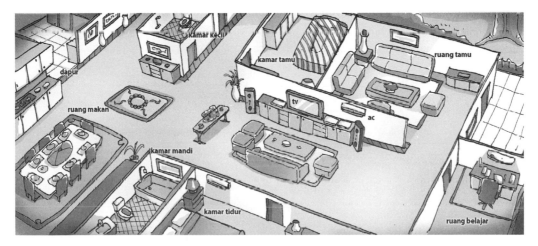

E. Rumah saya

■ *Gambarlah skétsa rumahmu dengan isinya seperti rumah keluarga Schroeder!*

The Interview
Wawancara

Beberapa kawan Sari ingin bertemu dengan Joel. Joel akan diwawancarai untuk majalah mahasiswa dalam bahasa Indonesia. Tetapi meréka merasa malu, lalu kata meréka kepada Sari: "Bagaimana kalau Joel kamu ajak saja? Dia pasti setuju déh!"

Joel tidak suka ditertawakan. "Jangan lucu-lucu, ya. Harus ada pertanyaan yang bermakna. Minta diberi daftar masalah téma wawancara sebelumnya, kalau dapat. Mudah-mudahan nanti berlangsung dengan lancar."

Joel dikerumuni mahasiswa, dipimpin Sari. Jawabannya akan meréka rekam. Misalnya:
S. "Apa yang Joel paling suka tentang Indonesia?"
J. "Ya, sulit kalau disuruh memilih. Mungkin sifat orang Indonesia yang ramah-tamah dan terbuka terhadap orang dari luar…"
S. "Apa yang Joel paling benci tentang Indonesia?"
J. "Jelas, polusi udara dan eksploitasi lingkungan. Kami sayang pada alam, dan tidak suka kalau dirusakkan untuk mencari keuntungan berlebih-lebihan."
S. "Sebenarnya, ada kawan-kawan yang ingin melanjutkan studinya ke luar negeri. Apakah dapat diurus Joel? Bagaimana caranya?"
J. "Ada cukup banyak jalan yang bisa ditempuh. Misalnya untuk penelitian pasca sarjana, dibimbing oléh ahli di Australia atau Amerika. Tetapi selalu ada syarat: bahasa Inggris harus bagus, supaya lancar berkomunikasi."
S. "Barangkali sudah cukup, terima kasih banyak, Joel."
J. "Sama-sama!"

WORDLIST

ahli	expert	**bimbing: dibim-**	supervised
alam	nature	**bing**	
benci	to hate	**daftar**	list
berkomunikasi	to communicate	**déh**	(colloquial particle, em-
berlangsung	to proceed, go ahead		phasizing that something is
berlebih-lebihan	excessive		right)
bermakna	meaningful	**eksploitasi**	exploitation

faédah	benefit	**sekian**	this much, as much as this
jawaban	answer	**setuju**	to agree
kerumun: dikeru-	crowded, surrounded	**sifat**	character
muni		**supaya**	so that
kesediaan	willingness	**suruh: disuruh**	told, ordered
keuntungan	profit	**syarat**	condition
lingkungan	environment	**téma**	theme, subject
lucu	funny	**tempuh: menem-**	to enter on, follow (a way)
malu	shy, embarrassed	**puh**	
pasca sarjana	postgraduate	**tentang**	about
penelitian	research	**terbuka**	open
pilih: memilih	to choose	**terhadap**	towards
pimpin: dipimpin	led	**tertawa: diterta-**	laughed at, made fun of
polusi	pollution	**wakan**	
ramah-tamah	friendly, warm, cordial	**urus: diurus**	arranged, organized
rekam: meréka	recorded by them	**wawancara**	interview
rekam		**wawancara: diwa-**	interviewed
rusak: dirusakkan	destroyed, ruined	**wancarai**	
sayang pada	to love, be fond of		

LANGUAGE NOTES

The passive

The difference between active and passive verb forms is very important in Indonesian, as the passive is much used. To understand the difference, it might be useful to start from an example in English:

> Many people read this book. [ACTIVE]

Compare:

> This book is read by many people. [PASSIVE]

In the first sentence, the subject is "many people", and in the second "this book"—a change of focus. At the same time, the form of the verb has also changed, from "read" to "is read", and with other words we see the ending –ed. (In different examples, "is" might of course be replaced with "am", "are", "was", "were"; and the –ed here is the past participle, and has nothing to do with the past tense.)

The situation in Indonesian is very similar, in that with the passive the focus of the sentence is different, and the form of the verb changes too.

A normal active structure is: Subject – **meN**-verb – Object. But in Indonesian it is very common to highlight the object, by making it the subject, that is, by putting it first in the sentence and changing the verb into a passive form. Somehow, it seems less personal. But the old subject, now termed Agent, still has to be accommodated.

By using the example above and putting it into Indonesian, we can illustrate the transformation and at the same time introduce the first pattern:

Banyak orang membaca buku ini. [ACTIVE]   Many people read this book.
Buku ini dibaca oléh banyak orang. [PASSIVE] This book is read by many people.

Regarding form, we note that the prefix **meN-** has disappeared and has been replaced by the prefix **di-**.[3] Further, the "agent", that is, those doing the action, is introduced by the word **oléh**, "by". Whenever the agent is a noun we will find the **di-** form of the verb. Even when no agent is actually present, as sometimes happens, we still have the prefix **di-**, e.g.

Buku ini sering dibaca. This book is often read.

In a somewhat informal style, the word **oléh** can be omitted, but only if it follows its verb directly, thus:

Buku ini dibaca banyak orang. This book is read by many people.
(In translation we have to keep the "by".)

But when the agent is the third person pronoun, **dia**, there is a change: we still have **di-**, but **dia** takes the form **–nya**, which is suffixed to the verb, as in:

Buku ini dibacanya. This book is/was read by him/her.

By the way, this translation may not sound very idiomatic in English, so one may choose to reproduce it in the active: "He/she read this book".
With the pronoun "they", **meréka**, we have to use **oléh**:

Buku ini dibaca oléh meréka. This book was read by them.

So far, with a noun or pronoun we have seen only third person agents (he, she, they, it, or a thing). With first and second person agents, the pattern changes: the **di-** does not occur, and the agents are put in a different place, namely in front of the verb in its base-word form, thus:

Saya membaca buku ini. [ACTIVE]   I read this book.
Buku ini saya baca. [PASSIVE]   This book was read by me.

---

3   Please observe that this is a prefix, that is, is written joined to the base-word, and has nothing to do with the preposition **di**, which has a completely different function and is always written separately.

The pronouns **kamu**, "you", **kita** and **kami**, "we", work in exactly the same way as **saya**.

Kamu membaca buku ini. [ACTIVE]	You read this book.
Buku ini kamu baca. [PASSIVE]	This book is read by you.

But if the agent pronoun is **aku** or **engkau**, it is written in a shortened form and prefixed:

Buku ini kubaca.	This book is read by me.
Buku ini kaubaca.	This book is read by you.

These forms are more likely to be found in literature or songs.
Even with third person agents, **dia** and **meréka**, this pattern can be used and is considered correct:

Buku ini dia baca.	This book is read by him/her.
Buku ini meréka baca.	This book is read by them.

In the examples given here using the verb **membaca**, we have no suffix, but the same applies to any verb, also ones with **-i** or **-kan**; these are unaffected by the change to a passive form, e.g.

menyirami	to water	→	**disirami**	watered
mendengarkan	to listen to	→	**didengarkan**	listened to

Care should be taken with the pronoun "it", because this sometimes occurs in an impersonal sense, and is associated with a passive verb in Indonesian, but without any separate word for "it", e.g. **Perlu diingat…** "It is necessary to recall…", even where it may look like an active in English translation.

Finally, we should mention that there are other kinds of passive, featuring the affixes **ke- -an** and **ter-**, which will be discussed in Lessons 21 and 22.

LATIHAN 18 EXERCISE 18

Wawancara
The Interview

A. Pertanyaan untuk bacaan

■ *Bacalah isi bacaan baik-baik dan jawablah pertanyaan-pertanyaan di bawah ini!*

1. P: Siapa yang ingin mewawancarai Joel?

   J: _____

2. P: Pertanyaan yang bagaimana yang dikehendaki Joel?

   J: _____

3. P: Apa yang disukai Joel tentang Indonesia?

    J: _____

4. P: Apa yang paling tidak disukai Joel tentang Indonesia?

    J: _____

5. P: Pertanyaan apa lagi yang diajukan kepada Joel?

    J: _____

6. P: Syarat utama apa yang harus dipunyai oléh mahasiswa Indonesia untuk belajar ke Australia atau Amerika menurut Joel?

    J: _____

7. P: Mengapa kemampuan berbahasa Inggris sangat penting menurutmu?

    J: _____

8. P: Mahasiswa apa dari Indonesia yang kebanyakan belajar di luar negeri?

    J: _____

B. Menyimak

■ *Simaklah baik-baik Tape Latihan 18 kemudian jawablah pertanyaan-pertanyaan berikut ini!*

1. P: Sebutkan contoh kegiatan-kegiatan mahasiswa UI di luar kuliah meréka!

    J: _____

2. P: Bagaimana pendapat orang tua Sari terhadap kegiatan-kegiatan ékstra kurikulér tersebut?

    J: _____

3. P: Mengapa Sari dan Joel menganggap kegiatan tersebut sama pentingnya dengan kuliah meréka?

    J: _____

4. P: Apakah Joel sangat tertarik dengan organisasi mahasiswa peduli lingkungan yang ada di kampus? Mengapa? Jelaskan!

    J: _____

5. P: Kegiatan apa yang diikuti Sari dan kakaknya?

    J: _____

6. P: Menurut Joel apa perbédaan utama antara mahasiswa Indonesia dan mahasiswa Australia?

    J: _____

7. P: Apa artinya keberadaan majalah yang ditulis mahasiswa di kampus menurut Agus?

    J: _____

8. P: Menurut Sari satu kemampuan apa yang harus dipunyai oléh mahasiswa Indonesia?

J: _____

C. Tata bahasa

■ *Carilah lima kalimat pasif di dalam bacaan lalu terjemahkanlah ke dalam bahasa Inggris yang baik!*

1. In :_____
    Eng:_____

2. In :_____
    Eng:_____

3. In :_____
    Eng:_____

4. In :_____
    Eng:_____

5. In :_____
    Eng:_____

D. Membuat pertanyaan

■ *Tulislah satu pertanyaan untuk tokoh-tokoh terkenal di bawah ini:*

1. Nelson Mandela
    Q: _____?

2. Tiger Woods
    Q: _____?

3. J K Rowling
    Q: _____?

4. Einstein
    Q: _____?

5. Marie Curie
    Q: _____?

6. Mother Theresa
    Q: _____?

7. R.A. Kartini
    Q: _____?

8. Helen Keller

   Q: _____?

9. Aung San Suu Kyi

   Q: _____?

10. Bill Gates

   P: _____

E. Siapakah saya?

■ *Bacalah keterangan singkat yang disediakan kemudian jawablah pertanyaan di bawah ini*

1. Saya berasal dari salah satu negara di Asia yang paling padat penduduknya. Perawakan saya kecil, tanpa rambut dan saya selalu memakai kaca mata. Saya dikenal dengan pendekatan politik anti kekerasan. Nama keluarga saya sama dengan salah satu dinasti politik ternama di negara saya.

   P: Siapakah saya?
   J: _____

2. Saya seorang laki-laki dan nama depan saya dimulai dengan huruf W. Saya lahir di Inggris dan karya tulisan saya dianggap memberi pengaruh besar terhadap perkembangan bahasa Inggris. Karya tulisan saya dianggap klasik dan sudah sering kali diangkat menjadi filem atau drama. Hampir semua orang di seluruh dunia pernah mendengar nama saya. Salah satu karya saya yang paling banyak dikenal orang adalah tentang kisah cinta sepasang anak muda yang tragis.

   P: Siapakah saya?
   J: _____

3. Saya berasal dari sebuah negara yang dikenal sebagai negara matador. Selain matador, orang-orang juga mengenal negara saya sebagai tempat diadakannya festival tomat besar-besaran. Hobi saya melukis tetapi lukisan-lukisan saya sama terkenalnya dengan kumis saya.

   P: Siapakah saya?
   J: _____

4. Karena tradisi yang sangat kolot dari kecil saya sudah dipingit di rumah. Semua anak perempuan dilarang untuk keluar rumah apa lagi pergi ke sekolah untuk mendapat pendidikan. Pada zaman itu tidak ada persamaan hak untuk wanita. Saya tidak setuju dengan pandangan yang menurut saya sangat merendahkan derajat kaum wanita. Léwat surat-surat yang saya tulis dan kirim kepada sahabat saya di negara Belanda, saya ungkapkan ketidaksetujuan saya terhadap perlakuan yang diterima oléh kebanyakan perempuan Indonesia pada jaman itu.

   P: Siapakah saya?
   J: _____

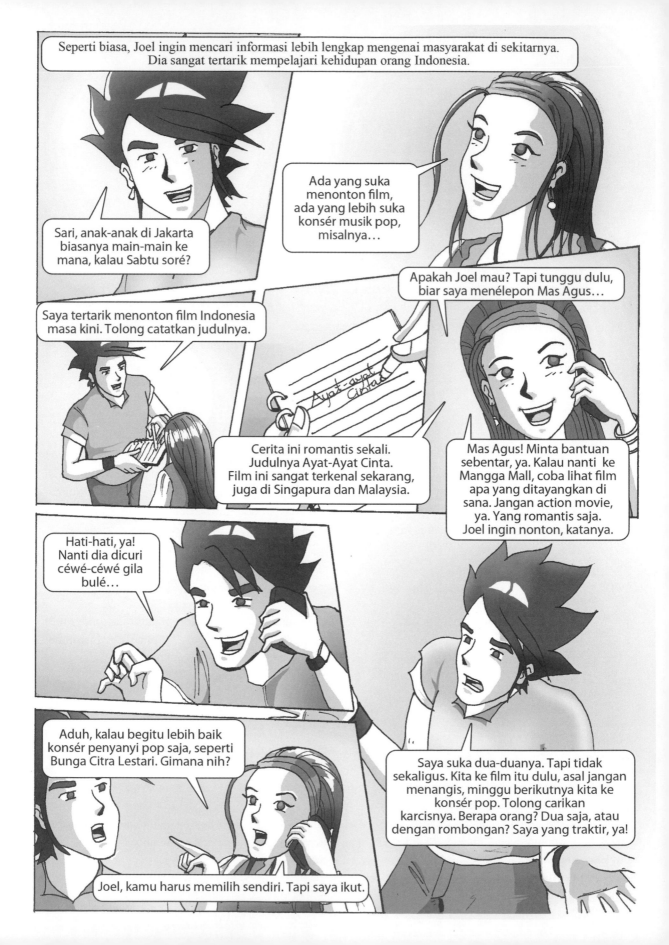

LESSON 19

What Will We Watch?
Menonton Apa?

Seperti biasa, Joel ingin mencari informasi lebih lengkap mengenai masyarakat di sekitarnya. Dia sangat tertarik mempelajari kehidupan orang Indonesia.

Dia berkata kepada Sari: "Sari, anak-anak di Jakarta biasanya main-main ke mana, kalau Sabtu soré?"

Sari: "Ada yang suka menonton film, ada yang lebih suka konsér musik pop, misalnya…"

Joel: "Saya tertarik menonton film Indonesia masa kini. Tolong catatkan judulnya."

(Sari mencatat judul film:) "Cerita ini romantis sekali. Judulnya Ayat-Ayat Cinta. Film ini sangat terkenal sekarang, juga di Singapura dan Malaysia. Apakah Joel mau? Tapi tunggu dulu, biar saya menélepon Mas Agus…

(Sari menélepon:) Mas Agus! Minta bantuan sebentar, ya. Kalau nanti ke Mangga Mall, coba lihat film apa yang ditayangkan di sana. Jangan action movie, ya. Yang romantis saja. Joel ingin nonton, katanya."

Agus: "Hati-hati, ya! Nanti dia dicuri céwé-céwé gila bulé…"

Sari: "Aduh, kalau begitu lebih baik konsér penyanyi pop saja, seperti Bunga Citra Lestari. Gimana nih?"

(kepada Joel) "Joel, kamu harus memilih sendiri. Tapi saya ikut."

Joel: "Saya suka dua-duanya. Tapi tidak sekaligus. Kita ke film itu dulu, asal jangan menangis, minggu berikutnya kita ke konsér pop. Tolong carikan karcisnya. Berapa orang? Dua saja, atau dengan rombongan? Saya yang traktir, ya!"

WORDLIST

asal	provided, on condition that	gimana	(coll. = **bagaimana**)
berikutnya	following (that), next	info	(informal) information
berminat	to be fond of, interested in	judul	title, name
biar	let	karcis	ticket
bulé	white person	konsér	concert
catat:	to note down for	masa kini	contemporary
mencatatkan		masyarakat	society, community
céwé	girl	musik pop	pop music
curi: mencuri	to steal	nih	(coll. = **ini**)
dua-duanya	both of them	nonton	(coll. = **menonton**)
gila	crazy about	penyanyi	singer

romantis	romantic	**tangis: menangis**	to cry
rombongan	group, gang	**terkenal**	well known, famous
sekaligus	at the same time	**tinggal:**	to leave behind
sekitarnya	surrounding	**meninggalkan**	

LANGUAGE NOTES

Orders, requests, prohibitions

Sometimes we use language to persuade others to do something or not do something, in accordance with what we want. But in order to have the desired effect, such utterances have to take account of what the relationship between the speaker and addressee is, and in what circumstances they are communicating. In some situations it may be acceptable to be blunt, whereas in others we have to be very careful not to offend somebody's feelings, and so quite a different form of expression has to be used.

Beginning with the most abrupt, we have different forms of the relevant verb, where a distinction should be made between intransitive and transitive verbs.

1. With intransitive verbs, there is no change in form, e.g.

    Duduk di sini! Sit here!
    (As is usual in imperatives, a second person pronoun, "you", is not found.)

2. With transitive verbs, the prefix **meN-** is dropped, provided the action refers to a specific object, e.g.

    Tutup jendéla itu! Close that window!

    The same applies even if the object is only implied, e.g.

    Dengarkan baik-baik! Listen carefully (to what I'm going to say)!

3. Otherwise the **meN-** is retained, that is, if there is no object or a non-specific object, e.g.

    Membaca dengan teliti! Read carefully!

    In this case, the verb has an intransitive sense, such as "Do reading", rather than "Read it".

4. Prohibitions (negative orders) are formed with the word **jangan**, "don't". Just as with orders, this can be used:

    With an intransitive verb, e.g.

    Jangan duduk di situ! Don't sit there!

    Or with a transitive verb with a specific object, e.g.

    Jangan tutup jendéla itu! Don't close that window!
    (N.B. No **meN-**, and one particular window.)

Or with a transitive verb with a non-specific object, e.g.

> **Jangan memasang iklan pada témbok ini!** Don't post ads on this wall!
> (N.B. No particular ad, just ads in general.)

5. An order with a transitive verb is often expressed by using a passive with **di-**. This is good, idiomatic Indonesian. It has the effect of focusing on the object concerned, which is found first, without mentioning an agent ("you"). In other words, it is impersonal and feels less blunt, like "let it be …-ed". For example:

> **Pakaian ini dicuci, ya!** Would you wash these clothes, please!
> (lit. "Let these clothes be washed, okay").

The same can be done with **jangan**, e.g.

> **Hadiahmu jangan dibuka dulu!** Don't open your present yet!
> (lit. "Don't let your present be opened first").

Note how the noun concerned comes first in these two sentences: this is the focus.

6. Other impersonal prohibitions are expressed with passives, using the word **dilarang** "forbidden", e.g.

> **Dilarang masuk.**   No entry (lit. "It is forbidden to enter")
> **Dilarang merokok.**   No smoking (lit. "It is forbidden to smoke")

Both of these verbs are of course intransitive.

7. The particle **-lah** is sometimes found in association with orders and prohibitions. It is suffixed to the verb, which occupies an initial position. Normally its function is to mark or highlight a word. Here it has the effect of making the order less abrupt, probably because the word is lengthened by one syllable. For example:

> **Berdirilah!**   Stand up! (Not just "Stand!")
> **Makanlah!**   Eat up!

There exist several words which serve to soften an order, making it more like an invitation. These are:

(a) **Silakan** "please". This is used only to invite someone to do something for their own benefit, e.g.

> **Silakan masuk!** Please come in!

Also by itself:

> **Boléh saya masuk?** May I come in? **Silakan!** Please!

But if the verb is transitive, the prefix **meN-** is dropped, e.g.

Silakan ambil kuéh ini! Please take one of these cakes!

(b) **Tolong** (lit. "help"). This has the effect of asking someone to do something for you, as in English "Kindly…" or "Would you mind…", e.g.

Tolong tuliskan nama anda. Kindly write your name for me. (N.B. No **meN-** here.)

(c) **Coba** (lit. "try"). This has the effect of urging someone to make an effort. As such it is more likely to be addressed to someone of equal or lower status (like "Do me a favour and…"), e.g.

Coba bersihkan méja ini. Clean up this table, please. (N.B. No **meN-**.)

(d) **Harap** (lit. "hope"). This forms a formal, impersonal way of asking for something to be done, often found in official notices, e.g.

Pintu harap dikunci sebelum pergi.   Kindly lock the doors before leaving.
Harap tenang pada jam tidur.   Kindly be quiet at rest times.

Polite requests can be formed with:

(a) **Minta** (lit. "ask"). This forms a polite request to do something for one, e.g.

Minta disambung dengan Pak Yoto.
Please connect me with Pak Yoto.
(Note the impersonal form, without the use of **saya** (I, me).)

(b) **Mohon** (lit. "request"). This functions in the same way as **minta**, but is more likely to be used to address someone of high status. For example,

Mohon surat ini ditandatangani di bawah ini.
Would you kindly sign the letter here at the bottom.

(c) **Perkenankanlah** (lit. "graciously permit"). This is used in a formal situation, for example when giving a speech in front of highly esteemed persons, e.g.

Perkenankanlah saya memperkenalkan Dékan Fakultas kami.
Please allow me to introduce the Dean of our Faculty.

Menonton Apa?
What Will We Watch?

A. Pertanyaan untuk bacaan

■ *Jawablah pertanyaan-pertanyaan di bawah ini sesuai dengan isi bacaan!*

1. P: Selain bahasa Indonesianya menjadi lebih baik, apa yang ingin diketahui oléh Joel selama tinggal di Indonesia?

    J: _____

2. P: Hari ini apa yang ingin diketahui oléh Joel?

    J: _____

3. P: Menurut Sari apa kegiatan anak muda pada akhir pekan?

    J: _____

4. P: Apa yang ingin dilakukan Joel?

    J: _____

5. P: Apa judul filem Indonesia yang ingin ditonton Joel?

    J: _____

6. P: Selain filem Indonesia yang tengah popular apa lagi yang ingin ditonton Joel?

    J: _____

7. P: Minggu ini Joel ingin memilih kegiatan apa dulu?

    J: _____

8. P: Siapa yang ingin membayar karcis filem dan konsér musik? Mengapa?

    J: _____

B. Menyimak

■ *Dengarkan baik-baik isi Tape Latihan 19 dan jawablah pertanyaan-pertanyaan berikut!*

1. P: Menurut Joel cara apa yang paling éféktif untuk mempelajari sebuah budaya?

    J: _____

2. P: Jelaskan cara yang paling éféktif untuk menguasai bahasa menurut ibu Joel?

    J: _____

3. P: Sejak tiba di Jakarta apa yang membuat Joel terhéran-héran?

    J: _____

4. P: Bahasa Indonesia macam apa yang dipelajari Joel di universitasnya di Australia?

    J: _____

5. P: Selain menonton sinétron dengan Bu Tuti di rumah kosnya, apa yang dilakukan Joel untuk mempelajari bahasa gaul?

    J: _____

6. P: Bagaimana perfileman di Indonesia sekarang ini?

    J: _____

7. P: Sebutkan beberapa judul filem Indonesia yang dianggap popular karena kualitasnya yang bagus!

    J: _____

C. Pertanyaan umum (Kuis)

1. P: Sebutkan salah satu nama anggota kelompok Beatles!

    J: _____

2. P: Siapa nama petinju légéndaris berkulit hitam dari Amerika?

    J: _____

3. P: Dari mana grup musik ABBA berasal?

    J: _____

4. P: Apa nama album Michael Jackson yang paling suksés?

    J: _____

5. P: Grup musik apa yang menyanyikan lagu 'We are the Champions'?

    J: _____

6. P: Dari negara mana Van Beethoven berasal?

    J: _____

7. P: Siapa nama pelukis 'Mona Lisa'?

J: _____

8. P: Angklung adalah alat instrumén musik yang terbuat dari apa?

J: _____

9. P: Samba adalah jenis tarian dari negara mana?

J: _____

10. P: Siapakah pengarang drama yang berjudul 'Waiting for Godot'?

J: _____

11. P: Sebutkan salah satu filem yang dibuat oléh Woody Allen.

J: _____

12. P: Siapa nama bintang filem yang berperan sebagai Forrest Gump?

J: _____

13. P: Filem yang berjudul 'Schindler's List' bertéma apa?

J: _____

14. P: Siapa nama bintang filem yang memérankan tokoh James Bond yang pertama?

J: _____

15. P: Siapakah nama pengarang Indonesia yang menulis novel 'The Glass House'?

J: _____

Twilight in Jakarta
Senja Di Jakarta

Setelah mandi soré, sambil minum kopi tubruk di beranda, Joel membaca-baca majalah Gatra yang tadi dibelinya di toko buku. Harganya Rp 24.500. Ada rubrik bermacam-macam, seperti politik, hukum, bisnis, kedokteran dan olahraga. Yang paling berguna bagi Joel ialah politik dan hukum.

Misalnya, ada artikel mengenai prosés pemilihan présidén. Pengarangnya berpendapat bahwa "pemilu yang kolosal itu membutuhkan persiapan yang matang dan cermat dari penyelenggara". Semua peraturan harus selesai sebelumnya. Kalau tidak, dapat menyulitkan pelaksaanan. "Harus ada pemahaman atas kondisi géografis, karakter demografis…"

Tetapi Joel sudah mulai mengantuk. Matanya capai. Sebentar lagi, tahu-tahu sudah gelap, jam kecoa main-main di lantai kamar mandi. Timbul minatnya untuk makan. Makan apa? Ayam goréng atau pizza? Ya, ayam goréng saja! Jadi Joel keluar, menuju ke KFC yang paling dekat, di pojok jalan besar. Ayamnya énak, dan di réstoran lebih ramai daripada duduk-duduk sendirian di rumah. Mungkin bisa bertemu dengan teman baru. Nah, di mana daftar makanannya?

WORDLIST

artikel	article	**kantuk:**	to feel sleepy, be drowsy
atas	for, regarding	**mengantuk**	
atur: peraturan	regulation	**karakter**	character
ayam goréng	fried chicken	**karang:**	author, writer
bagi	for	**pengarang**	
beranda	veranda	**kecoa**	cockroach
berguna	useful	**kedokteran**	medicine, medical matters
bisnis	business	**kolosal**	huge, large-scale
capai	tired	**kondisi**	conditions
cermat	careful, accurate	**kopi tubruk**	coffee prepared by pouring
daftar makanan	menu		boiling water on ground
démografis	demographic		coffee beans
duduk-duduk	to sit around	**laksana:**	implementation
gelap	dark	**pelaksanaan**	
géografis	geographical	**main-main**	to come out to play

matang	mature, well thought out	selenggara:	organizer
olahraga	sport	penyelenggara	
paham:	understanding	selesai	finished, ready
pemahaman		sendirian	alone
pemilu	general election	senja	twilight
pilih: pemilihan	choosing, election	siap: persiapan	preparations
politik	political; politics	tahu-tahu	suddenly, before he knew it
réstoran	restaurant	timbul	to arise
rubrik	column	tuju: menuju	to head (for)

LANGUAGE NOTES

Nouns and the link with verbs

Apart from the many simple nouns that have already been used, Indonesian has also large numbers of nouns that are the product of various processes of affixation (just as in English, e.g. to emend: emendation; to repair: repairer, etc.). Several of these processes will be mentioned here, in particular ones which demonstrate interesting links with verbs.

It is useful to be able to observe these links, as this helps us to understand the meanings of such nouns better. As well as the regularities that we can point out, there are of course also irregularities and odd cases where we may not be able to predict a meaning. The only way to be sure is to check the dictionary and see what forms and meanings actually occur.

The affixes *peN-* and *-an*

Nouns formed with these two affixes (in combination) can be compared with verbs with the prefix **meN-**, without a suffix, with the suffix **-kan**, or with the suffix **-i**. However, we observe that the suffix **-an** replaces **-kan** or **-i**, where these occur. All of these verbs will be transitive. The corresponding nouns also have a "transitive" meaning, that is, "the act of doing (whatever the base-word indicates)".

meN-		peN-~-an	
menulis	to write	**penulisan**	writing (the act, process, way of writing something)
membuat	to make	**pembuatan**	making (production, manufacture, construction)
membangun	to build	**pembangunan**	development (building, construction)

meN-~-kan		peN-~-an	
mengembangkan	to expand	**pengembangan**	expansion, development
mengumumkan	to announce	**pengumuman**	announcement
menyelesaikan	to finish	**penyelesaian**	completion
melaksanakan	to carry out	**pelaksanaan**	implementation

meN-~-i		peN-~-an	
mengairi	to irrigate	**pengairan**	irrigation
menyirami	to water	**penyiraman**	watering

As examples of interesting variations, we can mention:

penerangan	1. informing, clarifying 2. illumination, lighting (corresponding to the verbs)
menerangkan	"to make clear", and **menerangi** "to light up" respectively
penemuan	discovery, invention, find, finding (in the senses of both "the act of finding" and "what is found")
penginapan	which corresponds to the verb **menginap** "to lodge, spend the night", but means "place for lodging", not "the act of lodging"

The affixes *per-* and *-an*

Many nouns with these affixes correspond to intransitive verbs with the prefix **ber-**. They have the meaning of either the act or the result of the act referred to by the verb. For example:

ber-		per-~-an	
bekerja	to work	**pekerjaan**	work (Note the form here)
belajar	to study	**pelajaran**	lesson (Note the form)
berjanji	to promise	**perjanjian**	promise, agreement
bertemu	to meet	**pertemuan**	meeting
berkembang	to develop, widen, grow	**perkembangan**	development, growth, expansion (cf. **pengembangan** on p. 152)

However, there are also some nouns with **per- -an** that correspond to transitive verbs, and indicate the act of doing what the base-word indicates, e.g.

meN-		per-~-an	
menolong	to help	**pertolongan**	help
mengingatkan	to warn, remind	**peringatan**	warning, reminder
mencoba	to try, test	**percobaan**	test, trial, attempt
memohon	to ask for, request	**permohonan**	request, appeal

Verbs with the prefix **memper-** also have related nouns with **per-~-an**, e.g.:

memper-		per-~-an	
memperbaiki	to repair, improve	**perbaikan**	repairs, improvement
memperhatikan	to heed, pay attention to	**perhatian**	attention
mempertimbangkan	to weigh up, consider	**pertimbangan**	consideration, judgement

Nouns with *per-~-an* and a noun as base-word

As well as the above, where the base-word was verbal, there is another, quite different, group of nouns, also featuring the affixes **per-** and **-an**, but this time with a noun as base-word. Some examples are found as attributes, following another noun, and so are usually translated adjectivally. These have the meaning of "matters relating to whatever the base-word refers to". (A similar meaning can be found with some nouns with **ke- -an**, see Lesson 21.) Other examples have a more general meaning, or apply to a wider area, as compared to their base-word. Examples:

		per-~-an	
bank	bank	**perbankan**	banking" (e.g. **séktor perbankan** the banking sector)
ékonomi	economy	**perékonomian**	economic (affairs)
industri	industry	**perindustrian**	industrial
istilah	term	**peristilahan**	terminology
kamus	dictionary	**perkamusan**	lexicography

Nouns with the prefix *peN-*

Firstly, nouns with this prefix attached to a verbal base-word can indicate the person who carries out the action, e.g.

		peN-	
menonton	to watch	**penonton**	spectator, viewer
menulis	to write	**penulis**	writer
menganut	to follow	**penganut**	follower, adherent
menumpang	to ride in/on	**penumpang**	passenger
menduduki	to occupy	**penduduk**	inhabitant

Secondly, these nouns can also refer to inanimate objects that carry out the action. These are often found in apposition to another noun, qualifying it in such a way as to tell us what it does. Combinations with **alat**, "instrument, tool", are common. Examples:

		peN-	
mendengar	to hear	**alat pendengar**	listening device, earphones
mendinginkan	to cool	**pendingin**	coolant; **alat pendingin ruangan** room air conditioner
menenangkan	to soothe	**obat penenang**	tranquillizer
menyegarkan	to refresh	**obat penyegar**	tonic

And thirdly, there are a few **peN-** nouns based on adjectives, referring to someone or something characterized by the base-word, e.g.

		peN-	
jahat	bad, evil, wicked	**penjahat**	criminal
muda	young	**pemuda**	youth, young person
sakit	sick	**penyakit**	illness
besar	big	**pembesar**	big-shot, VIP

Nouns with the prefix *pe-*

Nouns formed with **pe-** refer to persons who carry out the action indicated by the verb. This verb is often one with the prefix **ber-**. For example:

		pe-		
bekerja	to work	**pekerja**	worker	
berdagang	to trade	**pedagang**	trader	
berjalan	to walk	**pejalan (kaki)**	pedestrian	
beserta	to accompany	**peserta**	participant	
berenang	to swim	**perenang**	swimmer	
bertinju	to box	**petinju**	boxer	
main bulu tangkis	to play badminton	**pebulu tangkis**	badminton-player	

And finally, there are few cases where both **peN-** and **pe-** occur, with similar meanings, e.g.

		peN- and pe-		
mencintai	to love	**pencinta** and **pecinta**	lover, fan, devotee
menyaingi	to compete with, rival	**penyaing** and **pesaing**	competitor, rival

LATIHAN 20 EXERCISE 20

Senja Di Jakarta
Twilight in Jakarta

A. Pertanyaan untuk bacaan

■ *Jawablah pertanyaan-pertanyaan berikut ini berdasarkan isi bacaan!*

1. P: Apa yang dilakukan Joel pada soré hari ketika dia di rumah kosnya?

   J: _____

2. P: Apa itu 'Gatra'?

   J: _____

3. P: Apa artinya 'rubrik'?

   J: _____

4. P: Rubrik apa yang paling dicari Joel ketika dia membaca majalah Gatra?

   J: _____

5. P: Apa isi artikel yang dibaca Joel soré ini?

   J: _____

6. P: Apakah Joel selesai membaca artikel itu?

   J: _____

7. P: Apa yang ingin dimakan Joel petang ini?

    J: _____

8. P: Mengapa Joel suka makan di réstoran KFC dekat rumah kosnya?

    J: _____

B. Menyimak

■ *Simaklah baik-baik Tape Latihan 20 dan cobalah menjawab pertanyaan-pertanyaan berikut!*

1. P: Menurut kamu apa itu 'kopi tubruk'?

    J: _____

2   P Majalah Gatra bergaya seperti majalah internasional apa?

    J: _____

3. P: Bahasa Indonesia gaya apa yang dipakai dalam majalah seperti Gatra?

    J: _____

4. P: Topik hangat apa sekarang ini yang sering dibahas di majalah-majalah di Indonesia?

    J: _____

5. P: Apa manfaatnya membaca majalah popular untuk kemampuan bahasa Indonesia Joel?

    J: _____

6. P: Selain hukum rubrik apa yang sering dicari Joel?

    J: _____

7. P: Mengapa Joel berfokus pada dua topik itu?

    J: _____

C. Tata bahasa

■ *Tulislah kata benda sebanyak mungkin dari kata dasar dari kolom sebelah kiri!*

Kata dasar	Kata benda
CONTOH (EXAMPLE) Kerja	Pekerjaan, pekerja, pengerjaan
Bantu	
Janji	
Tonton	
Jalan	

Kata dasar	Kata benda
Terang	
Renang	
Tenang	
Ingat	
Selesai	
Baca	
Ajar	
Sabar	
Hukum	

D. Pertanyaan umum (kuis)

■ *Jawablah pertanyaan-pertanyaan di bawah ini!*

1. P: Berapa kira-kira jumlah penduduk Jakarta?

    J: _____

2. P: Apa nama lama kota Jakarta?

    J: _____

3. P Kota New York juga sering dikenal sebagai kota yang?

    J: _____

4. P: Di kota mana taksi berwarna hitam?

    J: _____

5. P: Di kota mana alat angkutan umum disebut tuk-tuk?

    J: _____

6. P: Di kota mana terdapat gondola yang terkenal?

    J: _____

7. P: Di kota mana para umat Islam menunaikan ibadah Haji?

    J: _____

8. P: Apa nama kota di Eropa yang terkenal sebagai 'kota romantis'?

    J: _____

Going to the Doctor
Ke Dokter

Pada suatu pagi Joel sedang léwat halte bis, kebetulan tepat di depan Kedutaan Besar Australia. Ada banyak orang menunggu kedatangan bis, lalu ketika bis mérah itu tiba di situ meréka mendorong-dorong mau naik. Ada beberapa pemuda datang berlari-lari, mendorong Joel dari belakang, lalu naik bis. Baru sesudah bis berangkat Joel meraba sakunya: kosong. Dia kecopétan. Untunglah, tidak banyak yang hilang, hanya dompét berisi uang kecil saja.

Tetapi mulai saat itu, perasaannya berubah. Dia mengalami rasa ketakutan, kekecéwaan dan kegagalan, seakan-akan peristiwa itu mempengaruhi sikapnya terhadap lingkungannya. Mengapa begitu? Sari menyadari ada sesuatu yang tidak bérés. Dia bilang kepada Joel: "Joel, kamu mau saya bawa ke dokter, supaya diperiksa, ya."

Joel tidak berkeberatan. Mereka berdua hadir pada jam bicara di prakték Dr Lim, jam enam soré. Tidak perlu menunggu lama. Joel menerangkan kepada dokter: "Saya selalu merasa kecapaian dan lelah. Ada apa kiranya, dokter?"

Dr Lim berkata, "Ya, Joel, mukamu agak pucat. Ada kemungkinan kamu "kurang darah". Artinya, darah kekurangan zat besi. Istilah Inggrisnya anaemia. Disebabkan perubahan iklim, atau kurang makan yang bergizi. Kalau dapat, nasihat saya kamu berlibur, ke Puncak misalnya. Di sana kamu bisa mengaso di tempat sejuk. Di samping itu, saya akan menulis resép untuk tablét yang mengandung zat besi. Oké?"

Joel dan Sari: "Terima kasih banyak, dokter."

WORDLIST

agak	rather	**berlibur**	to take a holiday
artinya	that means	**berubah**	to change
aso: mengaso	to take a rest	**bilang**	to say, tell
bawa: membawa	to take	**darah**	blood
bérés	in order	**dompét**	purse, wallet
bergizi	nutritious	**dorong: mendorong**	to push
berisi	to contain	**hadir**	to be there, present
berkeberatan	to have an objection	**halte bis**	bus stop

jam bicara	consulting hours	**periksa: memeriksa**	to examine
kandung: mengandung	to contain	**prakték**	practice
kecapaian	exhausted, worn out	**pucat**	pale
kecopétan	to have one's pocket picked	**raba: meraba**	to feel, touch
		resép	prescription
kegagalan	failure	**sadar: menyadari**	to realize, be aware
kekecéwaan	disappointment	**saku**	pocket
ketakutan	fear	**seakan-akan**	as if
kosong	empty	**sikap**	attitude
lama	for long, a long time	**supaya**	so that
lelah	tired	**tablét**	tablet
muka	face	**terang: menerangkan**	to explain
nasihat	advice	**zat besi**	iron (as a chemical substance)
oké	okay		
pemuda	youth, boy		

LANGUAGE NOTES

Nouns, verbs and adjectives with the affixes *ke-* and *-an*

I Nouns

1. In Lesson 20 we have shown how certain nouns correspond to particular verbs. In a similar way, we can observe how nouns are derived from adjectives, using the prefix **ke-** and suffix **-an** in combination. These nouns have an abstract meaning (cf. English nouns with the ending –ness, -ity), relating to the quality expressed by the adjective. Some simple examples are:

		ke-~-an	
senang	happy	**kesenangan**	happiness
cantik	pretty	**kecantikan**	prettiness, beauty
jelas	clear	**kejelasan**	clarity

2. Note that sometimes when an adjective is negated with **tidak** or **tak** the abstract noun is formed with both words as its base, e.g.

		ke-~-an	
tidak adil	unjust	**ketidakadilan**	injustice
tidak cocok	incompatible	**ketidakcocokan**	incompatibility
tidak jujur	dishonest	**ketidakjujuran**	dishonesty

3. Similarly, there is a small group of nouns formed on the basis of intransitive verbs, e.g.

		ke-~-an	
datang	to come	**kedatangan**	arrival
berangkat	to depart	**keberangkatan**	departure
naik	to go up	**kenaikan**	rise, increase
pergi	to go (away)	**kepergian**	trip, departure
jadi	to become	**kejadian**	event, incident

4. Further, the base-word can sometimes be a word which is itself the result of derivation, e.g.

		ke-~-an	
terbuka	open, outgoing	**keterbukaan**	openness (on the prefix **ter-**, see Lesson 22)
pemimpin	leader" (base-word **pimpin**)	**kepemimpinan**	leadership
berhasil	to succeed	**keberhasilan**	success

5. There is another important group of words with the affixes **ke-** and **-an**, formed on the basis of a noun. With regard to meaning, they can be compared to some of the nouns with **per- -an** mentioned in Lesson 20. These words have the meaning of "matters relating to… (whatever the base-word indicates)". Often they occur after another noun, and modify it, and so can be translated into English with an appropriate adjective. For example:

		ke-~-an	
masyarakat	society	**kemasyarakatan**	social, as in **ilmu kemasyarakatan** social sciences
héwan	animal	**kehéwanan**	relating to animals, as in **fakultas kehéwanan** faculty of veterinary science
doktor	doctor (medical)	**kedokteran**	medical, as in **fakultas kedokteran** medical faculty
hutan	forest	**kehutanan**	forestry, as in **departemen kehutanan** department of forestry
polisi	police	**kepolisian**	police, as in **akadémi kepolisian** police academy

A somewhat different type is found in the following examples, where the base-word indicates a rank or position, and the derived form "the area administered by…":

		ke-~-an	
menteri	minister	**kementerian**	ministry
duta	emissary	**kedutaan**	embassy
raja	king	**kerajaan**	kingdom
lurah	headman (of village)	**kelurahan**	the area headed by a Lurah

II Verbs

There are various groups of words which can be mentioned here, depending on the kind of base-word involved. But all these **ke-~-an** forms contain the idea of "suffering" from, or being adversely affected by something.

1. With an intransitive verb as base-word, many of these forms involve the use of a "complement", which completes the meaning, e.g.

		ke-~-an	
mati	to die	**kematian**	to suffer a bereavement, e.g. **kematian ayah** to lose one's father

hilang to be gone, lost   **kehilangan**   to suffer a loss, e.g. **kehilangan dompét** to lose one's wallet

2. Another group has a noun as a base-word. For example:

		ke-~-an	
copét	pickpocket	**kecopétan**	to be the victim of a pickpocket
banjir	flood	**kebanjiran**	to get flooded, caught in a flood
hujan	rain	**kehujanan**	to get caught in the rain
malam	night	**kemalaman**	to be overtaken by night, out after dark
siang	daylight	**kesiangan**	to wake up after daylight, oversleep

3. The next group is based on an adjective, thus:

		ke-~-an	
dingin	cold	**kedinginan**	to feel cold, too cold
haus	thirsty	**kehausan**	to suffer from thirst
lapar	hungry	**kelaparan**	to be starving
panas	hot	**kepanasan**	to feel too hot, suffer from the heat
sepi	lonely, deserted	**kesepian**	to feel lonely; too quiet

4. A further group corresponds to a passive verb with **di-** and **-i**. The meaning here is also passive, but with an added adverse, unintentional or accidental meaning. An agent can occur, introduced by **oléh** if it is a person. For example:

di- and -i		ke-~-an	
didatangi	visited	**kedatangan**	to be visited unexpectedly, to have unwelcome visitors
diketahui	found out	**ketahuan**	found out, caught in the act
dijatuhi	dropped on	**kejatuhan**	to have something fall on one
ditulari	spread (disease)	**ketularan**	to get infected
dimasuki	entered	**kemasukan**	possessed; entered accidentally; contaminated

5. There are two verbs that should also be listed here; these do not have the meaning of "suffering from", but "able to be....":

me-		ke-~-an	
melihat	to see	**kelihatan**	able to be seen, visible; it looks, seems…
mendengar	to hear	**kedengaran**	able to be heard, audible

The unusual form **kebetulan** means "to happen to…; coincidentally, by chance".

III Adjectives

There is another derivation using the affixes **ke-** and **-an** which has an adjective or noun as its base-word, but in a reduplicated form, providing an adjective with as meaning "resembling, having the quality of the base-word only to a certain degree". For example:

	ke-~-an	
barat west	**kebarat-baratan**	Westernized; overly Westernized
ilmu science	**keilmu-ilmuan**	pseudo-scientific
kanak-kanak young child	**kekanak-kanakan**	childish, puerile
kuning yellow	**kekuning-kuningan**	yellowish (and other colours similarly)

Emergencies

Ambulance! **Ambulans!**	I'm lost! **Saya tersesat!**
Careful! **Hati-hati!**	I'm sick! **Saya sakit!**
Doctor! **Dokter!**	Just a moment! **Nanti dulu!**
Don't! **Jangan!**	Look out! **Awas!**
Emergency! **Darurat!**	One moment, please! **Sebentar, ya.**
Enough! **Cukup!**	No! (= it's not like that): **Bukan!**
Excuse me (drawing attention): **Maaf,...**	Police: **Polisi!**
Excuse me (trying to get past): **Permisi...**	Stop! **Stop!**
Excuse me? (I didn't understand you): **Maaf?**	Taxi! **Taksi!**
	Thief! **Maling!**
Fire! **Kebakaran!**	Toilet?! **Ada kamar kecil?**
Help! **Tolong!**	Water! (Need a glass of water!) **Air minum!**
I'm allergic! **Saya alérgi!**	Wrong! **Salah!**

LATIHAN 21 EXERCISE 21

Ke Dokter
Going to the Doctor

A. Pertanyaan untuk bacaan

■ *Bacalah isi bacaan baik-baik lalu cobalah menjawab pertanyaan-pertanyaan di bawah ini!*

1. P: Di mana Joel berjalan waktu itu?

   J: _____

2. P: Mengapa banyak orang di tempat itu?

   J: _____

3. P: Bagaimana orang-orang naik bis di Indonesia?

   J: _____

4. P: Apa yang terjadi dengan Joel setelah bis berangkat?

   J: _____

5.   P: Bagaimana perasaan Joel setelah kejadian itu?

     J: _____

6.   P: Menurut Sari Joel harus melakukan apa?

     J: _____

7.   P: Apa yang dikatakan Joel kepada Dokter Lim?

     J: _____

8.   P: Apa diagnosa Dokter Lim?

     J: _____

B. Menyimak

■ *Dengarkan baik-baik isi Tape Latihan 21 lalu jawablah pertanyaan-pertanyaan di bawah ini!*

1.   P Menurut teman Joel apa yang harus dia coba selama tinggal di Jakarta?

     J: _____

2.   P: Mengapa banyak orang naik bis di Jakarta?

     J: _____

3.   P: Bis bisa menjadi salah satu cara mengurangi dampak kerusakan lingkungan. Jelaskan!

     J: _____

4.   P: Sebutkan bis macam apa saja yang ada di Jakarta!

     J: _____

5.   P: Apa penyebab utama anemia?

     J: _____

6.   P: Bagaimana mengatasi anemia?

     J: _____

C. Tata bahasa

■ *Bacalah bacaan dengan teliti, lalu:*

1.   Carilah dua kata benda dengan imbuhan (**ke-** dan **-an**):

     a. _____

     b. _____

2. Carilah dua kata kerja dengan imbuhan (**ke-** dan **-an**)

   a. _____

   b. _____

3. Carilah dua kata sifat dengan imbuhan (**ke-** dan **-an**)

   a. _____

   b. _____

D. Pertanyaan umum (Kuis)

■ *Apa profesi saya? Jawablah pertanyaan-pertanyaan kuis di bagian B dengan memakai daftar profési di bagian A!*

A. Daftar profcsi

a. Ahli tusuk jarum.	g. Pawang hujan
b. Dokter jiwa	h. Ahli bedah plastik
c. Tukang pijat	i. Ahli gizi
d. Dokter mata	j. Dokter anak
e. Psikolog	k. Ahli otak
f. Dukun bayi	l. Perawat

B. Pernyataan dan jawaban

1. Pernyataan: Saya memakai banyak jarum untuk merawat pasién saya.

   Jawaban: Saya _____

2. P: Di daérah-daérah terpencil di Indonesia saya masih diperlukan untuk membantu ibu-ibu melahirkan.

   J: Saya _____

3. P: Tugas saya membantu orang untuk mengerti makanan-makanan yang baik untuk keséhatan meréka.

   J: Saya _____

4. P: Katarak adalah salah satu kondisi yang sering saya tangani.

   J: Saya _____

5. P: Tugas saya membantu dokter-dokter di rumah sakit untuk merawat pasién.

   J: _____

6. P: Saya sering diundang sebelum pésta atau acara diadakan untuk mencegah atau mengalihkan hujan ke tempat lain.

   J: _____

7. P: Di negara-negara besar seperti Amerika saya sering melakukan operasi untuk memperbaiki penampilan seseorang.

   J: _____

8. P: Di jaman modérn ini banyak orang yang menderita déprési sering memerlukan bantuan saya.

   J: _____

9. P: Saya banyak menangani masalah keséhatan yang dialami oléh anak-anak.

   J: _____

10. P: Tugas utama saya adalah memahami bagaimana otak bekerja.

    J: _____

11. P: Kondisi méntal pasién saya menjadi fokus utama profési saya.

    J: _____

12. P: Saya bisa membantu orang merasa riléks dengan sentuhan-sentuhan secara fisik dengan tujuan mengendurkan otot-otot yang tegang.

    J: _____

E. Teka-teki

■ *Carilah kata-kata berikut dalam kolom di bawah!*

1. Lengan	6. Kepala	11. Kaki
2. Bahu	7. Ketiak	12. Hati
3. Léhér	8. Paha	13. Mata
4. Rambut	9. Perut	14. Hidung
5. Tengkuk	10. Telinga	15. Dagu

L	E	N	G	A	N	S	E
T	E	N	G	K	U	K	T
B	A	H	U	A	E	E	U
T	I	M	E	T	H	P	R
E	R	N	I	R	A	A	E
L	U	A	P	A	T	L	P
I	K	A	K	M	I	A	D
N	E	K	A	B	S	N	A
G	H	I	D	U	N	G	G
A	A	M	A	T	A	I	U

F. Mencocokkan

■ *Cocokkan nama-nama penyakit di bagian A dengan kosa kata yang berhubungan di bagian B.*

A. Nama kondisi	B. Kosa kata
1. Melanoma	a. Kurang darah
2. Diabetes	b. Pening/pusing berat
3. Vertigo	c. Kadar gula
4. Anemia	d. Kanker kulit
5. Insomnia	e. Usus buntu
6. Diménsia	f. Mata
7. Apéndik	g. Kesulitan tidur
8. Katarak	h. Pikun
9. Sinusitis	i. Radang hidung
10. Wasir	j. Sakit perut
11. Asma	k. Kekebalan tubuh
12. Bronkitis	l. Tenggorokan
13. HIV/AIDS	m. Pernafasan
14. Amandel	n. Batuk
15. Parkinson	o. Gusi
16. Hepatitis	p. Pembuluh darah kaki
17. Sariawan	q. Otak
18. Varises	r. Keropos tulang
19. Thalasémia	s. Sél-sél darah
20. Rematik	t. Hati

International Relations
Hubungan Internasional

Sejak kecil Sari sudah tertarik dengan cerita tentang negeri jauh di seberang, seperti yang terdapat dalam buku anak-anak. Dia ingin menjelajahi dunia sendiri. Orang tuanya menyarankan Sari untuk mengambil jurusan Ilmu Hubungan Internasional di Fakultas FISIPOL, sekurang-kurangnya sebagai langkah pertama. Setelah itu jalan karir akan terbuka ke Departemen Luar Negeri, misalnya dalam bidang diplomatik, atau ke dunia bisnis.

Sambil mempelajari perkembangan di Asia Timur, Sari mendapat tugas membaca bahan kuliah termasuk buku dan artikel jurnal yang kebanyakannya dalam bahasa Inggris. Buku tersebut dicari-carinya di perpustakaan, tapi jarang ketemu. Frustrasinya tidak terkatakan! Akhirnya dia teringat: Saya punya teman, si Joel. Mungkin dia bisa membantu.

Sari: "Anu Joel. Saya kerépotan mencari sumber untuk karangan yang ditugaskan oléh dosén saya. Di mana kiranya bisa mendapat buku itu?"

Joel: "Coba lihat judulnya, ya. Buku macam itu mesti terdapat di perpustakaan Monash. Ha! Saya punya akal! Kakak saya sebentar lagi akan berkunjung ke Indonesia, antara lain untuk menéngok saya. Bagaimana kalau buku itu dipinjamnya, lalu bagian yang paling penting kita fotokopi di sini? Tidak boléh memfotokopi semuanya, jadi kita pilih bab-bab yang perlu saja. Setuju?"

Rasa terima kasih Sari tidak terkira. Pipi Joel lalu diciuminya.
Joel: "Ah, ini yang namanya 'hubungan internasional'?"
Sari dan Joel tertawa-tawa…

CULTURAL NOTE

The kind of kiss alluded to here, **cium**, consists of sniffing the cheek. Hence another meaning of the same word, "to smell", e.g. flowers. Another term is **sun** (from Dutch *zoen*), European-style; but a noisy smacker is considered disgusting.

WORDLIST

akal	idea, plan	**kerépotan**	to be having trouble
ambil: mengambil	to take	**langkah**	step
antara lain	among other things	**namanya**	they call
bab	chapter	**negeri**	land, country
bagian	part, section	**orang tua**	parents
bahan	materials	**perkembangan**	developments
bidang	field, area	**perlu**	necessary
cium: menciumi	to kiss (repeatedly)	**pinjam: meminjam**	to borrow
diplomatik	diplomatic	**pipi**	cheek
dunia	world	**saksi: menyaksikan**	to see, experience, witness
fotokopi: memfotokopi	to photocopy		
frustrasi	frustration	**saran: menyarankan**	to suggest
jelajah: menjalajahi	to explore, roam	**sebagai**	as
jurnal	scholarly journal	**seberang**	the other side (of the world)
jurusan	course of study		
kanak-kanak	children	**sumber**	source
karangan	composition	**téngok: menéngok**	to visit (to see how s.o. is)
karir	career	**ternyata**	to turn out (that)
kebanyakan	majority	**tugas**	task, assignment
kecil	small, young		

LANGUAGE NOTES

The prefix *ter-*

There are in fact two prefixes with this form, associated with verbs and with adjectives. The former is more important, and so we will deal with it first.

Ter- with verbs

These verbs have a passive meaning. There are three distinct areas of meaning to be described here:

1. Stative. These verbs denote a state, and so they contrast with a passive with **di-**, which denotes an action done by somebody. Note that there are no suffixes here. Some examples:

terletak	located (cf. **diletakkan** placed (by someone))
tertulis	written (not oral) (cf. **ditulis** written (by someone))
terbuat	made (cf. **dibuat** made (by someone))
terbuka	open (cf. **dibuka** opened (by someone))
tertutup	shut (cf. **ditutup** closed (by someone))

Some common words belonging in this group which are worth remembering and describe a state (without any agent) are:

terkenal	well-known
tersebut	abovementioned (quite frequent, pointing to what has just been said)

tercatat	noted
tertanggal	dated (e.g. a letter)
tercantum	included, inserted, specified, stated (in a document)
terlibat	involved
tertarik	interested (not to be confused with **menarik** "interesting")
terjamin	guaranteed
terhormat	respected (especially in the opening of a letter)

The following are unusual but important cases:

terdiri	consisting (of: **atas** or **dari**)
tergantung	depending (on: **pada** or **dari**)
termasuk	including

2. Accidental. The term "accidental" indicates that an action occurs unintentionally, unexpectedly or suddenly. This suggests an action that contrasts with a deliberate one, with the prefix **di-**, e.g.

Uangnya tertinggal di rumah.	Her money was (got) left behind at home. (That is, she forgot it.)
(Cf. **Uangnya ditinggalkan di rumah.**	Her money was left behind at home. (That is, deliberately, so that it would be safe.))

Among accidental actions a distinction can be made between "intransitive" ones and "transitive" ones.

a) Here are some examples of verbs indicating accidental actions or states:

tertidur	to fall asleep (not just **tidur** to sleep, go to sleep, but to doze off when one did not intend to)
terbangun	to wake up (suddenly, unintentionally)
terjadi	to happen, take place, occur, come about
terkejut	to be startled
tergelincir	to slip, skid

b) And here are some examples of verbs that can be compared with transitive ones; sometimes here the prefix **ter-** means "to get …-ed by mistake". For example:

terbawa	taken by mistake
termakan	eaten by mistake

These verbs can have an agent, which has to be introduced by **oléh** ("by") when it is a pronoun; otherwise **oléh** is optional. As an example:

Biji itu tertelan oléh saya.
I swallowed the seed by mistake. (lit. "The seed was swallowed by mistake by me.)

Other verbs that belong here are:

tertangkap	captured
terpengaruh	influenced
tertipu	tricked, deceived
terancam	threatened

Some more interesting cases are:

teringat	to recall, remember, have something suddenly come to mind
terasa	(base-word: **rasa**) to feel, have a sensation in a part of the body; to be felt, noticed

3. Abilitative. This term indicates verbs having the meaning "able to be …-ed". For example:

terjual	able to be sold, salable
terdengar	able to be heard, audible
terlihat	able to be seen, visible
terdapat	able to be obtained, available

Many of these verbs are negated, that is, they mean "not able to be …-ed". With these, if a suffix **-kan** or **-i** occurs, it is retained in the **ter-** form. Examples:

tidak terduga	unable to be guessed, unexpected, unpredictable (cf. **menduga** to guess, surmise, assume, suppose)
tidak terkira	unable to be estimated, incalculable (cf. **mengira** to think, guess, imagine, calculate)
tidak terélakkan	unavoidable, ineluctable (cf. **mengélakkan** to shun, avoid, evade)
tidak terkendalikan	uncontrollable (cf. **mengendalikan** to control, restrain)
tidak terkatakan	indescribable, inexpressible (cf. **mengatakan** to tell, inform)
tidak terobati	incurable (cf. **mengobati** to treat)

4. Others. There are also some words with **ter-** that do not seem to fit into the groups mentioned. For example the verbs:

tersenyum	to smile
tertawa	to laugh

Are these to be viewed as unintentional actions? There are no corresponding forms **menyenyum** or **menawa**.

And finally, there are some words which are not verbs at all:

terhadap	towards, with regard to
terlalu	too (to an excessive degree)
terlambat	late (past the right time)
terutama	especially

Ter- with adjectives

Not related to the above is the use of **ter-** with adjectives. Here this prefix serves to form a superlative, "the most, -est", but this only occurs with adjectives of two syllables, e.g.

> **mahal** expensive → **termahal** most expensive, dearest
> **indah** beautiful → **terindah** most beautiful, loveliest

In the case of longer adjectives, or other words that function adjectivally (e.g. **menghérankan** "amazing"), the word **paling** has to be used, thus:

> **paling menghérankan**   most amazing

LATIHAN 22 EXERCISE 22

Hubungan Internasional
International Relations

A. Pertanyaan untuk bacaan

■ *Jawablah pertanyaan-pertanyaan di bawah ini sesuai dengan isi bacaan!*

1. P: Apa ketertarikan Sari sejak kecil?

    J: _____

2. P: Dari mana dia mendapat gagasan untuk menjadi penjelajah dunia?

    J: _____

3. P: Apa yang dilakukannya untuk mewujudkan cita-citanya?

    J: _____

4. P: Pekerjaan macam apa yang dia bisa coba setelah lulus universitas?

    J: _____

5. P: Apa yang menjadi salah satu kesulitan Sari dalam kuliahnya?

    J: _____

6. P: Siapa yang bisa membantu dia dan bagaimana caranya?

    J: _____

7. P: Kebanyakan buku-buku yang diperlukan Sari ditulis dalam bahasa apa?

    J: _____

B. Menyimak

■ *Simaklah baik-baik isi Tape Latihan 22 dan cobalah menjawab pertanyaan-pertanyaan di bawah ini!*

1. P: Apa singkatannya FISIPOL?

   J: _____

2. P: Pekerjaan apa saja yang bisa dilakukan oléh lulusan HI?

   J: _____

3. P: Mengapa Sari memutuskan untuk kuliah di Jurusan HI?

   J: _____

4. P: Mengapa kemampuan berbahasa Inggris sangat penting untuk mahasiswa seperti Sari?

   J: _____

5. P: Apa tujuan utama studi Hubungan Internasional?

   J: _____

6. P: Apakah Sari menyukai kuliah HI?

   J: _____

C. Tata bahasa

■ *Carilah kata dengan awalan **ter-** di dalam bacaan, kemudian sebutkan arti dan fungsinya!*

Kata	Arti/fungsi
1. _____	_____
2. _____	_____
3. _____	_____
4. _____	_____
5. _____	_____
6. _____	_____
7. _____	_____
8. _____	_____

D. Pertanyaan umum (kuis)

■ *Jawablah pertanyaan-pertanyaan kuis politik di bawah ini!*

1. P: Siapa nama dinasti politik terkenal di India?

    J: _____

2. P: Siapa nama présidén pertama Amerika Serikat?

    J: _____

3. P: Di mana konferénsi Asia-Afrika yang pertama kalinya diadakan?

    J: _____

4. P: Apa nama kcbijakan politik pemerintah Australia dulu yang dianggap diskriminatif terhadap orang yang bukan kulit putih?

    J: _____

5. P: Siapa nama wakil présidén RI yang pertama?

    J:

6. P: Siapakah nama seorang Raja Jawa yang pernah menjadi wakil présidén RI?

    J: _____

7. P: Siapakah nama présidén wanita pertama Indonesia?

    J: _____

8. P: Siapakah nama présidén Filipina yang masuk ke dunia politik setelah pembunuhan suamin-ya?

    J: _____

E. Singkatan

■ *Tulislah kepanjangan dan arti singkatan-singkatan berikut!*

1. UN

    Singkatan: _____

    Arti: _____

2. G20

    Singkatan: _____

    Arti: _____

3. UNESCO

Singkatan: _____

Arti: _____

4. UNDP

Singkatan: _____

Arti: _____

5. ILO

Singkatan: _____

Arti: _____

6. NATO

Singkatan: _____

Arti: _____

7. CIA

Singkatan: _____

Arti: _____

8. EU

Singkatan: _____

Arti: _____

9. ASEAN

Singkatan: _____

Arti: _____

10. RI

Singkatan: _____

Arti: _____

11. APEC

Singkatan: _____

Arti: _____

12. PDIP

    Singkatan: _____

    Arti: _____

13. OPEC

    Singkatan: _____

    Arti: _____

A Trip to Yogyakarta

Perjalanan Ke Yogyakarta

Di luar dugaan Joel mendapat kesempatan berkunjung ke kota Yogyakarta, pusat kebudayaan Jawa yang termasyhur.

Sari memberi tahu kepada Joel: "Liburan seméster ini kami punya rencana ke Yogya,* karena ingin menéngok nénék, yaitu ibu dari ibu, yang tinggal di sana. Apakah Joel mau ikut? Kami tidak akan lama, hanya kira-kira lima hari saja."

Joel: "Ya, tentu saja saya mau! Saya sudah lama ingin melihat-lihat peninggalan purbakala yang ada di daérah itu. Tapi kita akan naik apa ke sana?"
Sari: "Ada bis malam, ada keréta, dan ada pesawat terbang…bis malam dan keréta menghabiskan waktu, dan sangat berat untuk badan kita. Jadi pilihan kami pesawat terbang saja…"
Joel: "Ya, jelas lebih cepat dan nyaman. Mari kita cari jadwal dan harga tikét, ya."

Pengeras suara: "Para penumpang dipersilakan naik ke pesawat udara, dengan nomer penerbangan GA 210."
Pramugari: "Kenakan sabuk pengaman, menegakkan sandaran kursi dan melipat méja. Baju pelampung ada di bawah kursi anda…"

Dalam témpo 60 menit meréka sudah dekat tujuan. Gunung Merbabu dan Gunung Merapi sudah kelihatan di sebelah kiri, Laut Hindia dan Pegunungan Menoréh kelihatan di sebelah kanan. Pesawat membélok ke utara, lalu mendarat dengan lancar di Bandara Adi Sutjipto.

Keluarga dari Jakarta dijemput keluarga Yogya di luar pengambilan bagasi. Meréka tidak perlu ke hotél, sebab ada tempat yang cukup luas di rumah nénék. Joel diperkenalkan kepada nénék Sari: "Mbah, ini teman saya, orang Australia yang belajar di UI. Namanya Joel."

Nénék: "Apa padha slamet?"
Sari: "Inggih, Mbah, pengèstunipun".

Joel amat terkesan. Bahasa Jawa ini, alangkah halus dan merdu bunyinya!

*Catatan: Singkatan dari Yogyakarta; ucapan sehari-hari "Jogya".

WORDLIST

apa padha slamet?	(Jav.) Are you well?	**nikmat**	pleasant
alangkah	how!	**nomor**	number
amat	very	**para**	(word indicating collectivity)
badan	body	**pegunungan**	mountain range
baju pelampung	life vest	**penerbangan**	flight
bandara	airport	**pengambilan**	baggage collection
beri tahu:	to inform, tell	**bagasi**	
memberi tahu		**pengeras suara**	loudspeaker
bis malam	night bus	**pengèstunipun**	by/through your blessing
catatan	note	**peninggalan**	remains, ruins
diperkenalkan	introduced	**penumpang**	passenger
dipersilakan	invited	**pesawat**	aircraft
dugaan	guess, expectation	**(terbang/udara)**	
gunung	mountain	**pilihan**	choice
habis:	to use up, waste	**pramugari**	flight attendant, stewardess
menghabiskan		**purbakala**	ancient, archaeological
halus	smooth; refined	**sabuk pengaman**	seatbelt
inggih	(Jav.) yes	**sandaran**	back (of seat)
jadwal	timetable, schedule	**singkatan**	abbreviation
kebudayaan	culture	**tegak: menegakkan**	to put in an upright position
kenakan:	to fasten	**témpo**	(space of) time
mengenakan		**terbang**	to fly (N.B. no prefix **ter-**)
keréta	train (= **keréta api**)	**terkesan**	impressed
liburan	vacation, break	**termasyhur**	famous, renowned
lipat: melipat	to fold, close; to stow	**tikét**	ticket
mbah	(Jav.) grandmother/father	**tujuan**	destination
méja	table, tray-table	**ucapan**	pronunciation
merdu	sweet, melodious, soft		
nénék	grandmother		

CULTURAL NOTES

The city of Yogyakarta has at its heart the Kraton or royal residence of Sultan Hamengkubuwono X. It has been noted as a centre of the Javanese classical arts, such as dance, shadow theatre and of course the **gamelan** orchestra, but today it is crowded with students attending the many educational institutions located there, with Gadjah Mada University as the largest and oldest. Apart from this, it is a modern city with large shopping malls, many hotels, and busy traffic.

The "archaelogical remains" that Joel alludes to are, of course, the ancient temples (**candi**) to be found in Central Java, the best known ones being Borobudur, located about 30 km to the north-west and Prambanan not far to the east of Yogyakarta – although there are many more that are also well worth visiting. These were built from the 8th to the early 10th century, and are visible witnesses to a civilization of surprising sophistication which is called Hindu-Javanese, but was in fact inspired by both Hinduism and Buddhism. Following this period, it was continued in East Java.

Sari's family are ethnic Javanese and, as such, they speak the Javanese language in normal situations. Joel is pleasantly surprised to hear it, although he may already have heard it at Sari's home in Jakarta, without being fully aware of the distinction between Indonesian and Javanese.

LANGUAGE NOTES

Various suffixes *-an*

At first sight, when looking at an Indonesian text we might say that the suffix **-an** is quite common. But in fact there are several different processes here, since **-an** can be found with various nouns, some adjectives, and even numerals. In some cases it is combined with reduplication. Let us review the possibilities.

Nouns

1. The suffix **-an** with verbal base-word

a) With words in this group, there is a corresponding transitive verb, so that the noun formed in this way indicates the result of the action, and can be explained as "**apa yang di-...**" ("what is ....-ed"). So the noun has a "passive" feeling, in contrast to ones with an "active" feeling (mentioned in Lesson 20). Some of these nouns are the product of the action, and others are what is worked on by the action. Some examples are:

makan	to eat	→	**makanan**	food (**apa yang dimakan**)
minum	to drink	→	**minuman**	drink
memilih	to choose	→	**pilihan**	choice
menanam	to plant	→	**tanaman**	crop
meminjam	to borrow	→	**pinjaman**	loan
menyumbang	to contribute	→	**sumbangan**	contribution

b) An interesting subset of the above type consists of words that act as modifiers of another noun, telling us what is or has been done with it. For example:

menyimpan	to save up	→	**simpanan**	what is saved, as in: **uang simpanan** savings
membeli	to buy	→	**belian**	what is bought, as in: **barang belian** purchases
meninggalkan	to leave behind	→	**tinggalan**	what is left behind, as in e.g. **buku-buku tinggalan kakék** books inherited from Grandfather
menyéwa	to rent	→	**séwaan**	what is rented, as in: **rumah séwaan** a rented house

c) Another group of nouns formed with **-an** and a verbal base-word indicates more the action than its result, although it is sometimes difficult to distinguish them. For example:

melatih	to train	→	**latihan**	training, practice, exercise
melayani	to serve	→	**layanan**	service
menjawab	to answer	→	**jawaban**	answer
berpikir	to think	→	**pikiran**	thought

mengingat	to remember	→	**ingatan**	memory
memandang	to view	→	**pandangan**	view, opinion

d) And with some verbal base-words the suffix **-an** forms nouns which indicate either the instrument with which, or the place where, the action occurs, e.g.

menggiling	to mill	→	**gilingan**	mill (the machine or the place where rice is milled)
membendung	to dam	→	**bendungan**	dam
menyalur	to channel	→	**saluran**	channel
menyaring	to filter, strain	→	**saringan**	filter, strainer, sieve
menimbang	to weigh	→	**timbangan**	scales, weighing machine

2. The suffix **-an** can also occur with noun base-words. In this case, we find nouns that have a meaning quite similar to the base-word, or which form an expansion or development from it. For example:

akhir	end	→	**akhiran**	suffix
jalan	road	→	**jalanan**	roadway
laut	sea	→	**lautan**	ocean
pasar	market	→	**pasaran**	the market (in an abstract sense)
peran	actor, character	→	**peranan**	role, part
pinggir	edge	→	**pinggiran**	outskirts

3. There are several nouns with **-an** that indicate a quantity or piece of something, e.g.

jajaran	a row, line, rank
pasangan	a pair, couple
rangkaian	a series, chain
timbunan	a heap, pile

4. The suffix **-an** combined with reduplication of a noun base-word can be seen in words of two kinds:
a) Words which indicate variety or generality of what is indicated by the base-word, e.g.

buah	fruit	→	**buah-buahan**	fruits (of various kinds)
daun	leaf	→	**daun-daunan**	foliage, leaves
pohon	tree	→	**pohon-pohonan**	trees, vegetation
sayur	vegetable	→	**sayur-sayuran**	vegetables (of various kinds)
tari	dance	→	**tari-tarian**	dances (of various kinds)

In one or two cases we get what could be called a "partial reduplication", thus:

dedaunan for **daun-daunan** (foliage, leaves), and **pepohonan** for **pohon-pohonan** (trees, vegetation), but with the same meaning.

b) Words that indicate either a miniature version or an imitation of what the base-word indicates, e.g.

burung	bird	→	**burung-burungan**	toy bird
kapal	ship	→	**kapal-kapalan**	toy ship
mobil	car	→	**mobil-mobilan**	toy car

5. With adjectival base-words, the suffix **-an** derives nouns that indicate something characterized by that quality, e.g.

asam	sour	→	**asaman**	pickles (in vinegar)
kotor	dirty	→	**kotoran**	dirt, excrement
manis	sweet	→	**manisan**	sweets, preserved fruits, candy

Adjectives

1. In a few cases, the suffix **-an** can extend or modify the meaning of an adjective, e.g.

murah	cheap	→	**murahan**	of low quality, common
rendah	low	→	**rendahan**	of low rank, subordinate

And reduplication can also occur, e.g.

besar	big	→	**besar-besaran**	on a big scale, grand
habis	used up	→	**habis-habisan**	completely, to the utmost, all-out

2. With measures of time, weight or distance, adjectives are formed which mean "by the …", e.g.

bulan	month	→	**bulanan**	monthly
kilo	kilogram	→	**kiloan**	by the kilo
méter	metre	→	**méteran**	by the metre
minggu	week	→	**mingguan**	weekly
tahun	year	→	**tahunan**	yearly, annual

but:

jam	hour	→	**jam-jaman**	by the hour, hourly

3. With noun base-words that indicate some sort of affliction, the adjective with **-an** means to be suffering from that, e.g.

cacing	worms	→	**cacingan**	infested with worms
jamur	fungus	→	**jamuran**	mouldy
jerawat	pimple	→	**jerawatan**	pimply, suffering from acne
kudis	scabies	→	**kudisan**	suffering from scabies, mangy
kutil	wart	→	**kutilan**	suffering from warts, warty

Numerals

The suffix **-an** occurs with group numbers, with several meanings:

1. An indefinite number:

puluh	group of ten	→	**puluhan**	tens; decades (of years)
ratus	group of 100	→	**ratusan**	hundreds
ribu	group of 1,000	→	**ribuan**	thousands

Also: **belasan** an indefinite number between ten and twenty

2. To indicate bank-notes, e.g.:

   (uang) sepuluh ribuan   a bank-note of Rp. 10,000

3. To indicate an approximate number, e.g.

   (berumur) delapan puluhan aged around 80
   lima ratusan   about 500
   (tahun) tiga puluhan   the (nineteen) thirties

LATIHAN 23 EXERCISE 23

Perjalanan Ke Yogyakarta
A Trip to Yogyakarta

A. Pertanyaan untuk bacaan

■ *Bacalah isi bacaan baik-baik dan jawablah pertanyaan-pertanyaan di bawah ini!*

1. P: Bagaimana perasaan Joel ingin melihat kota Yogyakarta?

   J: _____

2. P: Yogyakarta dikenal sebagai kota apa?

   J: _____

3. P: Siapa yang tinggal di Yogyakarta?

   J: _____

4. P: Ada berapa cara untuk pergi ke Yogyakarta?

   J: _____

5. P: Mengapa meréka memilih naik pesawat terbang? Jelaskan!

    J: _____

6. P: Perusahaan penerbangan apa yang meréka pakai?

    J: _____

7. P: Bahasa Indonesia macam apa yang dipakai oléh pilot dan awak pesawat ketika mereka menyampaikan pengumuman?

    J: _____

8. P: Bahasa apa yang dipakai nénék Sari?

    J: _____

B. Menyimak

■ *Dengarkanlah baik-baik isi Tape Latihan 23 dan cobalah jawab pertanyaan-pertanyaan di bawah ini!*

1. P: Mengapa Sari dan keluarganya sering pergi ke Yogyakarta?

    J: _____

2. P: Siapa yang lahir dan besar di Yogyakarta?

    J: _____

3. P: Propinsi Yogyakarta juga sering disingkat apa?

    J: _____

4. P: Berapa kira-kira jumlah penduduk DIY?

    J: _____

5. P: Siapa yang menjadi gubernur DIY sekarang ini dan mengapa dia dianggap sebagai sosok yang istiméwa?

    J: _____

6. P: Selain terkenal sebagai pusat budaya Jawa, Yogyakarta juga terkenal sebagai apa?

    J: _____

7. P: Sebutkan beberapa candi yang terletak di sekitar Yogyakarta!

    J: _____

8. P: Bahasa apa yang dipakai oléh kebanyakan warga Yogyakarta?

    J: _____

C. Tata bahasa

■ *Jenis kata: Carilah 8 kata benda dengan akhiran **-an** dalam bacaan!*

a. _____   e. _____

b. _____   f. _____

c. _____   g. _____

d. _____   h. _____

D. Pertanyaan umum (kuis)

1. P: Yogyakarta terletak di pulau apa?

    J: _____

2. P: Sebutkan nama beberapa candi yang ada di sekitar Yogyakarta!

    J: _____

3. P: Apa nama gunung berapi yang masih aktif yang terletak di dekat Yogyakarta?

    J: _____

4. P: Bahasa apa yang menjadi bahasa daérah Yogyakarta?

    J: _____

5. P: Siapakah nama raja Jawa terkenal dari Yogyakarta?

    J: _____

6. P: Apa nama univérsitas tertua dan terbaik di Yogyakarta?

    J: _____

7. P: Apakah nama makanan khas dari Yogyakarta yang bahan utamanya buah nangka?

    J: _____

8. P: Apakah nama pantai terkenal di Yogyakarta?

    J: _____

9. P: Pakaian warna apa yang tidak boléh dipakai oléh pengunjung pantai itu dan mengapa?

    J: _____

10. P: Apa nama pasar tradisional yang terletak di jantung kota Yogyakarta?

    J: _____

E. Kosa kata yang berhubungan dengan Yogyakarta

■ *Jelaskan kosa kata di bawah ini!*

1. Stasiun Lempuyangan: _____

2. Tamansari: _____

3. Sekatén: _____

4. Selokan Mataram: _____

5. Pakualaman: _____

6. Kaliurang: _____

7. Léséhan: _____

8. Borobudur: _____

9. Prambanan: _____

10. Gunung Merapi: _____

11. Tugu: _____

12. Kali Codé: _____

13. Alun-Alun Lor: _____

14. Malioboro: _____

15. Muséum Affandi: _____

To the Market
Ke Pasar

Joel: "Mau ke mana, Sari?"
Sari: "Saya mau mampir di Pasar Beringharjo. Ayo!"

Di pasar buah-buahan dan sayur-sayuran bertimbun-timbun. Orang berdesakan, mencari yang paling murah. Ada yang membeli beras, bumbu-bumbu, pakaian, sepatu…

Sari: "Di pasar kita boléh tawar-menawar. Malah harus. Tidak seperti toko. Di toko harga pas saja."

Sementara itu ada dua penjual tua yang berbantah-bantahan:
Penjual 1: "Lihat sana, ada putri cantik berpacaran dengan raksasa! Raksasa bermuka mérah!"
Penjual 2: "Aduh, jangan begitu! Nanti kepalamu dipukuli, otakmu bersérakan, lalu dikasi bumbu pedas gaya Minang…"
Penjual 1: "Iri hati kamu. Aku yang dilarikannya nanti!"
Penjual 2: "Ih masa! Dengan mukamu itu, seperti kripik kentang!"

Sari: "Hati-hati, ya, Joel. Kakimu jangan sampai bersentuhan dengan barang-barang yang di lantai itu. Mari, durian yang saya cari, supaya Joel berkenalan dengan buah yang terkenal itu. Nah, ini apa… Yu, durian berapa harganya?"

Joel melihat buah besar itu yang berwarna hijau kecoklat-coklatan dan berkulit seperti duri.
Sari: "Ini yang namanya durian. Énak sekali rasanya! Kami suka."
Joel diam saja. Dia bertemu mata dengan Sari. Sari baru mengerti bahwa Joel kurang suka baunya. Tentu saja bau itu menyengat. Joel menjauhi timbunan buah itu.

Sari: "Janganlah kuatir. Kalau sudah saya buka di rumah nanti, Joel akan saya beri sedikit untuk dicicipi. Sedikit saja! Kata orang, darah kita bisa bertambah panas…"

WORDLIST

ayo	come on!	**kulit: berkulit…**	to have a … skin
bantah: berban-tah-bantahan	to quarrel with each other	**lari: dilarikan**	run away with
		malah	on the contrary
barang-barang	(various) wares	**mampir**	to drop in, call in
beras	uncooked rice	**Minang**	Minangkabau, West Sumatra
bumbu	spices		
cantik	pretty	**murah**	cheap
coklat: kecoklat-coklatan	brownish	**otak**	brains
		panas	hot; passionate
diam	to say nothing, be quiet	**pedas**	hot (spices)
duri	thorn	**putri**	princess
iri hati	envious	**raksasa**	giant
jauh: menjauhi	to keep away from	**sementara itu**	meanwhile
kasi: dikasi	(coll.) to be given, have s.t. added	**sengat: menyengat**	pungent
		sérak: bersérakan	to lie scattered about
kentang	potato	**tambah: bertambah**	to become more…
kepala	head	**timbunan**	pile, heap
kripik	fried chip	**yu**	(Jav.) elder sister
kuatir	to worry, be anxious		

CULTURAL NOTE

Indonesians in general are proud of the fruits that happen to grow in their particular district, and are keen for the guest or visitor to try them. There are of course a wide variety of fruits, depending on the season, and many of them are really delicious. If you do try them and show your appreciation, you'll make a friend! So asking about the local fruits is a splendid way to start up a conversation.

Examples of local fruit: **pisang raja**, **pisang Ambon**, **pisang susu**; **nangka**, **mangga**, **manggis**, **rambutan**, **sawo**. Check your dictionary!

It is interesting to note that in Indonesian we have three terms for rice: **padi** for the plant growing in the field or when harvested but still unmilled; **beras** when milled; and **nasi** when cooked. (And in Javanese there is even a fourth one, **gabah**, which refers specifically to grains loose from the ear but not yet milled.) All this seems to indicate the cultural importance of this food-plant.

LANGUAGE NOTES

More intransitive verbs with *ber-*

There are a number of interesting formations all featuring the prefix **ber-**, some with a suffix, and of course all intransitive, that we need to present in order to complete the discussion. These have no object, and thus no passive forms.

1. Reciprocity
   These verbs mean doing a particular action "to each other".

a) The main type is marked by the affixes **ber-** and **-an**. For example, showing corresponding **meN-** forms:

mendesak	to push	→	**berdesakan**	to push each other
memandang	to look at	→	**berpandangan**	to look at each other
menabrak	to collide with	→	**bertabrakan**	to collide with each other

Naturally, the various base-words involved here have other derived forms as well, which can all be found in the dictionary.

b) Several words in this group feature reduplication, as well as the above affixes, without a perceptible difference in meaning, except the idea of repetition, e.g.

mengejar	to chase	→	**berkejar-kejaran**	to chase each other
memeluk	to hug	→	**berpeluk-pelukan**	to hug each other
memukul	to hit	→	**berpukul-pukulan**	to hit each other

c) In some cases we find a word added to complete the sense, which we can call the "complement" and which would be the object of the corresponding **meN-** form, e.g.

mengirim surat	**meréka berkirim-kiriman surat**
to send a letter	they sent letters to each other, corresponded
memegang tangan	**meréka berpegangan tangan**
to hold a hand	they held hands
menukar cincin	**meréka bertukaran cincin**
to exchange rings	they exchanged rings with each other, that is, got engaged

d) Commonly, these reciprocal forms refer to a mutual relationship or a spatial position, e.g.

berhadapan	to face each other, be facing
bertentangan	to be face to face, opposite, be in conflict
berdampingan	to be alongside each other, adjacent
berdekatan	to be close to each other
berjauhan	to be far from each other
berkenalan	to be acquainted with each other
berbatasan	to border on, adjoin
bermusuhan	to be enemies
berpacaran	to be boy/girlfriend
berkenaan	to concern, be related to
berhubungan	to be related to, connected with
bertalian	to be related to, linked with

Note that all these words take the preposition **dengan** "with", in order to introduce the person or thing related to.

For the sake of completeness, we should mention that there are two more ways to express reciprocity. Firstly, there is a construction using the word **saling** with the **meN-** form of the verb, e.g.

saling mencintai   to love each other
saling menghormati to respect each other

Secondly, there is a rare form, consisting of the base-word combined with the **meN-** form of the verb. A well-known example is:

tawar-menawar   to bargain, haggle with each other

(But the form **karang-mengarang** does not belong here; this is in fact a noun, meaning "writing, in general," as a subject or activity.)

2. Random action
Completely separate from the above, but also with the affixes **ber-** and **-an**, are the intransitive verbs that indicate action in a random or confused way, always with a plural subject. Some examples are:

berdatangan   to come from all directions
berlarian   to run in all directions
berkeliaran   to roam, wander, cruise about
bermunculan to turn up from all directions
bersérakan   to be scattered all about

3. The affixes **ber-** and **-kan**
Verbs with these affixes have as their meaning "to have (something) as (whatever the noun base-word indicates)". This something is the complement of the verb, not an object. Some examples are:

asas	principle, basis	→	**berasaskan**	to have… as principle, be based on the principle of…
cita-cita	ideal	→	**bercita-citakan**	to have… as ideal, aspire to…
dasar	basis, foundation	→	**berdasarkan**	to be based on…
isi	contents	→	**berisikan**	to have … as contents, contain…
sumber	source	→	**bersumberkan**	to have… as source, be based on…

A few examples have a verbal base-word:

mandi	to bathe	→	**bermandikan**	to have… as a bath, bathe in…
tulis	write	→	**bertuliskan**	to have… as inscription, be inscribed with….
tutup	cover	→	**bertutupkan**	to have… as covering, be covered in…

4. Numerals with the prefix **ber-**
Cardinal numbers prefixed with **ber-** form qualifying words that refer to a group, e.g.

berdua   (to be, form) a group of two; two together;
            e.g. **meréka duduk berdua** the two of them sat together

bertiga   (to be, form) a group of three; three together;
   e.g. **kami bertiga** the three of us; **berempat** all four, in a group of four

But with reduplication as well, we have words that mean "acting in a group of…", for example:

berdua-dua   (to do something) in twos, two-by-two
bertiga-tiga   (to do something) in threes, three at a time
berempat-empat (to do something) in fours

And with reduplicated numbers or measures, we find words that indicate forming or being in in-definite multiples of them, as in:

puluh	(group of) ten	→	**berpuluh-puluh**	in tens, by the tens, dozens
ratus	(group of) a hundred	→	**beratus-ratus**	by the hundreds, hundreds and hundreds of…
ribu	(group of) a thousand	→	**beribu-ribu**	by the thousands, thousands and thousands of…
kilo	kilogram	→	**berkilo-kilo**	in kilos, kilos and kilos of…
timbun	heap	→	**bertimbun-timbun**	in heaps, heaps and heaps of…

LATIHAN 24 EXERCISE 24

Ke Pasar
To the Market

A. Pertanyaan untuk bacaan

■ *Jawablah pertanyaan-pertanyaan berikut sesuai dengan isi bacaan!*

1.   P: Hari ini Sari ingin pergi ke mana?

   J: _____

2.   P: Apa saja yang dijual di Pasar Beringharjo?

   J: _____

3.   P: Apa bédanya berbelanja di pasar dan di toko?

   J: _____

4.   P: Ketika Sari dan Joel masuk ke pasar apa yang dilakukan oléh penjual 1 dan 2?

   J: _____

5.   P: Buah apa yang ingin 'dikenalkan' kepada Joel?

   J: _____

6. P: Apakah Joel suka durian?

    J: _____

7. P: Apa yang tidak disukai Joel?

    J: _____

8. P: Apa rencana Sari kalau sudah sampai di rumah nénék nanti?

    J: _____

B. Menyimak

■ *Simaklah baik-baik isi Tape Latihan 24 dan jawablah pertanyaan-pertanyaan berikut!*

1. P: Mengapa kita harus mengunjungi Pasar Beringharjo kalau kita pergi ke Yogyakarta?

    J: _____

2. P: Dagangan apa yang paling sering dicari orang?

    J: _____

3. P: Apakah Pasar Beringharjo menjadi tersingkir karena adanya pusat perbelanjaan modérn seperti Malioboro Mall?

    J: _____

4. P: Mengapa banyak pedagang yang berjualan di PB memakai bahasa Jawa?

    J: _____

5. P: Aspék apa yang disukai orang ketika berbelanja di pasar tradisional seperti PB?

    J: _____

6. P: Apa yang membuat Joel terkesan dengan suasana di PB?

    J: _____

7. P: Apakah para penjual itu juga bisa berbahasa Indonesia?

    J: _____

C. Tata bahasa (awalan *ber-*)

■ *Jelaskan kata-kata berawalan **ber-** dari bacaan!*

1. Bertimbun-timbun: _____
2. Berdesakan: _____
3. Berbantah-bantahan: _____
4. Berpacaran: _____

5. Bersérakan: _____

6. Berkenalan: _____

7. Berwarna: _____

8. Bertambah: _____

D. Terjemahan

■ *Terjemahkanlah kata-kata ini ke dalam bahasa Inggris!*

1. Kunir: _____
2. Jahé: _____
3. Temu giring: _____
4. Temu lawak: _____
5. Jcruk purut: _____
6. Kayu manis: _____
7. Ketumbar: _____
8. Pala: _____
9. Merica: _____

10. Cabé: _____
11. Asam: _____
12. Daun salam: _____
13. Laos: _____
14. Bawang putih: _____
15. Bawang mérah: _____
16. Terasi: _____
17. Kclapa: _____
18. Cengkih: _____

E. Berbelanja

■ *Jawablah pertanyaan-pertanyaan di bawah ini!*

1. P: Sari membeli mangga 3 kilo. Satu kilo harganya Rp 3000. Berapa rupiah Sari harus membayar semuanya?

   J: _____

2. P: Beras berkualitas paling baik harganya Rp 12.000 per kilo. Satu kwintal berarti berapa harganya?

   J: _____

3. P: Satu liter minyak tanah harganya Rp 3200. Pak Slamet mempunyai uang Rp 225.000. Berapa liter minyak tanah yang dia bisa beli?

   J: _____

4. P: Setiap minggu Bu Darmi menghabiskan dua setengah liter minyak goréng. Berapa liter minyak goréng yang dia habiskan dalam satu bulan?

   J: _____

5. P: Satu potong ayam berukuran besar harganya Rp 23.000, sedangkan ukuran kecil berharga RP 18.000. Bu Rusti memerlukan tiga potong ayam ukuran besar. Dia mempunyai uang sebesar Rp 178.000. Setelah membeli tiga potong ayam ukuran besar, berapa ayam ukuran kecil bisa dibeli dengan sisa uang itu?

   J: _____

National Days
Hari Nasional

Hanafi dan Joel sedang mengobrol di Coffee Shop Espresso di Jalan Margonda.

HANAFI Joel, apakah Australia punya Hari Nasional, seperti Hari Kemerdékaan kami pada tanggal 17 Agustus? Di sini setiap tahun ada upacara besar-besaran di mana-mana.

JOEL Ya, pasti ada. Namanya Australia Day, pada tanggal 26 Januari. Ada upacara juga, dan ada kembang api. Pada hari itu, tahun 1788, armada terdiri dari sebelas buah kapal layar berlabuh di pelabuhan Sydney. Pendatang Inggris yang pertama itu turun dari kapal, lalu mendarat di situ. Jadi yang dirayakan ialah didirikannya penetapan pertama orang Eropa, bukan proklamasi kemerdékaan, misalnya.

HANAFI Tapi apakah tidak ada penduduk sebelumnya, orang yang disebut penduduk asli alias aborijin? Meréka sudah lama menetap di tanah itu, selama puluhan ribu tahun, menurut artikel yang pernah saya baca.

JOEL Ya, benar. Penduduk asli itu pasti tertegun waktu menonton kapal itu belayar masuk, lalu memuntahkan ratusan orang kulit putih. Dan meréka pasti tidak senang kalau tanahnya direbut. Karena tidak membangun rumah dari batu, menanam tanaman atau menggembalai héwan, meréka disangka primitif, sehingga tidak perlu diperhitungkan. Sedangkan peradabannya terletak pada aspék batin...

HANAFI Apakah tidak ada konflik?

JOEL Timbulnya perselisihan tidak terélakkan. Di samping itu, penyakit-penyakit yang dibawa orang Inggris menular pada orang aborigin. Meréka tidak kuat menolak penyakit itu, sehingga banyak yang mati. Maka itu, masa kini ada yang berpendapat bahwa Australia Day itu jangan dirayakan, karena memperingati bencana. Negara yang betul-betul bersatu lebih baik memilih hari lain, yang menyatukan segala golongan masyarakat, serta menghormati préstasinya masing-masing, termasuk penduduk asli dan semua gelombang imigran yang tiba sejak tahun 1788...

HANAFI Wah, menarik sekali! Saya tidak membayangkan adanya sejarah seperti itu. Barangkali saya harus mendaftarkan diri untuk kuliah di jurusan Australian Studies!

WORDLIST

adab: peradaban	culture, civilization	**kapal layar**	sailing ship
alias	also known as	**kembang api**	fireworks
armada	fleet	**kemerdékaan**	independence
asli	original	**konflik**	conflict
aspék	aspect, side	**labuh: berlabuh**	to anchor
barangkali	perhaps	**labuh: pelabuhan**	harbour
batin	inner, spiritual	**maka itu**	and so
batu	stone	**masa kini**	nowadays
bayang: memba-yangkan	to imagine	**mati**	to die
		muntah: memuntahkan	to spew out
bencana	disaster	**préstasi**	achievement
daftar: mendaftar-kan diri	to enroll	**primitif**	primitive
		proklamasi	proclamation
darat: mendarat	to land, go ashore	**rebut: direbut**	seized
datang: pendatang	newcomer	**sakit: penyakit**	disease
duduk: penduduk	inhabitant	**sangka: disangka**	thought (wrongly)
élak: tidak teré-lakkan	inevitable	**satu: bersatu**	to unite, come together
		satu: menyatukan	to unite, bring together
gelombang	wave	**sebelumnya**	beforehand, previous
gembala: meng-gembalai	to tend, herd	**sedangkan**	whereas
		sejarah	history
golongan masya-rakat	social grouping	**selisih: perselisihan**	dispute, disagreement
		tanah	land
héwan	animals, livestock	**tanam: menanam**	to plant
hitung: diperhi-tungkan	taken into account	**tanam: tanaman**	crop
		tegun: tertegun	astonished
hormat: meng-hormati	to honour, respect	**tetap: menetap**	to settle
		tetap: penetapan	settlement
imigran	immigrant	**tolak: menolak**	to ward off, resist
ingat: memperin-gati	to commemorate	**tular: menular**	to spread (a disease)
		upacara	ceremony

CULTURAL NOTE

It has been observed that Indonesians who know anything about Australia have a tendency to take a special interest in the aboriginal inhabitants. Perhaps this has to be seen in the light of their own experience of colonization by Europeans, leading to exploitation and eventually to a struggle for independence, rather than to any cultural affinity. On the other hand, the history of European settlement is also worthy of attention, leading up to the creation of a truly multicultural society, in which a range of Asian immigrants play an increasingly important part.

By the way, a Department of Australian Studies does exist at the University of Indonesia.

Nominalization

This term means "turning something into a noun", and refers to verbs and adjectives. In other words, it is possible to make a verb or adjective into a noun. Whereas verbs and adjectives normally function as a predicate, by means of this process they can work in the same way as a noun, for example as a subject, an object, after a preposition or in a possessive relation.

This is a very useful process, and is found frequently in journalistic Indonesian prose, so anyone reading newspapers or magazines is sure to come across it and must understand it. The purpose of making such a construction is to highlight the action of the verb or the quality of the adjective, and say something about that.

It is possible to distinguish two types of nominalization.

The verbs involved here can be in a derived form, as well as their simple form. In this way we can take verbs with **ber-**, **ter-**, **meN-** or **di-**, and then give them the suffix **-nya**. This suffix has the effect of linking the new noun with a following noun. The same applies to any adjective. The following examples will illustrate this:

With the adjective **buruk** "bad":

> **Kabar burung tentang buruknya hubungan Sultan dengan isterinya sudah lama berédar.**
> Rumours about the bad relations between the Sultan and his wife have been circulating for a
> > long time.

The quality of the adjective **buruk** has been changed by giving it the suffix **-nya**, so that it can be joined with another noun, **hubungan**, so that the sentence is now talking about "the badness of the relations", which can follow the preposition **tentang** "about".

With the adjective **penting** "important":

> **Gubernur Jawa Timur menekankan pentingnya jalan tol untuk industrialisasi.**
> The Governor of East Java stressed the importance of the toll road for industrialization.

Here **pentingnya** is the object of the verb **menekankan** and can be linked with the noun **jalan tol**. In the following example we have both a nominalized verb and adjective:

> **Dipilihnya Désa Manunggal Jaya didasarkan pada besarnya potensi membangun désa
> > tersebut.**
> The choice of the village of Manunggal Jaya was based on the size of the potential to develop
> > this village.

The verb **dipilih** "chosen" has been turned into a noun with **-nya**, and now means literally "the being chosen", and can have something following in a possessive relation, namely the Desa Manunggal Jaya. (Of course this has nothing to do with the passive form with **di-** and **-nya**.)

In this example, the nominalized form functions as an object:

> **Menteri menuntut ditaatinya UU tentang lingkungan.**
> The Minister demanded obedience to (lit. the being obeyed of) the regulations regarding the
> > environment.

We could also translate as:

The Minister demanded that the regulations regarding the environment be obeyed.

Similarly, there are many examples with intransitive verbs, such as **Menurunnya** " The decline in…"; **Jatuhnya** " The fall of…"; **Meningkatnya** "The rise of…"; **Adanya** "the existence of…".

Some, but not all, such nominalized verbs and adjectives can be substituted with a noun with **peN-~-an** or **ke-~-an**, forms which were discussed earlier.

There is a second type of nominalization, in which no change in form takes place. Here we are dealing with intransitive and active transitive verbs only. Such verbs refer to a general activity and do not have a subject. For example:

Menganggur adalah keadaan yang menyiksa. Being unemployed is a painful condition.

We could compare this with:

Pengangguran bisa menimbulkan berbagai penyakit sosial.
Unemployment can give rise to various social ills.

Reduplication of verbs
All verbs can undergo this process.

The commonest meaning conveyed by reduplication is repetition or continuation of the action. With simple verbs there is no change in form, for example:

batuk to cough   →   **batuk-batuk** to keep coughing

With derived forms, however, not the whole word is doubled, only the base. But with the prefix **meN-** the nasal sound is retained in cases where this replaces the initial consonant. For example:

berteriak to scream   →   **berteriak-teriak** to keep screaming
mencari   to search   →   **mencari-cari**   to search about repeatedly
menulis   to write   →   **menulis-nulis**   to keep writing

In some cases, the reduplicated form contains the idea of making an effort or attempting to achieve an aim, e.g.

menghubungkan to connect   →   **menghubung-hubungkan** to attempt to make a connection, try to implicate

membesarkan to enlarge   →   **membesar-besarkan** to exaggerate, overemphasize, blow out of all proportion

With the negatives **tidak** or **belum** the reduplicated form suggests that the action still has not happened, contrary to expectation, e.g.

muncul   to appear, turn up   →   **tidak muncul-muncul** to still not turn up (no matter how long one waits).

With some verbs, though, reduplication gives a meaning of performing the action is a relaxed, casual, non-directed way, e.g.

berjalan	to walk	→	**berjalan-jalan**	to go for a stroll
duduk	to sit	→	**duduk-duduk**	to sit around and relax
membaca	to sit	→	**membaca-baca**	to have a relaxed read
melihat	to see	→	**melihat-lihat**	to have a look around, browse around

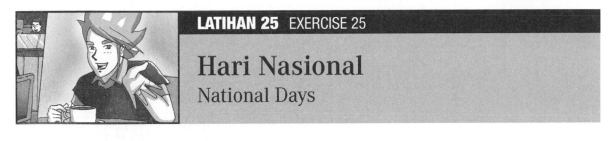

LATIHAN 25 EXERCISE 25

Hari Nasional
National Days

A. Pertanyaan-pertanyaan untuk bacaan

■ *Jawablah pertanyaan-pertanyaan ini berdasarkan isi bacaan!*

1. P: Hari ini Joel di mana dan dengan siapa?

    J: _____

2. P: Apa yang ditanyakan Hanafi kepada Joel?

    J: _____

3. P: Kapan dan bagaimana Hari Australia dirayakan?

    J: _____

4. P: Sebenarnya menurut Joel apa yang dirayakan pada Hari Australia?

    J: _____

5. P: Bagaimana nasib orang asli Australia menurut Joel?

    J: _____

6. P: Apakah Joel setuju Hari Australia dirayakan pada tanggal 26 Januari?

    J: _____

7. Kalau Joel tidak setuju apa gagasannya? Jelaskan!

    J: _____

8. P: Apa yang akan dilakukan Hanafi setelah mendengar cerita Joel?

    J: _____

B. Menyimak

■ *Dengarkanlah baik-baik isi Tape Latihan 25 dan jawablah pertanyaan-pertanyaan berikut!*

1. P: Apa yang terjadi menjelang tanggal 17 Agustus di Indonesia?

    J: _____

2. P: Apa yang terjadi pada tanggal 17 Agustus tahun 1945?

    J: _____

3. P: Apa saja yang dilakukan masyarakat Indonesia untuk merayakan kemerdékaannya?

    J: _____

4. P: Apa yang membuat Joel terkesan dengan suasana pada bulan Agustus?

    J: _____

5. P: Mengapa Joel tidak setuju dengan pemilihan tanggal 26 Januari sebagai Hari Australia?

    J: _____

6. P: Pihak-pihak siapa lagi di Australia yang kurang setuju dengan Hari Australia?

    J: _____

C. Pertanyaan umum (kuis)

■ *Jawablah pertanyaan-pertanyaan dari kuis di bawah ini!*

1. P: Kapan hari kemerdékaan Amerika Serikat diperingati?

    J: _____

2. P: Setiap tanggal 1 Mei orang di seluruh dunia memperingati hari apa dan untuk siapa?

    J: _____

3. P: Tanggal 25 Desember diperingati sebagai hari apa dan mengapa?

    J: _____

4. P: Sebutkan kapan Perang Dunia Pertama berlangsung.

    J: _____

5. P: Kapan Perang Dunia Kedua terjadi?

    J: _____

6. P: Kapan révolusi di Perancis berlangsung?

    J: _____

D. Menulis

■ *Tulislah sebuah kalimat untuk menerangkan nama tokoh terkenal berikut ini!*

1. George Washington: _____

2. Napoleon: _____

3. Marie Antoinette: _____

4. Mao Tse Tung: _____

5. Ho Chi Minh: _____

6. Helen Keller: _____

7. RA Kartini: _____

8. Martin Luther King: _____

9. Michael Gorbachov: _____

10. Soekarno: _____

Wall Lizards
Cicak

Di Jakarta Joel sering melihat cicak yang keluar soré hari dan berkeliaran di témbok rumah, terutama dekat lampu di luar, mengejar-ngejar serangga kecil yang tertarik oléh nyala lampu itu. Pikirnya, alangkah manis binatang itu, teman serumah dengan manusia. Sewaktu-waktu terdengar suaranya: cek cek cek...

Sari bercerita: "Menurut kepercayaan orang Bali, kalau kita dalam keadaan ragu-ragu, lalu mendengar cicak berbunyi tiga kali, maka kita diberi kepastian. Cicak adalah manifestasi Déwi Saraswati, déwi yang melindungi wacana dan tulisan..."

Mas Agus menyela: "Ah, gugon tuhon, takhayul itu! Kok percaya pada bunyi binatang! Lebih baik percaya pada penalaran sendiri, berdasarkan pengamatan dan penelitian terhadap fakta-fakta."

Ayah Sari menambah: "Menurut beberapa umat Muslim, cicak harus diberantas. Karena pada waktu Nabi Muhammad SAW dikejar oleh kaum musyrikin Arab, dan bersembunyi di gua Hiro, tiba-tiba ada cicak memberitahu meréka dengan bunyinya bahwa ada orang di dalam gua."

Lalu pada hari berikutnya di rumah kos Joel terkejut. Ada keributan di luar, seakan-akan diserang badai besar. Apa itu? Ternyata tetangga minta pengasapan untuk membasmi nyamuk. Kebetulan Joel baru saja membaca laporan di surat kabar Kompas, bahwa kasus demam berdarah di DKI Jakarta cenderung meningkat dan mulai membawa korban jiwa. Jumlah penderita DBD di Dépok meningkat sebanyak 29 persén saat itu.

Menurut Kepala Bidang Pengendalian Penyakit dan Penyéhatan Lingkungan Dinas Keséhatan Kota Dépok, pasién terbanyak dirawat di RS Bhakti Yudha sebanyak 55 orang. Seiring bertambahnya penderita DBD, bertambah pula permintaan warga untuk dilakukan pengasapan, menurut laporan itu.

Dengan demikian sudah ada yang bertanggung jawab mengawasi keséhatan penduduk di daérah itu. Tetapi Joel teringat pada cicak. Kalau nyamuk semua nanti habis, meréka mencari mangsanya di mana? Dan kalau cicak ikut kena asap itu, bagaimana akibatnya?

GRAMMATICAL NOTE

Note the difference between **bertambahnya** and **bertambah**, and note the word-order **dilakukan pengasapan**, not **pengasapan dilakukan**! See the Language notes on nominalization.

WORDLIST

akibat	result	**pasién**	patient
amat: pengamatan	observation	**pasti: kepastian**	certainty
asap	smoke, vapour	**percaya**	to believe
asap: pengasapan	fogging	**percaya: kepercayaan**	belief
awas: mengawasi	to keep watch over		
badai	gale, storm, tempest	**persén**	percent
basmi: membasmi	to exterminate	**tanggungjawab: bertanggungjawab**	responsible
binatang	animal, creature		
berantas: diberantas	wiped out	**pula**	also
cenderung	to have a tendency to	**ragu-ragu**	in doubt, uncertain
cicak	wall lizard	**rawat: dirawat**	nursed, treated
demam berdarah (DBD)	dengue fever	**ribut: keributan**	loud noise, tumult
		RS (Rumah Sakit)	hospital
dengan demikian	in this way	**SAW (Ar. Salallahu Alaihi Wassalam)**	May the blessing of God and peace be upon him
derita: penderita	sufferer		
DKI (Daerah Khusus Ibukota)	Special Capital Region	**sebanyak**	to the number of, by…
		séhat: keséhatan	health
fakta	fact	**séhat: penyéhatan**	improving health conditions
gua	cave		
gugon tuhon	(Jav.) superstition, nonsense	**seiring**	in keeping with, in line with
kaum	group, party	**sela: menyela**	to interrupt, butt in
kejar: mengejar	to chase, pursue	**sembunyi: bersembunyi**	to hide, conceal oneself
kena	affected by		
kendali: pengendalian	control	**serang: diserang**	assailed
		serangga	insect
korban jiwa	casualties, deaths	**takhayul**	superstition
lantas	then, next	**teliti: penelitian**	research
lindung: melindungi	to protect, be a patron of	**témbok**	wall
mangsa	prey, food	**tingkat: meningkat**	to increase, rise
manusia	humans, people	**tulisan**	writing
minta: permintaan	request	**umat**	members of a religious group
musyrikin	polytheists		
nabi	prophet	**wacana**	speech; discourse
nalar: penalaran	reasoning, logic	**warga**	resident, member of the community
nyamuk	mosquito		

CULTURAL NOTES

The **cicak**, wall lizard (also called **cecak**), is very common not only in Jakarta, but everywhere in the country. Newcomers are sometimes surprised to see a number of them hunting the little flying insects, mainly mosquitoes, on the walls of buildings, attracted by lights at night. They are quite different from the bigger lizard called **tokék** which lives in roofs and produces its typical loud **tok-kék** sound a number of times.

Traditional beliefs and customs are sometimes termed "superstition" by people who want to be seen as modern and science-minded, but such ideas are still in the back of the mind, as in any society, modern or otherwise. An example is the Indonesian fondness for ghost stories, also found in a printed form or even in TV dramas.

LANGUAGE NOTES

More about *yang*

The word **yang** was already mentioned in Lesson 13, and was described as a relative pronoun. As such, it can be translated with "who, which, that", where it introduces a clause giving extra information about the noun which precedes it. Note that there is no connection with the question-words "who?" and "which?", and also that "who", "which" or "that" are sometimes omitted in English in a less formal style, but always have to be inserted in Indonesian.

The following sentence provides an example:

> **Artikel yang dikarang Pak Sastro belum terbit.**
> The article (that) Pak Sastro wrote hasn't appeared yet.

Here the main information is: **Artikel belum terbit** ("The article has not yet appeared."); the extra information is placed after **artikel**, and is introduced with **yang**. It is worth noting that the Indonesian verb **dikarang** is passive, even though the English "wrote" may look like an active verb. This is because the Indonesian is focusing on **artikel**, and the clause means literally "which was written by Pak Sastro", so a passive is needed.

There are two more major uses of **yang** which should now be introduced. The first is a construction where it functions to nominalize a verb or an adjective, that is, turn it into a noun phrase which can serve as a subject or an object. A literal translation is "the one which", or "the thing that", or we might translate with "what" in the same sense. This is quite different from the use of **yang** as a relative pronoun, as there is no antecedent. Some examples:

...kasi' yang paling murah...

Minta apa?	What do you want?
Minta yang murah saja.	Just give me a cheap one.

Here we do not know what object is being referred to, only that a choice is being made.
A sentence of a somewhat different kind is the following:

> **Yang saya maksudkan, ialah pengangkatan guru baru.**
> What I meant was the appointment of new teachers.

Here a topic is stated, then a clarification is given.
Closely related to this is a construction where **yang** is inserted between the subject and its verb, in order to foreground that noun or pronoun. In order to translate this correctly, we have to say either "It is… which" or "I (he, etc.) am the one who…". Some examples are:

Dia yang saya pilih, bukan orang lain. She is the one I chose, not someone else.

The particle **-lah** is also sometimes found here, with the function of adding further emphasis. This is written suffixed to the noun, pronoun or word-group that heads the sentence, e.g.

Agama Islamlah yang dianut kebanyakan orang Indonesia.
It is Islam that the majority of Indonesians follow.

The effect of this sentence is to suggest that Islam is one out of a range of possibilities: it is Islam, and not some other religion. The words **agama Islam** are given a degree of emphasis. So we do not simply translate: "The majority of Indonesians follow Islam".

Noun clauses

This term is used to refer to clauses which follow a verb of saying, asking or ordering, and which are introduced by a certain conjunction and contain the contents of the statement, question or order. Let us illustrate this:

1. Following verbs of saying, telling or thinking, we use the conjunction **bahwa**, "that". (It will be clear that **yang** would be out of the question here, because it has a totally different usage.) However, it is true that in modern journalistic prose, writers sometimes omit **bahwa**, just as one can leave out "that" in English. (Is this influence from English, or just a wish to be concise?). Example:

   Dalam pidatonya Présidén menyatakan bahwa hubungan antara Amérika dan Cina sangat penting.
   In his speech the President stated that relations between America and China are very important.

2. Following verbs of asking, the clause containing the content of the question is introduced with **apakah**, "whether, if". (This use of **apakah** is of course somewhat different from the one we saw marking a question.) Note that if you see "if" in English you have to check: Does it mean "whether", or "on condition that"? In the latter case it must be rendered with Indonesian **kalau** (see Lesson 27). Example:

   Joel ingin tahu apakah emailnya diterima oléh Sari.
   Joel is wondering whether Sari has received his email.

3. Following verbs of ordering, urging or appealing, we use the conjunction **supaya** or **agar** (there is no difference), "that" (in the sense of "so that", please see Lesson 27). Example:

   Pak Diréktur menghimbau karyawannya supaya ikut memelihara lingkungan kerja.
   The Director called on his personnel to join in caring for the work environment.

Cicak
Wall Lizards

A. Pertanyaan untuk bacaan

■ *Jawablah pertanyaan-pertanyaan di bawah ini sesuai dengan isi bacaan!*

1. P: Binatang apa yang sering dilihat Joel di rumah-rumah di Indonesia?

    J: _____

2. P: Apakah Joel takut pada cicak? Mengapa tidak?

    J: _____

3. P: Apa yang diceritakan Sari kepada Joel tentang cicak?

    J: _____

4. P: Siapa itu Dewi Saraswati?

    J: _____

5. P: Apa kata kakak laki-laki Sari?

    J: _____

6. P: Apa yang diceritakan ayah Sari tentang umat Muslim dan cicak?

    J: _____

7. Kalau menurut Joel cicak tidak membahayakan, bagaimana halnya dengan nyamuk?

    J: _____

B. Menyimak

■ *Dengarkan baik-baik isi Tape Latihan 26 dan jawablah pertanyaan-pertanyaan berikut!*

1. P: Apa makanan utama cicak?

    J: _____

2. P: Selain cicak Joel juga pernah melihat binatang yang bentuknya sama tetapi lebih besar ukuran-
    nya. Binatang apakah itu?

    J: _____

3. P: Bagaimana orang akan beréaksi ketika pertama kali pergi ke rumah di Indonesia dan melihat banyak cicak di dinding rumah?

    J: _____

4. P: Sebelum pergi ke Indonesia Joel sudah diperingatkan oléh orang tuanya tentang bahaya nyamuk. Apakah meréka memberitahu Joel tentang cicak?

    J: _____

5. P: Mengapa banyak penderita penyakit demam berdarah di Jakarta?

    J: _____

6. P: Apa yang biasa dilakukan oleh pemerintah lokal untuk mengatasi demam berdarah?

    J: _____

7. P: Cara pencegahan yang bagaimana selain pengasapan untuk mengatasi penyakit demam berdarah?

    J: _____

C. Menulis

■ *Mengarang: tulislah sebuah karangan dengan cara pandang cicak dengan memakai kosa kata di bawah ini:*

Dinding	Panas	Lampu
Merayap	Ekor	Rumah
Tinggi	Orang-orang	Pintu
Nyamuk	Jendéla	
Hujan	Atap	

_____

_____

_____

_____

_____

_____

_____

_____

D. Pertanyaan umum (kuis)

■ *Jawablah pertanyaan-pertanyaan kuis di bawah ini!*

1. Q: Binatang ini dipakai sebagai lambang negara Republik Indonesia.

   A: _____

2. Q: Binatang ini dianggap langka, hanya makan sejenis bambu dan berasal dari Cina.

   A: _____

3. Q: Binatang ini bentuknya seperti cicak tetapi ukuran sangat besar, sangat berbahaya dan penghuni asli sebuah pulau di Indonesia timur.

   A: _____

4. Q: Binatang apakah yang dianggap sakti bagi masyarakat Hindu India?

   A: _____

5. Q: Platypus adalah binatang yang berasal dari negara mana?

   A: _____

6. Q: Almarhum Steve Irwin dikenal sebagai pemburu binatang apa?

   A: _____

E. Nama binatang dan negara asal

■ *Sebutkan nama negara asal binatang-binatang yang ada di bawah ini!*

Nama binatang	Negara
1. kangguru	_____
2. panda	_____
3. gajah	_____
4. tasmanian devil	_____
5. komodo	_____
6. burung kiwi	_____
7. burung cendrawasih	_____
8. unta	_____
9. beruang	_____
10. elang gundul	_____
11. anjing bulldog	_____

Demonstrations
Unjuk Rasa

Pada suatu hari, Joel sampai di kampus pagi-pagi. Dia terkejut melihat keadaan luar biasa: ratusan mahasiswa sudah berkumpul di depan gerbang utama. Ada kendaraan pick-up dengan beberapa mikrofon, dan sejumlah spanduk sudah dipasang di sepanjang jalan.

Setelah bertemu dengan temannya, Hanafi, Joel bertanya: "What's going on today?" Hanafi bingung sejenak...to die? pikirnya, lalu menjawab: "Jangan takut. Tidak ada bahaya. Tidak ada yang akan mati. Ini yang disebut démo dalam bahasamu, bukan? Indonesianya "unjuk rasa". Maksudnya, memberi tahu kepada pihak berkuasa tentang rasa, misalnya rasa kurang puas. Ini salah satu aspék kebébasan beréksprési. Sudah umum di Indonesia, terutama sejak jatuhnya rézim Soeharto tahun 1998. Unjuk rasa terjadi hampir setiap hari, khususnya di Jakarta. Baru-baru ini pernah ada tujuh unjuk rasa pada hari yang sama, di berbagai bagian kota, sehingga lalu lintas mengalami kemacetan di jalur utama, dan mengganggu pemakai jalan."

Joel: "Mengapa ada begitu banyak unjuk rasa?"

Hanafi: "Biasanya dilakukan oléh mahasiswa yang menentang kebijakan pemerintah, atau para buruh yang tidak puas dengan perlakuan majikannya."

Joel: "Apa ada gunanya?"

Hanafi: "Ya, coba. Pihak Réktor sudah mengeluarkan Surat Keputusan, dengan tujuan memungut uang pangkal Rp 5 juta sampai Rp 25 juta per mahasiswa baru. Aksi kami menuntut pencabutan SK itu. Kesempatan belajar harus merata bagi semua mahasiswa yang berpréstasi, jangan dijual kepada siapa pun yang berani membayar uang masuk!"

Sekitar pukul 10.00 massa bergerak memblokir pintu masuk kampus, sehingga mendapat réaksi dari pihak keamaman setempat. Pemimpin-pemimpin mengadakan orasi dari atas pick-up selama dua jam, yél-yél diteriakkan, dan semua sudah berkeringat. Joel ingin tahu apakah nanti ada hasilnya. Sudah ada pengumuman bahwa dialog dijadwalkan oléh pihak Réktorat dengan pihak mahasiswa, bertempat di kampus Salémba bésok pagi 9.00 WIB. Tinggal menunggu kabar.

Note: Trying saying "today" with an Australian accent.

WORDLIST

ada: keadaan	situation	**bébas: kebébasan**	freedom
aksi	campaign, action	**berani**	(coll.) able to
aman: keamanan	security	**bijak: kebijakan**	policy
bahaya	danger	**bingung**	confused

blokir: memblokir	to block	**pungut: memungut**	to charge, collect
buruh	worker	**putus: keputusan**	decree, decision
cabut: pencabutan	withdrawal, revocation	**rata: merata**	to be shared equally
dialog	dialogue	**réaksi**	reaction, response
éksprési: beréksprési	to express oneself	**réktor**	Rector (= president of a university)
gerak: bergerak	to move		
gerbang	gate	**réktorat**	Rector's office
guna	use	**rézim**	regime
jadwal: dijadwalkan	scheduled	**sejenak**	for a moment
jalur	(traffic) artery	**siapa pun**	anybody
jatuh	to fall	**spanduk**	banner
keluar: mengeluarkan	to issue	**surat keputusan (SK)**	decree, directive
kendara: kendaraan	vehicle	**tempat: bertempat**	to take place
keringat: berkeringat	sweaty	**tentang: menentang**	to oppose
khususnya	in particular, specifically	**teriak: diteriakkan**	shouted (out)
laku: perlakuan	treatment	**tinggal**	the only thing left to do is…
luar biasa	unusual, extraordinary		
macet: kemacetan	blockage, jam	**tuju: tujuan**	aim, object
majikan	employer, boss	**tuntut: menuntut**	to demand
massa	the mass, crowd	**uang pangkal**	admission fee (school, college)
mikrofon	microphone		
orasi	(public) speech	**umum: pengumuman**	announcement
pagi-pagi	early in the morning	**utama**	main
pasang: dipasang	set up	**WIB = Waktu Indonesia Barat**	West Indonesia Time
pihak	side, party		
pihak berkuasa	the authorities	**yél**	slogan
puas	satisfied		

CULTURAL NOTES

The extent of student activism in Indonesia is striking. Much energy is expended in pushing social or political causes that seem worthwhile to students and their organizations. It is true that the fall of the repressive Soeharto regime was at least in part due to pressure from this quarter, showing that the exercise of this kind of power is not futile. In fact, since that time, the freedom of expression enjoyed by students and workers has been much exercised.

However, this is not a new phenomenon, when one recalls how it was the Indonesian youth which promulgated the **Sumpah Pemuda** (Oath of the Youth) as long ago as 1928, and which also played a key part in the Proclamation of Independence in 1945.

LANGUAGE NOTES

More about conjunctions

Apart from the ones already mentioned in Lesson 26, Indonesian has a wide range of conjunctions, which serve to link clauses in the process of building up longer sentences. Alongside a main clause, we can add further information or modify it in several different ways. The clause introduced by the conjunction can occur either before or after the main clause; if it is placed in front, it receives more attention. We can list several types of conjunction; ones listed on the same line have the same meaning, and can be varied for stylistic reasons.

1. Time
   Conjunctions of time are:

ketika, waktu	when
sebelum	before
sesudah, setelah	after
sejak	since
sampai	until

An important point to note here is that **ketika** and **waktu**, "when", refer to an event in the past. If "when" refers to something yet to happen (in the future), it must be translated with **kalau** (etc.) (see below). And naturally this "when" has nothing to do with the question-word "when?", which is **kapan?**.

2. <u>Condition</u>

Conjunctions of condition allude to events that have not yet occurred, but may or will occur, provided a certain condition is fulfilled. They include:

kalau, jika, jikalau	if, when
bila, apabila, bilamana	when, whenever, if
asal, asalkan	provided that
seandainya, andaikata, sekiranya	supposing that, if

One observes that "when" and "if" are quite close in Indonesian.

3. <u>Reason</u>

Conjunctions of reason include:

karena, oléh karena	because, because of the fact that (*but in Malaysian*: **kerana**)
sebab, oléh sebab	because
lantaran, gara-gara	because (*journalistic style only*)

4. <u>Purpose</u>

The conjunctions are:

    supaya, agar   so that

Supaya and **agar** are followed by a full clause, the subject of which is usually different from that of the main clause; if the subject is the same, it can be omitted.

5. <u>Concession</u>

There are a number of conjunctions all of which can be translated with "although, even though":

meskipun

walaupun

sekalipun

biarpun

sungguhpun

kendati, kendatipun (*journalistic style*)

6. <u>Others</u>

kalau-kalau	lest, in case, (in the hope/fear) that
sehingga	so that, to the extent that, as a result of which (N.B. not to be confused with **supaya**, which is also translatable with "so that")
padahal	whereas, whilst, notwithstanding the fact that
seakan-akan, seolah-olah	as if, as though

Finally, there are a few cases where a word looks like a conjunction, but is in fact a preposition, preceding a word-group consisting of a nominalized verb and other words dependent on it, for example:

With **untuk**:

Kita akan berusaha untuk mengatasi segala kesulitan.
We will endeavour to overcome every difficulty.
(Cf. the use of **untuk** in the sense of "for".)

With **dengan**:

Dia berhasil meraih gelar dengan memperhatikan petunjuk-petunjuk dosénnya.
She succeeded in attaining the degree by paying attention to her lecturer's instructions.
(Cf. the use of **dengan** in the sense of "with".)

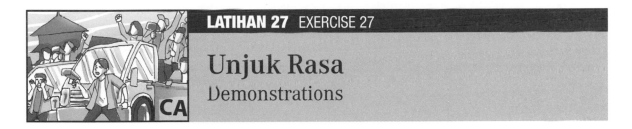

LATIHAN 27 EXERCISE 27

Unjuk Rasa
Demonstrations

A. Pertanyaan dari bacaan

■ *Jawablah pertanyaan-pertanyaan di bawah ini menurut isi bacaan*

1. J: Ke mana Joel pergi pada hari itu?

   J: _____

2. P: Mengapa dia terkejut? Apa yang terjadi?

   J: _____

3. P: Apa yang terjadi menurut Hanafi?

   J: _____

4. P: Apa tujuan dari unjuk rasa kali ini?

   J: _____

5. P: Biasanya kegiatan apa saja yang dilakukan di dalam sebuah unjuk rasa?

   J: _____

6. P: Apakah unjuk rasa kali ini berhasil? Apa indikasinya?

   J: _____

B. Menyimak

■ *Simaklah baik-baik isi Tape Latihan 27 dan jawablah pertanyaan-pertanyaan berikut!*

1   P: Apakah di Indonesia demonstrasi di kampus-kampus hal yang biasa?

J: _____

2.   P: Apa yang dilihat Joel pagi itu?

J: _____

3.   P: Menurut Hanafi apa tujuannya unjuk rasa?

J: _____

4.   P: Apa bédanya démo sebelum dan sesudah éra Suharto?

J: _____

5.   P: Apa dampak yang ditimbulkan démonstrasi yang sering terjadi di Jakarta menurut Hanafi?

J: _____

6.   P: Unjuk rasa yang disaksikan Joel hari ini tuntutannya apa? Jelaskan!

J: _____

7.   P: Gambarkan apa saja yang dilakukan oléh peserta unjuk rasa!

J: _____

8.   P: Dari unjuk rasa hari ini?

J: _____

C. Sebutkan nama negara asal para aktifis di bawah ini

Nama aktifis   **Negara**

1.   Che Guevara   _____

2.   Aung San Suu Kyi   _____

3.   Lech Walesa   _____

4.   Hlavac   _____

5.   Cut Nyak Dien   _____

6.   Gandhi   _____

7.   Martin Luther King   _____

8.   Nelson Mandela   _____

9.   Kemal Atatürk   _____

10. Norodom Sihanouk   _____

11. Ho Chi Minh   _____

D. Menulis (mengarang)

■ *Pilihlah salah satu nama aktifis dalam kolom di atas, lalu tulislah karangan tentang cerita hidupnya!*

_____

_____

_____

_____

_____

_____

_____

_____

_____

_____

LESSON 28

The Secret Trumpet
Trompét Rahasia

SARI	Joel, kalau akhir minggu soré hari begini di rumah, kamu biasanya sedang apa?
JOEL	Jarang ada waktu, tapi kalau mau relax saya meniup trompét saya. Kadang-kadang diundang main dengan beberapa teman. Kami punya band kecil. Namanya "Sticky and the Insects".
SARI	Hé, kita sudah berkenalan begitu lama, tapi baru sekarang saya dengar kamu bisa main trompét! Artinya, makin lama kenal, makin mendalam persahatannya, bukan? Jadi, musik macam apa?
JOEL	Ya, funky jazz, dan pernah main hip hop gaya Jamaika.
SARI	Mengapa trompetnya tidak dibawa ke sini?
JOEL	Takut mengganggu tetangga, lalu ditegur pak RT. Apalagi kalau meniup trompét untuk meniru suara gajah galak. Lucuuu sekali.
SARI	Mas Agus punya teman yang mempunyai trompét. Joel mau coba? Saya ingin dengar bunyinya bagaimana.
JOEL	Ah, lain kali saja, ya.
SARI	Ada program RCTI yang namanya Dahsyat, yang mengundang band. Musiknya hébat. Dahsyat belum lama ini mengundang Hillary Clinton, atas permintaan Kedubes Amerika Serikat. Sayangnya, Bu Hillary mengaku hanya kenal nama The Beatles dan The Rolling Stones saja.
JOEL	RCTI itu apa?
SARI	Artinya, Rajawali Citra Télévisi Indonesia, stasiun TV swasta terbesar di Indonesia.
JOEL	Anu, Sari, lagu apa yang kamu paling suka?
SARI	"Godai aku lagi", sebuah single dari Agnes Monica. Kalau mau, biar saya catat liriknya untuk Joel. Terus bisa dibawa pulang ke luar negeri, lalu dinyanyikan di sana.
JOEL	Apakah Dahsyat ada di Jakarta saja?
SARI	Tidak. Nanti Sahabat Dahsyat yang tinggal di Bali bisa menonton bintang tamu di sana, disiarkan langsung dari Hard Rock Kafé di Kuta. Aduh, saya ingin ke Bali. Bali dekat Australia, kan?
JOEL	Ya, dekat. Dan saya harap Sari akan ke Australia juga, menéngok orang tua saya di Geelong...

Sudah menjelang waktu untuk Joel pulang. Program studinya di Jakarta sudah selesai.

SARI	Kapan Joel kembali ke Jakarta?

JOEL	Belum tahu. Tapi jelas, saya ingin datang lagi, secepat mungkin.
SARI	Jauh di mata...
JOEL	Dekat di hati.

CULTURAL NOTES

The RT mentioned here is the smallest neighbourhood organization, consisting of a group of neighbours, headed by a "Pak RT", its elected chairman. A number of RT come under the RW (**Rukun Warga**, Citizens' Organization, formerly called RK, **Rukun Kampung**). The function of the RT is to promote social cohesion and deal with any causes of friction. Playing a trumpet loudly in the house would be likely to cause irritation with the neighbours, bearing in mind that their walls are very close. The system of RT and so on originates from the period of the Japanese occupation (1942–45), when it served as a means of surveillance.

WORDLIST

aku: mengaku	to admit, confess	**goda: menggodai**	to tempt
apalagi	especially	**hébat**	terrific
biar	let me	**jauh di mata dekat**	absence makes the heart
bintang tamu	guest star	**di hati**	grow fonder
dahsyat	awesome	**kedubes =**	embassy
dalam: mendalam	to become deeper	**kedutaan besar**	
gajah	elephant	**lagu**	song, melody
galak	fierce, wild	**langsung**	direct, straight

lirik	lyric	siar: disiarkan	broadcast, transmitted
lucu	funny	stasiun	station
main	to play	swasta	private
nyanyi: dinyanyikan	sung	tegur: ditegur	warned, criticized
punya: mempunyai	to own, possess	terus	and then
rahasia	secret	tiru: meniru	to imitate
RT = Rukun Tetangga	neighbourhood association	tiup: meniup	to blow
		trompét	trumpet
sahabat: persaha-batan	friendship		

LANGUAGE NOTES

Some other structures

1. **makin…makin…**

   Two adjectives can occur in what has been called a "correlative relationship" (Sneddon 1996:352). This means that as the degree of the first adjective increases, so too does the second. This can be trans- lated with: "The more…, the more…". Often the first clause contains the word **lama**, "long (of time)", suggesting that as time goes by, the degree of the second adjective increases. Some examples are:

   > **Anaknya makin besar makin pandai.**
   > The more his child grows up the cleverer he/she becomes.

   > **Penduduk Indonesia makin lama makin banyak.**
   > The inhabitants of Indonesia keep on increasing. (lit. "the longer the time, the more")

   > **Iklim Australia makin lama makin kering.**
   > The climate of Australia is getting drier and drier.

2. **baik… maupun…**

   This construction functions to link two nouns or phrases, in such a way as to suggest that what is said applies to both items. It is translated with "Both… and…", or, with a negative, "Neither… nor…" Examples:

   > **Baik di desa maupun di kota minyak tanah sudah mahal.**
   > Both in the country and in the city kerosene has become expensive.

   > **Baik prosa maupun puisi Indonesia énak dibaca.**
   > Both Indonesian prose and poetry are a pleasure to read. (Note the passive verb-form here, lit. "to be read".)

3. **baru**

   Apart from its common function as an adjective, meaning "new, recent, fresh, modern", this word also has an adverbial use which sometimes leads to confusion and is worth mentioning here. In this use it does not describe a noun, but modifies the verb, and can be translated with "only, not until, not before". For example:

Baru jam dua malam dia masuk kamar tidurnya.
She only entered her bedroom at 2 a.m.

And a well known advertising slogan runs:

Ini bir baru. Ini baru bir. This is a new beer. This is what you call beer.
(Lit. "only this is beer – everything till now wasn't real beer.")

4. Ways of opening a sentence

In both spoken and written Indonesian, there is a favoured method of opening a sentence, using one word (generally), following by a pause (or a comma), as an introduction to the main statement. There are several different types, e.g.

Suggesting a consequence from, or a contrast with, the preceding sentence:

Maka…, (or **Maka itu,…**)	Consequently…., And so,
Sebab, …	For that reason,… This is because…
Namun, …	Nevertheless, … Even so, …
Padahal, …	However, … All the same, …

With an adjective, nominalized by suffixation with **-nya**:

Anehnya,…	The funny (odd) thing is, …
Lucunya, …	The amusing thing is, …
Sayangnya, …	Unfortunately, ….

Or nominalized with **yang**:

Yang menghérankan, …	The amazing thing is, …

With a noun, again suffixed with **-nya**:

Soalnya, …	The problem is, …
Pokoknya, …	The main thing is, …
Misalnya, …	For example, … (an example is…)
Maksudnya, …	That is to say, … (the intention is…)
Alasannya, …	The reason (motive) for that is, …
Buntutnya, …	The result (outcome) is, ….

Using a verb without a subject, translated with an English present participle (-ing):

Mengingat …, …	Bearing in mind that …, ...
Melihat …, …	In view of the fact that …, …
Merasa …, …	Feeling that …, …

5. Foregrounding, or the "split subject"

When a subject consists of a group of words, sometimes this can be split up in such a way as to "foreground" part of it. This is done by placing the part to be highlighted at the beginning of the sentence in order to receive more attention, separating it from the rest of the subject with a pause or comma, which is then suffixed with the possessive **-nya** to preserve the link. We hear a rising intonation before the comma, suggesting "Wait, there's more!" Some examples:

Rumah ini, besarnya hanya 20 méter persegi.
The size of this house is only 20 square metres.
   (Cf. **Besar rumah ini hanya 20 méter persegi.**)

Orang kaya itu, rumahnya berjumlah dua puluh buah.
That rich man's houses are twenty in number.
   (Cf. **Rumah orang kaya itu berjumlah dua puluh buah.**)

Racun tadi, cara menghilangkannya begini.
The method of removing this poison is as follows.
   (Cf. **Cara menghilangkan racun tadi begini.**)

In each case, we could translate: "As for…, …" in order to render this foregrounding.

Common Signs about Town

Awas anjing galak	Beware of the dog
Bélok kiri jalan terus	Free left turn
Boléh putar balik	U-turn allowed
Dilarang masuk	No entry
Dilarang memakai sandal jepit	No thongs
Dilarang merokok	No smoking
Dilarang parkir	No parking
Harap antri	Please form a queue
Harap tenang	Quiet, please
Jalan buntu	No through traffic
Jalan pelan-pelan	Drive/ride slowly
Khusus busway	Bus lane
Pria	Gents
Satu arah	One way
Tamu harap lapor	Visitors must report
Tidak untuk minum	Not for drinking
Three in one	Only vehicles with at least three passengers
Uang pas	Exact money
Wanita	Ladies

LATIHAN 28 EXERCISE 28

Trompét Rahasia
The Secret Trumpet

A. Pertanyaan untuk bacaan

■ *Bacalah isi bacaan lalu jawablah pertanyaan-pertanyaan berikut!*

1. P: Apa yang dilakukan Joel pada akhir minggu di rumahnya di Australia?

   J: _____

2. P: Apakah Joel bisa bermain trompét dengan baik? Apa indikasinya menurutmu?

   J: _____

3. P: Apa nama kelompok musik Joel?

   J: _____

4. P: Gaya musik apa yang dimainkan Joel dan kelompok bandnya?

   J: _____

5. P: Jelaskan apa itu 'Dahsyat'!

   J: _____

6. P: Di mana acara télévisi Dahsyat disiarkan?

   J: _____

7. P: Apakah Joel masih akan lama tinggal di Jakarta?

   J: _____

8. P: Apakah dia ingin kembali lagi ke Indonesia? Kapan?

   J: _____

B. Menyimak

■ *Simaklah baik-baik isi Tape Latihan 28 dan jawablah pertanyaan-pertanyaan berikut!*

1. P: Selain bermain trompét apa lagi yang menjadi hobi Joel?

   J: _____

2. P: Selain Jazz gaya musik apa yang disukai Joel?

   J: _____

3. P: Apa koméntar Joel tentang perkembangan musik pop di Indonesia?

   J: _____

4. P: Mengapa Joel lebih tertarik kepada musik tradisional Indonesia seperti gamelan misalnya?

   J: _____

5. P: Alat instrumén apa yang ingin Sari pelajari?

   J: _____

6. P: Sewaktu masih remaja dan tinggal di Yogyakarta apa yang sering dilakukan ibu Sari?

   J: _____

7. P: Musik jenis apa yang disukai ayah Sari?

   J: _____

8. P: Siapa sekarang yang mewarisi hobi ibu Sari?

   J: _____

C. Pertanyaan umum (kuis)

1. P: Siapakah nama pemain drum sekaligus penyanyi kelompok musik Genesis?

   J: _____

2. P: Beatles berasal dari negara mana?

   J: _____

3. P: Siapakah nama penyanyi wanita terkenal dari Yunani?

   J: _____

4. P: Siapa nama grup band yang terkenal dengan lagunya 'Bohemian Rhapsody'?

   J: _____

5. P: Siapa nama penyanyi dangdut Indonesia yang mempopulérkan tarian 'ngebor'?

   J: _____

D. Sebutkan nama negara asal saluran televisi yang ada dalam daftar

Télévisi	Nama negara
1. SBS	
2. NBC	
3. TVRI	
4. NHK	
5. BBC	
6. Al Jazeera	
7. CBS	
8. AP	
9. CBC	
10. ORF	
11. RTHK	

E. Mengisi kalimat dengan kata kerja yang tepat.

Dipetik	Dipukul	Ditiup	Digésék	Digoyang	Ditekan

1. Seruling
2. Gitar
3. Kendang
4. Gong
5. Biola
6. Angklung
7. Piano
8. Sitar
9. Kulintang
10. Trompét
11. Saxophone
12. Keyboard
13. Didgeridoo

F.   Menulis (mengarang)

■ *Tulislah sebuah karangan yang menceritakan apa yang akan terjadi dengan Joel dan Sari sesudah Joel pulang ke Australia.*

_____

_____

_____

_____

_____

_____

_____

_____

_____

_____

Appendix

How do you say it in Indonesian?

This appendix contains a list of approximately 100 high-frequency English words with their Indonesian translations, covering a range of phrasal verbs and other idioms. It is, of course, not exhaustive. It aims to assist an English-speaking student who wants to know how to say or write a particular word in Indonesian. Experience in teaching has shown that it may be difficult to make a choice among the various renderings to be found in a dictionary, and there is often a tendency to be too literal when translating.

The method is to ask oneself: "What does this word actually mean?" When we reflect on this, several different meanings may present themselves, each with quite different translations into Indonesian. If you get it wrong, the results may be amusing or nonsensical! Of course, we encourage the learner always to double-check in a good dictionary, in order to survey all the possible forms. But in no circumstances should an electronic translation machine be used; as an experiment we looked up the English idiom "on the spur of the moment" – you know what that means ("without a second thought, spontaneously"), and certainly not the literal translation **di atas pacu saat**.

A final hint is to remember the subtle differences that may exist between colloquial and formal expressions, because we need to take these into consideration when choosing the best equivalent in good Indonesian.

Special thanks are due to Katherine Davidsen, Johansjah Sugianto and Linda Hibbs for reading this list and offering valuable suggestions.

A/AN

In many cases this has no translation, e.g. (where indefiniteness is intended): afflicted by an eye disease **diserang penyakit mata**
She's a clever girl. **Dia gadis pandai.**
But where it means 'one':
  Se-: Rp. 25,000 a packet **Rp 25.000 sebungkus**
  Seorang: a medical student **seorang mahasiswa kedokteran**
  Sebuah: a large truck **sebuah truk besar**
a kind of **sebangsa/semacam/sejenis**
it's a pity/shame **sayang**
it's a pleasure **senang sekali**
it's an honour **merupakan kehormatan**
it's an insult **kurang ajar!**

ABLE

See *can, could*: **bisa, dapat**.
Also: **mampu** able to afford: He can buy a car. **Dia mampu membeli mobil.**
  Sempat to get the chance, succeed in, get to, manage to, still be able to:
They were able to nab the thief at the crossroads.

Pencuri sempat diciduk di perempatan jalan.
able [adj.] 'having ability' **cakap, trampil, berbakat**

ABOUT

about (= approximately) **kira-kira**: about eleven o'clock **kira-kira jam sebelas**
  (= almost) **hampir**: It's about time. **Sudah hampir waktunya.**
about to (= going to, on the point of) **baru akan**;
  (= planning to) **berniat untuk**
(= concerning) **tentang, mengenai, perihal**
(= around, here and there) verb with **ber-~-an**:
  to wander about **berkeluyuran**
  to be spread about **berserakan**
  to cruise about **berkeliaran**
  to fly about **beterbangan**
  to run about **berlari-larian**
(= because of) **karena**
What about…? **Bagaimana kalau….?**
to set about (a job) **menggarap, mulai mengerjakan**

AFTER

after [adv., conj.] **sesudah, setelah**
(before verbs) **habis, selesai**
after all (= as you might expect) **nota béne**; (having considered) **akhirnya**; anyhow **bagaimana pun (juga), toh, toh ada gunanya**
to be after (= look for, pursue) **mencari, mengejar**
to take after (= resemble) **mirip**
to follow after **menyusul, mengikuti**
After you! **Silakan duluan!**

ALL

all alone **seorang diri**
all together **bersama-sama**
All right! (= okay!) **Baiklah!**
all over the place (= everywhere) **di mana-mana**
all gone **habis semuanya**
all the time **terus-menerus, selalu**
all at once (= suddenly) **tiba-tiba**
all but (= almost) **hampir, nyaris** (to give a negative connotation)
all over (= finished) **selesai**
in all (= in total) **semuanya**
most of all **paling**
Is that all? **Ini saja? Itu saja?**
at all: Can I help you at all? **Apakah (sekiranya) saya bisa bantu?**
not... at all **tidak...sama sekali**
all the more... **makin lama makin...**
all night **semalam suntuk**
all-important **terpenting**
all-Indonesia **se-Indonesia**

ANY

Sometimes not translated:
Are there any letters? **Apakah ada surat?**
I haven't got any. **Saya tidak punya / Tidak ada.**
In combinations:
anywhere (= in any place) **di mana saja**
anywhere (= to any place) **ke mana saja**
anything **apa saja**
anyone **siapa saja**
any one (out of several) **mana saja**
any time **kapan saja**
any time now (= very soon) **tidak lama lagi / dalam waktu singkat**

any more (= no longer) **lagi**: He doesn't work here any more. **Dia sudah tidak bekerja di sini lagi.**
Are you any better? **Apakah sudah merasa lebih baik?**

AS

as (= in the capacity of) **sebagai**: as a linguist... **sebagai ahli bahasa...**
(= like) **seperti**: as usual **seperti biasa**
(as... as, in comparisons) **se-**: as high as a mountain **setinggi gunung**
as far as (= until, up to) **sampai**: as far as the main road **sampai jalan besar**
as far as (= to the extent that) **se-**: as far as I know **setahu saya**
as for (= concerning) **kalau**
as good as (= almost) **praktis / boléh dikatakan**
as long as (= while) **selama**
as long as (while there's still time) **mumpung**
as one (= all together) **serentak / sekaligus**
as soon as **begitu**
as (= when) **ketika**
as (= because) **karena**
as though **seolah-olah / seakan-akan**
as to (= regarding) **tentang / mengenai**

ASK

to ask a question **tanya, bertanya**: May I ask your name? **Boléh tanya nama anda?**
to ask about **bertanya tentang / menanyakan**
to ask oneself **bertanya pada diri sendiri** (cf. to wonder **bertanya-tanya dalam hatinya**)
to ask out (= invite) **mengajak berkencan**
to ask for **minta** (= request) **mohon**
a big ask (= challenge) **tantangan besar**
for the asking **tinggal minta saja**
I ask you! (exclamation of amazement, = how is it possible!) **Bagaimana mungkin!**
to be asking for trouble **mengundang masalah (terlalu berani)**

BAD

bad (in general; evil, wicked) **buruk**: bad weather **cuaca buruk**
(= ugly) **jelék**
(= impolite) **tak pantas**
(= rotten) **busuk**
(= unwell) **kurang énak / kurang séhat**
(= naughty) **nakal**

(= criminal) **jahat**
bad luck **nasib malang**
not bad (= pretty good) **lumayan / boléh juga**
to be bad for (= disadvantage) **merugikan**
to be bad at **kurang pandai**
bad-tempered **cepat marah**

BEFORE

(time) **sebelum**
(in the past, formerly) **dulu**
before long (in the future, soon) **tidak lama lagi,
    sebentar lagi**
(in advance of) **lebih dulu / duluan**
(place, = in front of) **di depan / di muka**
    in the presence of **di hadapan**
to have before one (= face) **menghadapi, ber-
    hadapan dengan**

BIG

big (= large) **besar**
on a big scale **besar-besaran**
to think big **berpikir secara besar-besaran /
    mengejar ambisi**
(= grown up) **déwasa**
to talk big (= brag) **membual**
big (= elder) sister / big (= elder) brother **kakak**
big-hearted (magnanimous) **besar jiwa / pemur-
    ah**
too big **kebesaran**
a big shot **pembesar**
big-time criminal **penjahat kelas kakap**
big toe **jempol kaki, ibu jari kaki**

BOTH

both (of them) **kedua-duanya / dua-duanya /
    keduanya**
both (the group of two) **kedua**: both children **ke-
    dua anak itu**
both... and... **baik... maupun....**

BY

by (introducing the agent of a passive verb) **oléh**.
    For example: **Email Joel diterima oléh Sari.**
    Joel's email was received by Sari.
by (= at) **di**: by the side of the road **di pinggir
    jalan**
by (= via, by way of, through) **léwat**
by (= with) **dengan**: What do you mean by that
    expression? **Apa yang dimaksudkan dengan
    ucapan itu?**

by the hour **jam-jaman**
by the day **harian**
by the kilo **kiloan**
by law **menurut hukum**
by agreement **menurut persetujuan**
by oneself (= alone) **sendirian**
by the way, ... **omong-omong, ngomong-
    ngomong, ...**
by far **jauh**
by and large (= generally) **pada umumnya**
by degrees (= gradually) **sedikit demi sedikit**
by day **siang hari**; by night **malam hari**
by all means (= certainly) **pasti**
by no means (= definitely not) **sama sekali tidak**

CALL

to call (= summon) **memanggil**
to call (= telephone) **menélepon**
to call (= name) **menyebut**: What do you call this?
    Ini disebut apa?
to be called (= named) **bernama**
to call back **menélepon kembali**
to call for (= require) **memerlukan**; (= suggest,
    propose, call on) **menyerukan**
to call forth (= cause) **menimbulkan / menyebab-
    kan**
to call off (= cancel) **membatalkan**
to call in (= drop in) **mampir / singgah**
to call on (= visit) **mengunjungi / berkunjung ke**
to call out (= shout) **berteriak**
to call together (= gather) **mengumpulkan**
to call up (troops) **mengerahkan**
call-button **kenop panggilan**
call-girl **wanita panggilan**

CAN / COULD

can, able to, capable of; to know how to, manage
    to **bisa**
can, able to, capable of; -able, -ible **dapat**
    Note: These two 'modal words' are very close
    in meaning, and sometimes interchangeable, but
    not always. **Bisa** includes being mentally able,
    while **dapat** (perhaps influenced by its second
    meaning, 'to get, obtain') includes being physi-
    cally capable of doing something.
can, may, allowed to **boléh** (Note: This is quite dif-
    ferent from Malaysian Malay)
EXAMPLES:
    His grandchild can walk (already). **Cucunya su-
    dah bisa jalan.**

Were you able (did you manage) to sleep? **Bisa tidur?**

Of course you can (it's quite possible). **Bisa saja.**

It can be said that (we may say that)… **Boléh dikatakan (bahwa)…**

It can't be predicted. **Tidak dapat diramalkan.**

What can you do? **Apa boléh buat!** (idiom)

May I ask a question? **Boléh tanya, ya.**

Can do! **Bisa!**

CARE

to care about (= pay attention to) **mempedulikan**

to not care (= be indifferent to) **tidak peduli**

to care for (= take care of, keep) **memelihara**

to care for (= arrange, manage, run) **mengurus**

to care for (= keep an eye on, be responsible for) **menjaga**

to care for (= attend to, look after, tend) **mengasuh**

to care for (= nurse, treat) **merawat**

to care for (= like) **suka**: I don't care for dogs. **Saya tidak suka anjing.**

to take care (= be careful, attentive) **berhati-hati**

to not care (= not mind, have no objection) **tidak berkeberatan**

cares (= worries) **kesusahan**

with care (= accurately) **dengan teliti**

CARRY

to carry (in general) **membawa**
  (a heavy burden, with others) **menggotong**
  (a load, on the shoulder) **memikul**
  (on the back or hip) **menggéndong**
  (in the hand, hanging down) **menjinjing**

to carry (= transport) **mengangkut**

to carry off (= abduct, steal) **membawa lari**

to carry off (= seize, claim) **merebut**

to carry on (= continue) **meneruskan / melanjutkan**

to carry out (= implement) **melaksanakan**

to carry through (= complete) **menyelesaikan**

to get carried away (= forget oneself) **lupa diri**

CLEAR

clear (= distinct, explicit) **jelas**
  (= evident, obvious) **terang**
  (of weather) **cerah**
  (of road) **kosong**
  (of liquid, sky) **jernih**
  (= transparent, limpid) **bening**

to clear (clean up, rubbish) **membersihkan**
  (debts) **melunasi**
  (goods, in a sale) **mengobral**
  (= to approve) **mengesahkan**
  (the table) **mengangkat makanan**

to clear off (= run away) **membolos**

to clear up (weather, = stop raining) **menjadi terang**

COME

to come (= arrive) **datang**

to come about (= happen) **terjadi**

to come across (= find, meet) **menemukan**

to come along (= join in) **ikut**

to come back (= return) **kembali**

to come between (= separate) **memisahkan**

to come down (= descend) **turun ke bawah**;
  (= become less) **berkurang**

to come forward (= advance) **tampil ke muka**

to come from (= originate from) **berasal dari**

to come in (= enter) **masuk**

to come off (= come loose) **terlepas**; (= succeed) **berhasil / jadi**

to come out (= emerge) **keluar**; (of publications) **terbit**; (of flowers) **mekar**

to come to (= add up to) **berjumlah**; (= to become conscious) **sadar lagi**

to come within (= be included in) **tercakup**

Come on! (inviting, urging) **Ayo!**

Come on now! (protesting) **Jangan begitu! Sudahlah!**

DO

NOTE: Many different idioms as well as grammatical functions in English.

to be doing (= engaging in an activity): What are you doing? **Kamu sedang apa?/ Kamu sedang berbuat apa?**

to do (= work at) **bekerja**: What do you do? **Anda bekerja sebagai apa?**

to do about it (= tackle, deal with) **menggarap, menindak**: We should do something about it. **Harus kita garap, harus kita tindak.**

That will do (= be enough) **Sudah cukup**

do (emphatic function): You do understand, don't you? **Kamu mémang mengerti, kan?**
  It did turn up in the end. **Akhirnya muncul juga.**

In questions and negatives, no separate translation!

Do you understand? **Apakah mengerti?**

No, I don't. **Tidak (mengerti).**

to do away with (= remove) **menghilangkan**

to do up (= repair) **merénovasi**; done up (= decorated) **berhias**

could do with (= needs) **perlu / membutuhkan**: It could do with some paint. **Perlu dicat.**

to do without **berjalan tanpa, mengalami kekurangan**

done (food) **masak**

done in (= exhausted) **kecapaian**

to have to do with **berkaitan / berhubungan / bertalian dengan**

END

to end (= to come to an end) **berakhir**

to end (= bring to an end) **mengakhiri**

to end it all (= commit suicide) **membunuh diri**

end [noun] (= extremity) **ujung**: at the end of the street **di ujung jalan**

in the end (= finally) **akhirnya**

the end of the line **titik penghabisan**

the bitter end **saat terakhir**

at the end of one's tether **putus asa**

at the end of the day (= after considering everything) **setelah mempertimbangkan semuanya**

to make ends meet **belanja dengan uang seadanya**

for days on end **berhari-hari terus-menerus**

at a loose end, **tidak bertujuan / tidak tahu ke mana**

the ends of the earth **ujung dunia / ke mana saja**

That's the end of it! **Habis perkara!**

FEEL

to feel **merasa**: I feel quite well. **Saya merasa cukup séhat.**

I feel it's time to go home. **Saya rasa sudah waktunya untuk pulang.**

it feels... **rasanya**: It feels nice. **Rasanya énak.**

It feels as if it's going to rain. **Rasanya seperti akan hujan.**

to feel (= of an object) **berasa**: The kettle feels hot. **Téko berasa panas.**

to feel (= have a bodily sensation) **terasa**: Her feet feel cold. **Kakinya terasa dingin.**

to feel like (= want to) **ingin**

to feel (= touch, grope) **meraba**

to feel for (= sympathize with) **merasa kasihan pada**

to feel hurt (= offended) **tersinggung**

I feel (= think) that **saya kira...**

to feel at home **betah, kerasan**

FEW

few (= not many) **sedikit**

very few **sedikit sekali**

no fewer than **paling sedikit / tidak kurang dari**

a few (= several) **beberapa**

quite a few **cukup banyak**

few and far between **jarang sekali**

FOR

Time:

for a moment **sebentar**

for several months **selama /untuk beberapa bulan**

for eight years **selama delapan tahun**

for years **bertahun-tahun**

for a long time **lama**

for good **untuk selama-lamanya**

for the time being **untuk sementara**

for (= to, used for) **untuk**: money to buy food **uang untuk membeli makanan**

for (= for the sake of) **demi**: for your health's sake **demi keséhatanmu**

for (= on behalf of) **bagi**

for (= toward, of feelings) **terhadap**: feelings of respect for **rasa hormat terhadap**

as for (= regarding) **kalau / bagi**

word for word **kata demi kata**

for sale **akan dijual**

for fun **iseng**

for a joke **tidak sungguh-sungguh, bercanda**

for nothing (= without paying) **gratis / tanpa dibayar**; (= in vain) **dengan sia-sia**

thanks for **terima kasih atas**

to pay for **membayar**

to pay for schooling **membayar uang sekolah**

to hope for **mengharapkan**

to exchange for **menukar dengan**

FUN

to have fun (= to enjoy oneself, have a good time) **bersenang-senang / bermain-main**

just for fun (not serious) **main-main saja**

to be fun (= enjoyable) **menyenangkan**; (= exciting) **asyik** to make fun of (= mock) **mengolok-olokkan / mengéjék**

GET

to get (= obtain) **mendapat**

to get (= become) **menjadi**: To get dark **Menjadi gelap**

Movement in various directions:

to get in/on (modes of transport) **naik**

to get off/out (transport) **turun**

to get there (= arrive) **tiba / sampai**: We got there at 4. **Kita tiba (di sana) jam empat.**

to get back **kembali**

to get home **pulang / tiba di rumah**

to get away (= leave) **berangkat**; (= escape) **lolos**

to get across **menyeberang**

to get behind (= be late) **terlambat**

to get beyond **meléwati**

to be getting on (in years) **lanjut usia**

to get on **bagaimana**: How are you getting on? **Bagaimana kabarnya?**

How did you get on? **Bagaimana hasilnya?**

to get over (= recover from) **sembuh dari**; (= surmount) **mengatasi**

to get together **berkumpul**

to get up (= from sleep) **bangun**, (from a sitting position) **bangkit**

GIVE

to give (= grant, provide, add) **memberi**

to give (= contribute) **menyumbang**

to give (= pay) **membayar**

to give (= hold, a talk, party etc.) **mengadakan**

to give and take **saling mengalah**

to give away (= donate) **menghadiahkan / mendermakan, mengamalkan**

to give back (= return) **mengembalikan**

to give birth **melahirkan / bersalin**

to give in (= admit defeat) **menyerah / mengalah**

to give off (= emit) **mengeluarkan**

to give out (= distribute) **membagi-bagikan**

to give up (= stop, e.g. smoking) **berhenti**; (= abandon) **meninggalkan**

give or take a few (= approximately) **kurang-lebih**

given to (= have a tendency to) **cenderung**

given (= a certain) **tertentu**

I give up! (= to have learned one's lesson) **Kapok aku!**

GO

to go (general) **pergi**

to go (= leave) **berangkat**

to go (= be lost) **hilang**

to go (= travel, move) **berjalan**

to go (= be allowed) **boléh**

to go (= become) **menjadi**: S. is going mad. **S. menjadi gila.**

to go across **menyeberang**

to go after **mengikuti / menyusul**

to go along **ikut serta**

to go around [trans.] **mengelilingi / berédar, berkeliling** [intrans.]

to go away **pergi; berangkat; hilang**

to go back **kembali**

to go before **mendahului**

to go by **léwat**

to go down **turun**; (= become less) **berkurang**

to go in **masuk**

to go into **memasuki**

to go on with (= continue) **meneruskan**

to go out **keluar**; (= be extinguished) **padam**

to go through (= experience) **mengalami**

to go together/with (= fit) **cocok**

to go up **naik**; (= increase) **meningkat**

GOOD

good (general: quality, condition, character) **baik**

to taste, feel good **énak**

to have a good time **bersenang-senang**

How good to see you! **Senang sekali bertemu dengan kamu!**

to be good at **pandai**

to be good for **berguna untuk**

as good as (= almost) as good as new **dapat dikatakan baru**

good-hearted **baik hati**

good-looking **cantik** (girls), **ganteng, cakap** (boys)

Good luck! **Selamat! Sukses!**

Good morning **Selamat pagi!**

a good deal (= quite a lot) **cukup banyak**

Good heavens! (in surprise) **Aduh! Ya Allah!** (Isl.)

HAPPEN

to happen (= to occur) **terjadi**: What's happened? **Apa yang terjadi?**

(by coincidence) **kebetulan**: It happened to be a Friday. **Kebetulan hari Jumat.**

(possibly, might) **kiranya, barangkali**: Do you happen to know her name? **Apakah (kiranya) kamu tahu namanya?**

to happen on (= to find) **menemukan, kedapatan**

to have happen to one (= to experience something) **ditimpa, kena**: What happened to you? **Kamu kena apa? Kamu kenapa? (kena + apa)**; (= to get lost) What's happened to my watch? **Jamku hilang ke mana?**

as it happens…, **sebenarnya…kebetulan**

HARD

hard (not soft) **keras**: a hard mattress **kasur keras**

to work hard **bekerja keras**

hard liquor **minuman keras**

(difficult, troublesome) **sukar**: It's hard to find work. **Sukar mencari pekerjaan.**

(difficult, tough, complex) **rumit**

(complicated, intricate) **sulit**

(hard to find, get; burdensome, troublesome) **susah**

(hard to bear, serious, severe) **berat**

hard up **kekurangan uang / miskin**

hard and fast **mutlak**

hard cash **uang kontan**

hard-headed **keras kepala**

hard-hearted **keras hati**

hard luck **nasib malang**

hard of hearing **susah mendengar**

HAVE

to have (= to be there) **ada**: Do you have a cat? We do! **Apakah ada kucing? Ada!**
   Ber-: Do you have a family? (= are you married?) **Apakah sudah berkeluarga?**

to have (= own) **punya**: They have two cars. **Meréka punya dua buah mobil.**

the owner **yang punya**

to have (= possess) **mempunyai**: the ones who have the right… **yang mempunyai hak…**

to have (= cause, order) **menyuruh**: Just have it pulled out! **Suruhlah dicabut saja!**

NOTE: 'has/have…-ed' forms a past tense in English; use **sudah** in Indonesian: Have you eaten? **Sudah makan?**

Many idioms with 'have', e.g.
   to have breakfast **makan sarapan**
   to have a baby **melahirkan anak**
   to have a cold **pilek**
   to have a fright **terkejut**

to have a good time **bersenang-senang**

to have an inspiration **mendapat ilham**

HERE

here (= this place) **sini**; (= in this place) **di sini**; (= to this place) **ke sini**

Here you are! (giving something) **Silakan!**

Here's the room. **Ini kamarnya.**

Here it is! **Inilah dia!**

my friend here **teman saya ini**

here and there **sana-sini**

Here goes! **Mari! Coba saja!**

up to here in work **sampai tenggelam dalam kesibukan**

HOW

how? **Bagaimana?**: How does it work? **Bagaimana kerjanya?**

How are things going? **Bagaimana kabarnya?**

how (= the way, method) **caranya**: This is how you do it. **Begini caranya.**

how much? **Berapa?**: How much does it cost? **Berapa harganya?**

how many? **Berapa?**: How many are there? **Ada berapa?**

how often? (= how many times?) **Berapa kali?** How many times a week? **Berapa kali seminggu?**

How far? **Berapa jauhnya?**: How far is it from here? **Berapa jauhnya dari sini?**

How! (**betapa** adj. + **-nya**): How big he's grown! **Betapa besarnya!**
   Alangkah (adj. + **-nya**): How beautiful it is! **Alangkah indahnya!**

how much **betapa**: She doesn't know how much I love her. **Dia belum tahu betapa saya mencintainya.**

how is it that…, How come…? (= why?) **kenapa / mengapa?**

How about…? **Bagaimana kalau…**: How about we eat out tonight? **Bagaimana kalau kita makan di luar malam ini?**

How are you going? (= how are you?) **Apa kabar?**

How will we go? (= by what mode of transport?) **Kita naik apa?**

IF

if (= on condition that) **kalau, jika**: If I get the opportunity… **Kalau ada kesempatan …**

(= whether) **apakah**: It's not clear if the conference will go ahead or not. **Belum jelas apakah konferénsinya akan berlangsung atau tidak.**

If only! (= just imagine) **bayangkan!** (I wish it was) **mudah-mudahan**

if for instance (= supposing) **(kalau) seandainya, seumpamanya**

even if **kalau sekalipun**

a bit iffy **kurang meyakinkan**

See also *that*.

IN

in (location) **di**: in town **di kota**; in the country **di pedésaan**

(time) in time (= punctual) **pada waktunya**; (= gradually) **lama-kelamaan**

in a week's time (future) **seminggu lagi**

in two hours (time taken) **dalam waktu dua jam**

in the dry season **pada musim kering / kemarau**

in my opinion **menurut pendapat / hémat saya**

in case of fire **kalau ada pembakaran**

in these circumstances **dalam keadaan ini**

in the context/framework of **dalam rangka**

in the name of **atas nama**

in writing **secara tertulis**

to be in (= present, at home) **ada**; (= to have arrived) **sudah sampai/masuk**

ins and outs **seluk-beluk**

IT

Often no direct translation needed in Indonesian.
EXAMPLES:
It's hot. **Panas.**
It's raining. **Hujan.**
It's a pity. **Sayang.**
It hurts. **Sakit.**
It's a long way. **Jauh.**
It doesn't matter. **Tidak apa-apa.**
It's important. **Penting.**
How much is it? **Berapa harganya?**
Do you like it? **Apakah suka?**
I don't believe it! **Saya tidak percaya / masak!**
Drink it up! **Minumlah!**
Don't worry out it. **Jangan kuatir.**
What can you do about it? **Apa boléh buat?**

JUST

just (= only) **saja**: just a little/a bit **sedikit saja**;
Just joking! **Main-main saja!**

just **baru**: The program's just begun. **Acaranya baru mulai.**

just now (= a moment ago) **tadi / baru-baru ini**; (= only recently) **baru saja**

just (= exactly) **tepat**: Just in time. **Tepat pada waktunya.**

(= really) **benar-benar**: It's just great here! **Benar-benar senang di sini!**

(with imperative) **saja**: Just look! **Lihat saja!**

just [adj.] (= fair) **adil**

just as / like **seperti**

just in case, lest (= as a precaution) **untuk jaga-jaga / supaya jangan**

KNOW

to know (= be acquainted with) **kenal dengan** (a person); (= be familiar with) **kenal akan** (matters)

to get to know **mengenal**

to know (= identify, recognize) **mengenali**

known (= well known, recognized) **terkenal**

to know by sight **kenal tanpa tahu nama orang**

to know (= understand, be well informed) **tahu**; (= to find out about) **mengetahui**

to know no bounds (= unlimited) **tanpa batas**

to know the ropes (= be experienced) **berpengalaman**

to not want to know (= don't care) **tak peduli**

You-know (= can't mention the word) **anu**

Goodness knows! (= I have no idea) **Kurang tahu saya!**

LEARN

to learn ([intrans.], = to do study about) **belajar**: to learn Javanese **belajar bahasa Jawa**; ([trans.] = to study) **mempelajari**: to learn how to peel a mango **mempelajari caranya mengupas mangga**

(= hear, find out about) **mendapat kabar bahwa / mendengar / mengetahui**

(= learn by heart, memorize) **menghafalkan**

learned **terpelajar / berilmu**

learning (noun) (= science) **pengetahuan / ilmu pengetahuan**; (= being learned) **keterpelajaran**

LEAVE

to leave (= to depart, set out, go away) **berangkat, pergi, keluar dari**

(= to leave behind, abandon) **meninggalkan**

left behind (accidentally) **tertinggal**

the only thing left to do is… **tinggal…**

(= to allow) **membiarkan**: Don't leave the door open. **Janganlah membiarkan pintunya terbuka.**

(= to postpone) **menunda**: Leave it till next year. **Tundalah sampai tahun depan.**

(= to bequeath) **mewariskan**

(= to hand over, surrender) **menyerahkan**: I leave it to you! **Terserah kepada kamu!**

(= to leave over, remaining) **menyisakan**; left over **tersisa**

to take leave (= say goodbye) **minta diri, berpamitan**

(= to have a holiday) **mengambil cuti**

sick leave **cuti sakit**

by your leave (= permission) **dengan izin anda**

to leave off (= cease) **berhenti**

to leave out (= remove, omit) **menghapus**; (= neglect, fail to include) **mengabaikan, tidak memasukkan**

It leaves a lot to be desired! (= is very unsatisfactory) **sangat tidak memuaskan**

LET

to let (= allow) **membiarkan**: Let it be! (forget it) **Biarlah!**

let's… **Mari…**: Let us / me… **Biar kita / saya…**; (= come on!) **Ayo!**

to let be (= not interfere) **jangan diganggu**

to let down (= disappoint) **mengecéwakan**

to let fly (= explode, in anger) **meledak**

to let go (= release) **melepaskan**

to let off (= forgive) **memaafkan**; (fireworks) **menyalakan**

to let up (= subside, wind, rain) **reda**

let alone **apalagi / jangankan**

LIE

to lie (= be in a lying position) **berbaring / terbaring**

(= to be located) **terletak**

(= to be found) **terdapat**

(= to be present) **berada**

(= to be buried) **terkubur**

(= to tell a lie) **berbohong**

to lie in (= sleep late) **tidur sampai siang**

LIKE

to like **suka**: I like eating chocolate. **Saya suka makan coklat.**; I like you! **Saya suka kamu!**

(= be attached to, fond of, have a preference for) **menyukai**: whatever you like **sesuka hatimu**

like (= resembling) **seperti**: To swim like a fish. **Berenang seperti ikan.**

(= such as) **seperti**: a paper like Kedaulatan Rakyat **Surat kabar seperti K.R.**

like ([adj.] = of the same) **se-**: like-minded **sependapat**

and the like **dan lain-lain, dan sebagainya**

like this **begini**

like that **begitu**

LIVE

to live (= be alive) **hidup**: still living/ alive **masih hidup**

(= have a way of life) **hidup**: to live according to one's religion **hidup sesuai dengan agama**

(= to reside) **tinggal / bertempat tinggal**: Sari lives in Pasar Minggu. **Sari tinggal di Pasar Minggu.**

live [adj.] **hidup**: live fish **ikan hidup**; live music **musik hidup**

to live together **hidup bersama, tinggal bersama**

to live apart **hidup terpisah**

to live on **hidup dari / dengan**

to live through (= experience) **mengalami**

to live up to **hidup sesuai dengan**

to live from hand to mouth **hidup Senin-Kemis**

LOOK

to look (at) (= see) **melihat**

(= have the appearance of) **kelihatan**

(look at and notice; consider) **memandang**

to look about / around **melihat-lihat**

to look toward, in the direction of **menoléh** (back: **ke belakang**; to the right: **ke kanan** etc.)

to look for **mencari**

to look into (= examine) **memeriksa, mengusut**

to look on (= consider as) **menganggap**

to look up to (= respect) **menghormati, mencontoh**

Look, it's like this… **Begini, ya…**

Look out! **Awas!**

looks (noun) (= appearance) **rupa**: (= face) **wajah**

good looks (= smart appearance) **ketampanan**; (male) **kegantengan**; (female) **kecantikan**

LOVE

to love **cinta pada / mencintai**: (e.g. mother for child) **sayang pada**

to fall in love **jatuh cinta**

to be in love with **jatuh cinta dengan**

to make love (= have sex) **bersanggama / bersetubuh**

(= be in love with each other) **berkasih-kasihan, bercinta**

I'd love to! **Senang sekali!**

love [noun] **cinta**

(passion) **asmara**: love-song **lagu asmara, lagu cinta**

(affection, devotion) **kasih / kasih sayang**

(beloved) **kekasih**; (girlfriend, boyfriend) **pacar**

(abstract) **kecintaan** (e.g. for homeland)

(affair, romance) **percintaan**

'love' (term of address) **sayang(ku)**

(in tennis) **kosong**

MAKE

to make (general) **membuat**, (slang) **membikin**

(= build) **membangun**

(= create) **mengadakan**

(= cause to become) **menjadikan**

(= force) **memaksakan**

to make it (= arrive safely); **sampai dengan selamat**; (= succeed) **berhasil, mencapai cita-cita**

to make a noise **ribut**

to make a fuss (= be fussy, hard to please) **réwél**

to make haste **bergesa-gesa**

to make love **bercinta, bersanggama**

to make a mistake (= be wrong) **salah**

to make off with (= abduct) **melarikan**; (= steal) **mencuri**

to make up (after a quarrel) **rukun / damai lagi**

(= put on make-up) **berdandan / merias**

(= concoct) **mengarang / mengada-ada**

(= arrange) **membéréskan / mengatur**

(for time lost) **mengejar**

to make trouble **menghasut**

to make trouble for (someone) **membuat susah**

MATTER

matter [noun] (= case, instance) **hal, urusan**

(= substance) **zat**

(= material) **bahan**

(= article) **barang**

(= question, problem) **soal**

(= pus) **nanah**

to matter (= be important) **penting**; (= be meaningful) **berarti**

it doesn't matter **tidak apa-apa, tidak apalah**

no matter what **mau tak mau**

no matter how **bagaimana pun juga**

no matter when **kapan pun juga**

as matters stand,... **dalam keadaan begini...**

as a matter of course (naturally) **selayaknya**

in the matter of, re... **dalam hal...**

MEAN

to mean (= intend) **bermaksud, berniat**: to mean well **niatnya baik**

to mean (= signify, have meaning) **berarti**: What does this mean? **Ini apa artinya?**

to mean (= destine) **menakdirkan**

(= allot, assign) **memperuntukkan**

to mean it (= be sincere, honest) **bersungguh-sungguh**

mean [adj.] (= stingy) **pelit, kikir**

(= cruel) **kejam**

(= humble, low, degraded) **hina**

(= tricky) **licik**

(= average) **rata-rata**

MEANS

means [noun] (= tool, device, implememt) **alat**

(= method) **cara**: by fair means **dengan cara yang jujur**

by means of **dengan / memakai**

by all means (= definitely) **tentu saja**

by any means **dengan cara apa saja**

by no means **sama sekali tidak**

means of transport **alat pengangkutan**; by what means of transport? **Naik apa?**

(= property, wealth) **harta / kekayaan**

beyond one's means **di luar kemampuannya**

MUCH

much [adv.] (= a lot, many things) **banyak**: There is much to discuss. **Ada banyak yang harus dibicarakan.**

as much as possible **sebanyak mungkin, sebanyak-banyaknya**

much too... **jauh terlalu**: This sauce is much too spicy. **Sambal ini jauh terlalu pedas.**

twice as much **dua kali lebih banyak**

so much, as much as this **sekian**

not much **tidak begitu**: Do you like it? Not much. **Apakah kamu suka? Tidak begitu.**

very much **sekali**: He likes her very much. **Dia suka sekali padanya.**

much as... **walaupun**: Much as we tried, it still wasn't finished. **Walaupun kita berusaha keras, namun belum selesai juga.**

MUST, HAS TO, SHOULD, OUGHT TO

(general) **harus**: Tap water has to (should) be boiled before it can be drank. **Air keran harus direbus sebelum diminum.**

You ought to **haruslah!**

(= should have, but didn't) **seharusnya**

(= without fail, for sure, certainly; stronger than **harus**) **mesti**: If the traffic's as blocked as this, we're sure to miss the plane. **Kalau lalu lintas macet begini, kita mesti ketinggalan pesawat.**

(= should be) **semestinya** as it should be **seperti semestinya**

(= obligatory, required, compulsory) **wajib**: You must wear a safety belt. **Wajib mengenakan sabuk pengaman.**

(= must have, very likely) **pasti**: He must have caught it from another child. **Penyakit itu pasti ketularan dari anak lain.**

See also *need*.

NEED

to need (something) **membutuhkan**

(= require) **memerlukan**

to need to (= have to, ought to, do something) **perlu**: I need to get to the shops. **Saya perlu ke toko.**

(= should) **harus**: Do I need to wait? **Apakah saya harus menunggu?**

No need (= it's not necessary) **tidak usah**: There's no need to pay. **Tidak usah membayar.**

need [noun] **kebutuhan / keperluan**: He has few needs. **Kebutuhannya tidak banyak.**

the need for, (= necessity) **perlunya**: It is not yet clear whether it is necessary to get medicine. **Perlunya mencari obat belum jelas.**

NO

No (answer to question) **tidak** (coll. **nggak**)

(= not any) **tidak** (plus verb and noun): I have no money **Saya tidak punya uang.** There's no time. **Tidak ada waktu.**

No longer (= no more, not any more) **(sudah) tidak... lagi**: It's no longer raining / not raining any more. **Tidak hujan lagi.**

No (= not a) **bukan**: This is no goat! **Ini bukan kambing!**

No way! (= impossible) **Tak mungkin!**

No (= forbidden) **dilarang**: No entry. **Dilarang masuk.**

no good (= bad) **kurang baik**

(= a pity) **sayang**: That's no good! **Sayanglah!**

no go (= will not go ahead) **tidak jadi**

no one (= nobody) **tidak seorang pun**

No worries! **Oké! Bérés!**

OFF

to be off (a race) **mulai**

(= don't like any more) **tidak suka lagi**

(= going bad, rotten) **busuk**

(= cancelled) **dibatalkan**

(= taken off, clothes) **dibuka, dilepas, ditanggalkan**

(= turned off, switch) **mati, dimatikan**

(= loose, e.g. button) **lepas**

a day off **hari libur, tidak masuk**

on and off **sebentar-sebentar**

well off **makmur, mampu**; badly off **miskin**

off-colour (= not feeling well) **kurang énak badan**; (= blue) **cabul sedikit**

off-duty **bébas tugas**

off-season **musim sepi**

off-the-cuff (= spontaneously) **secara spontan**

off-the-record **secara tidak resmi**

ON

on (location) **di**

on top of **di atas**

on the right **di sebelah kanan**

on the plane **di dalam pesawat**

on Sunday **pada hari Minggu**

on (a date) **pada tanggal...**

on time **pada waktunya**

on that occasion **pada kesempatan itu**

Other idioms:

　on the condition that **dengan syarat**

　on condition (= provided) **asal**

　on the initiative of **atas prakarsa**

　on the authority of **atas kuasa**

　on behalf of **untuk, atas nama**

on (= after) **sesudah / setelah**: On arriving in Semarang,... **Sesudah tiba di Semarang....**

on and off (= from time to time) **sewaktu-waktu**

on and on (= continuously) **terus-menerus**

on the spur of the moment (= suddenly) **secara mendadak**

on the point of (= about to) **sebentar lagi / hampir akan**

on the subject of **tentang/mengenai**: Congratulations on **selamat atas**

on the program **di acara**

on the TV / radio **di TV / radio**

on this number **di nomor ini**

on the phone **sedang menélepon, sedang bicara**

on edge (= anxious, jumpy) **cemas / senéwen**

on the contrary **sebaliknya**

ONE

one [numeral] **satu**

the [adj.] one **yang**: the younger one **yang lebih muda**

one or other **salah satu**, (person) **salah seorang**

one day… **pada suatu hari**

one (somebody) **seorang**

not one (of them) **satu pun / seorang pun tidak…**

as one (= all together) **serentak**

at one (= agreed, in harmony) **setuju**

to become one, act as one **bersatu**

one by one, one at a time **satu demi satu, satu-satu**

the only one **satu-satunya**

one and all **semuanya / semua orang**

one and only **unik, satu-satunya**

one day (in future) **kapan-kapan, suatu hari**

one or two **satu dua**

the one (= same) **sama, se-**: from the one village **dari désa yang sama / sedésa dengan**

ONLY

only **saja** (after the word modified): He only eats vegetables. **Dia makan sayuran saja.**

Hanya (before the word modified): Adults only. **Hanya orang déwasa.**

Hanya… saja (both, for more emphasis): There is only one. **Hanya ada satu saja.**

only [adv.] **baru** (= just; with prospect of change): Their child is only five. **Anaknya baru lima tahun.** (but will get older)

Cuma (= just; no expectation of change): It only costs a thousand. **Harganya cuma seribu.**

Cuma (= but, except): You can play here, only don't be too noisy. **Boléh main-main di sini, cuma jangan terlalu ramai.**

the only one **satu-satunya**

an only child **anak tunggal**

If only! (= imagine how nice it would be!) **Bayangkan énaknya… Andaikan (saja)…**

ORDER

to order (= place an order) **memesan**

an order **pesanan**

on order **sedang dipesan**

to order **menurut pesanan**

to order (= give an order, command) **memerintah** (= tell, instruct, direct) **menyuruh**

an order **perintah**

by order of **atas perintah**

in order, in good order **bérés, rapi**

out of order **rusak / tidak beroperasi**

in order (= proper) **patut**

in order (= succession) **dalam urutan**

order **tata tertib, ketenteraman**

in order to **supaya / agar**

order (= regime) **orde**

(= arrangement, system, pattern) **tata** (in many compounds, e.g. **tata cara** etiquette, protocol)

OTHER

other **lain**

others (= other people) **orang lain**

the others **lainnya**

some… others… **ada yang…, ada yang**

some other time **lain kali saja**

on the other hand **sebaliknya / di pihak lain**

the other day **belum lama ini**

one after the other **satu demi satu**

among other things **antara lain**

and others (= et cetera) **dan lain-lainnya (dll.)**

in another place (= elsewhere) **di lain tempat**

other times, other manners **lain dulu, lain sekarang**

OUT

to go out **keluar**

to get out (= escape) **melepaskan diri**

(= disembark) **turun**

to take out **membawa keluar**

to throw out **membuang**

to send out **mengirimkan**

(= emit) **mengeluarkan**

to sort out (= arrange) **mengatur**

to put out (a fire) **memadamkan**

to help out **menolong / membantu**

to be out (= not at home) **sedang pergi / tidak ada**

di rumah

out of (= none left) **kehabisan / tidak ada**

out of (= made of, from) **dari**

out of (= because of) **karena**

out to it (= unconscious) **tidak sadar / pingsan**

out of town **di luar kota**

out of order (= not working) **rusak**

out of the way (= isolated) **terpencil**

Out of the (my) way! (= move aside) **Minggir!**

OVER

over (= above) **di atas**

over (= more than) **lebih / ke atas / léwat**

over here **di sebelah sini**

over there **di sana / di sebelah sana**

over (during the period of) **selama**

over the road **di seberang jalan**

to cross over **menyeberang**

to be over (= finished, ended) **selesai / berakhir**

to be over it (= better, recovered) **sembuh / pulih**

to be over the moon (= very happy) **luar biasa senang**

to do it over (= repeat) **mengulangi**

to think it over (= consider) **menimbang / memikirkan**

to move over (= shift) **bergésér**

to stay over (= spend the night) **menginap**

over the hill (= old) **lanjut usia**

overseas **di luar negeri**

PLEASE

to please (= make happy, content) **menyenangkan**; (= satisfy) **memuaskan**

pleased **senang / puas**

pleasing **menyenangkan**; (= interesting) **menarik**; (= pleasant, to hear, see) **énak didengar / dilihat**

hard to please (= fussy, choosy) **réwél**

As you please! (= please yourself) **Sesuka hatimu!**

Please! (inviting someone to do something) **silakan!**

(do something for me) **tolong...**

(formal) **harap**

(would you please, be so kind as to) **sudilah**; (would you please) **minta**

(kindly, formal) **mohon**

POLITE

polite (= civil, courteous, correct) **sopan**

(= refined) **halus**

(= ethical, decorous, correct) **sopan-santun**

(= proper, fitting, in good taste) **pantas**

(= with good manners, cultured) **beradab**

POSSIBLE

possible, possibly **mungkin**

impossible, out of the question **tidak mungkin**

very possible **mungkin sekali**

quite possibly **kemungkinan besar**

How is it possible? **Mana mungkin! Masa!**

as soon as possible **secepat, selekas mungkin**

to the fullest extent possible **sedapat-dapatnya, sebisa-bisanya**

PUT

to put (= place, lay) **menaruh**

(= assign a place, locate, deploy) **menempatkan**

(= lay, place, put down) **meletakkan**

(a question) **mengajukan pertanyaan**

(= express, put in words) **mengungkapkan**

(= estimate, guess at) **menaksir**

to put aside **menyisihkan**

to put away (= save up, store) **menyimpan**

to put down (= despise, hold in contempt) **menghinakan**

to put forward (= suggest, offer, propose) **mengemukakan**

to put on (clothes) **mengenakan pakaian, berbaju**; (weight) **bertambah gemuk**

to put out (fire) **memadamkan api / kebakaran**

to put together (= collect) **mengumpulkan**; (= compile) **menyusun**

to put up with (= be able to bear, endure) **tahan**

RATHER

rather (= quite, somewhat) **agak**: This book is rather boring. **Buku ini agak membosankan.**

(= quite, a lot) **cukup**: He's rather arrogant. **Cukup sombong orangnya.**

(= to prefer; would sooner) **lebih suka**: I'd rather just stay home. **Saya lebih suka tinggal di rumah saja.**

(= rather than, instead of) **daripada**

REMEMBER

to remember ([intrans.], = to be mindful) **ingat**

(= to be mindful of) **ingat akan**

([trans.], = to recall, recollect, keep in mind) **mengingat**

(= to have suddenly come to mind) **teringat**

(= to commemorate) **memperingati**

(= to convey greetings) **menyampaikan salam**: Remember me to your little sister. **Sampaikan salam kepada adikmu.**

(= to not forget) **jangan lupa**: Remember to lock the door. **Jangan lupa mengunci pintu.**

SAY

to say (= tell) **bilang**: Who says I'm stingy? **Siapa bilang saya pelit / kikir?**

to say (= speak) **berkata**

to say (= state, tell) **mengatakan** (with object, or **bahwa**, that…)

he said **katanya**: What did he say? **Apa katanya?**

it is said, they say **kata orang / kabarnya / konon**

the said (= aforementioned) **tersebut**

a say (= voice) **suara**: a say in the decision **suara dalam keputusan itu**

it goes without saying (= it is quite clear) **sudah cukup jelas**

to say the word **memberi ijin / perintah**

there's no saying **tak mungkin diramalkan**

when all's said and done **pada akhir perhitungan**

a saying (= proverb) **pepatah / peribahasa**

SEEM

it seems (= the appearance of it is…) **rupanya**

it seems (= the feeling of it is…) **rasanya**

it seems (= apparently) **kelihatannya / nampaknya / rupa-rupanya**

it seems to me (= in my opinion) **pada hémat saya, pada pendapat saya…**

it seems to be (= to have the look of, but not in fact) **kelihatannya**

it seems to be (= it is as if) **seolah-olah**

SET

to set (= place, put) **menaruh**

(= a clock, trap etc.) **memasang**

(= fix, determine) **menentukan**

(the table) **mengatur**

([intrans.], the sun) **terbenam**

to set apart **mengasingkan / menjauhkan**

to set aside (= save, money) **menyimpan / menabung**; (= put on the side) **mengesampingkan**

to set back (turn back, clock) **mengundurkan**

to set down (in writing) **menuliskan**; (= put down, place) **meletakkan**; (= disembark passengers) **menurunkan**

to set off (= leave) **berangkat**

to set up (= arrange, establish) **mengadakan / mendirikan**

to set out (= leave) **berangkat**; (= display) **memamérkan**

set [adj.] (= fixed) **tetap**

set (= ready) **siap**

SO

so (= very) **sekali / sangat**: I'm so tired. **Saya capai sekali.**

so (= like that) **begitu**: Of course it's so. **Mémang begitu.**

so (= as a result, consequently) **jadi…**

so (= also) **juga**: So am I. **Saya juga.**

so (= true) **benar**: It's not so. **Tidak benar.**

and so,… **maka, …**

so that (purpose) **supaya**

so… that (degree) **begitu…sehingga**

the so-called **yang dinamakan**

so-and-so **si anu**

so-so **lumayan**

So what? **lantas? terus?**

it so happened that… **kebetulan…**

so far (= till now) **sampai sekarang / selama ini**

So long! (= see you later) **Sampai jumpa!**

SOME

(Note: sometimes no separate translation.)

some (= a little, a certain quantity) **sedikit**: Do you want some sambal with that? **Mau pakai sambal sedikit?**; I've already got some. **Sudah ada.**

some (= several, a few) **beberapa**: some kilos of rice **beberapa kilo beras**

some…., others… **ada yang… ada yang…**: Some are old, others are young **Ada yang tua, ada yang muda**

some (indefinite) some… or other: some person or other **orang entah siapa**

some day (in future) **kapan-kapan**

at some length **agak lama**

at some distance **agak jauh**

someone, somebody **seseorang, ada orang**

somehow **bagaimana pun juga**

(= approximately) **kurang lebih**: some ten kilometres **kurang lebih sepuluh kilo.**

somewhere **di salah satu tempat / entah di mana**: She left her keys somewhere. **Kuncinya ketinggalan, entah di mana.**

STAND

to stand ([intrans.], = stand erect) **berdiri**

(= be there) **berada**

(= able to bear) **bertahan**

(= continue to be valid) **berlaku**

as things stand,… **dalam keadaan begini,…**

to stand aside **meminggir / mengundurkan diri**

to stand back **mundur**

to stand by (= be ready) **bersiap / siap-siaga**

to stand for (= mean) **berarti**

(= to allow) **membiarkan / memboléhkan**

to stand in for (= replace) **mengganti**

to stand on (= insist) **menuntut**

to stand out (= excel) **menonjol**

to stand over (= threaten) **mengancam**

to stand up (= rise) **berdiri**

SURE

sure 1. (= certain, positive, determined, proven); 2. (= for sure, surely, no doubt, certainly, of course) **pasti**

Also for a person: I'm sure. **Saya pasti.**

But: I'm not too sure. **Kurang tahu saya.**

There's sure to be another chance. **Pasti ada kesempatan lain.**

For sure! Sure! **Tentu! Tentu saja!**

surely (= certainly) **tentunya** (cf. not necessarily **belum tentu**)

to be sure of (= confident, certain, positive, convinced) **yakin**: sure of her love **Yakin akan cintanya**

sure enough (= it turns out that) **ternyata / nyatanya**

TAKE

to take (= get, fetch) **mengambil**; (= escort) **mengantar**

to take away **mengambil**; (= subtract) **mengurangi**; (= remove) **menghilangkan**

to take off (aircraft) **tinggal landas**; (clothes) **membuka**

to take up (= collect) **mengumpulkan**; (an offer) **menerima**; (space) **mengambil**; (topic) **membicarakan**

to take in (= trick) **menipu**

to take after (= resemble) **menyerupai / mirip dengan**

to take along **membawa (serta)**

to take back (= withdraw) **menarik kembali**

to take down (= note) **mencatat**

to take for (= guess) **mengira**

to take out **mengeluarkan**; (money from account) **mengambil**; (= extract, tooth) **mencabut**

to take up with **bergaul dengan**

to take it (= bear it) **tahan**

TALK

to talk **bicara** (more formal: **berbicara**)

(= to have a chat) **bercakap**

(= chat, converse) **ngomong**

to talk about (= discuss) **membicarakan**

to talk back (= dispute) **membantah**

to talk into (= persuade) **membujuk**

talk [noun] (= lecture) **ceramah**; (= rumours) **desas-desus, kabar burung**

talks (= discussions) **pembicaraan / négosiasi**

idle talk, nonsense **omong kosong**

to give a talking-to, talk like a Dutch uncle **menca-ci-maki / memarahi**

to talk big **menyombongkan diri**

TELL

to tell (= say) **bilang**: Don't tell anyone! **Jangan bilang, ya!**

to tell (= inform) **memberitahukan**

to tell ([trans.], = narrate) **menceritakan**; ([intrans.], = tell a story) **bercerita**

to tell (= order) **menyuruh**

to tell (= state) **mengatakan**

to tell (= know) **tahu**: How can I tell? **Bagaimana saya bisa tahu?**

to tell (= distinguish) **mengenali**

to tell (the difference) **membédakan**

to tell on (= make a complaint about) **mengadukan**

to tell off (= reprimand) **menegur**

to tell tales (= gossip) **bergunjing**

to tell the time **melihat jam**

You're telling me! **Tak usah bilang!**

all told (= taking account of everything) **kalau dihitung semuanya**

See also *say*.

THAT

that, those [demonstrative] **itu**: That becak's wrecked. **Bécak itu rusak.**

that, those ([pron.]: one, thing) **itu**: That's not very important. **Itu tidak begitu penting.**

that ([conj.], after verbs of saying etc.) **bahwa**: The lecturer said that his marks were excellent. **Bu** dosén mengatakan bahwa angkanya bagus.

that (after adjectives): zero, or **karena**
It's a pity that we can't meet again. **Sayang kita tidak bisa ketemu sekali lagi.**

amazed that **héran karena**

disappointed that **kecéwa karena**

happy that **senang karena**

sad that **sedih karena**

that perhaps, lest, in case **kalau-kalau**: She was afraid (that) there might be a cockroach in the bathroom. **Dia takut kalau-kalau ada coro dalam kamar mandinya.**

so that **supaya / agar**

like that, that way **begitu**

That's it! (the end of the matter) **Habis perkara!**

THE

In most positions, no translation, e.g.
  the State **negara**
  the middle class **golongan tengah**
  on the edge of the river **di tebing sungai**
But in other places, when specific, not general: **itu**
  There's a bird's nest in the mango tree. **Ada sarang burung di dalam pohon mangga itu.**
at the time **pada waktu itu**
the rich (= rich people) **orang kaya**
the … one(s) **yang**: the first (one) yang **pertama**; the last (one) **yang terakhir**
the… the… **makin… makin**: the more the merrier **makin banyak makin ramai**
the (a language) **bahasa**: borrowed from the Sanskrit **dipinjam dari bahasa Sanskreta**

THERE

there is / are (= exist) **ada**
to be there (= present) **hadir**
to be there (= at home) **ada di rumah**
there (= that place) **situ**; (= in that place) **di situ**
there (= that place over there, more distant) **sana**; (= in that place) **di sana**; (= to that place) **ke sana**
to be there (= arrive) **sampai / tiba (di tujuan)**: Are we there yet? **Sudah sampai belum?**
There you are! (= that's it) **Itu dia!**
there comes a time to… **tibalah waktunya untuk**

THING

thing (= object) **benda**
thing (= matter, case) **hal**: And another thing,.. **Dan hal lain lagi…**

thing (= problem, question, matter) **soal**: There's another thing that needs to be thought about… **Ada soal lagi yang perlu dipikirkan**
things (= luggage) **barang-barang**
things (= clothes) **pakaian**
things (= tools) **alat-alat**
things (= the situation) **keadaan**: Things are looking up! **Keadaannya membaik!**; How are things? **Bagaimana kabarnya?**
The thing is, … **Soalnya,…**
the … thing (adjective + -nya): The main thing is, … **Pokoknya, …**
the funny thing is, … **Anéhnya, …**
it's not the thing to do (= not polite) **tidak pantas**
Just the thing! **Ini dia! Tepat yang diinginkan!**

THINK

to think (= reflect, muse) **berpikir**
to think things over **berpikir-pikir**
to think about (someone or something) **memikirkan**
to think (= have occur to one) **terpikir**
to think of (= hold an opinion about) **berpendapat tentang**
without thinking **tanpa dipikir**
to think aloud **berpikir dengan suara keras**
to think back to **mengenang**
to think better of (= regret) **menyesal**; (= repent) **tobat**
to think big **mempunyai cita-cita tinggi**
to think nothing of **memberanikan diri / menganggap mudah**
to think out **memecah masalah**
to think over **mempertimbangkan**
to think through **memikirkan masak-masak**
to think up **mencari akal**

THROW

to throw **melémparkan** (e.g. ball, stone); **menyorotkan** (light)
to throw away (rubbish) **membuang**
to throw down **menjatuhkan**
to throw on (clothes) **memakai (baju) dengan tergesa-gesa**
to throw over (= abandon) **meninggalkan**
to throw out (= evict) **mengusir**; (= reject) **menolak**
to throw up (= vomit) **muntah**
to throw a party **mengadakan pésta**
to throw a fit **bertingkah / menunjukkan émosi**

TIME

time (= o'clock) **jam** [formal: **pukul**]: What time is it? **Jam berapa?**

time (general) **waktu**: I have no time! **Tidak ada waktu!**

at that time **pada waktu itu**

right on time **tepat pada waktunya**

from time to time **sewaktu-waktu / kadang-kadang**

at the same time **pada waktu yang sama / sekaligus**

time (= occasion) **kali**: every time **setiap kali**

time after time (= repeatedly) **berkali-kali**

time (= period, era) **jaman** (formal: **zaman**): in the time of the VOC **Pada jaman VOC**

any time **kapan saja**

all the time (= always) **selalu**

at no time (= never) **tak pernah**

for the time being **untuk sementara**

to take one's time (= not rush) **dengan santai / tidak terburu-buru**

to take time out (= have a break, rest) **beristirahat**

time off (= a holiday) **libur**

in quick time **cepat-cepat**: All in good time! (= be patient) **Sabarlah dulu!**

TO

to (direction toward, a place) **ke**

(to a person) **kepada**

(talking to) **dengan**

to (for, used for) **untuk**: money to buy food **uang untuk membeli makan**

to (up to, until, as far as) **sampai**

to (regarding, toward) **terhadap**: attitude toward corruption **sikap terhadap korupsi**

to (= before the hour) **kurang**: a quarter to one **jam satu kurang seperempat**

in order to **supaya**

> NOTE: the 'to' of the English infinitive (e.g. 'to give') has no Indonesian translation.

TOO

too (= excessive) **terlalu**: Your composition's too long. **Karanganmu terlalu panjang.**

That's too much! (= going too far) **Terlalu!**

too (= also) **juga**: Their cat's fat too. **Kucing meréka juga gemuk.**

pun He feels sad too. **Dia pun merasa sedih.**

too much (= in excess) **lebih**: This account's 100,000 too much. **Rékening ini 100.000 lebih**

Too bad! **Sayang sekali!**

all too soon **terlalu cepat**

TOUCH

to touch (= brush lightly against, come into contact with) **menyentuh**

to be touching, to touch each other **bersentuhan**

to touch (= feel, handle) **menjamah**

to touch (= grope, caress, fondle) **meraba**

to touch (up)on (a subject) **menyinggung**

to touch, be touching (the heart) **mengharukan**

to get in touch with (= contact) **menghubungi**

to keep in touch **tetap berhubungan**

to touch down (= land, aircraft) **mendarat**

TRUE

true (= right, correct, according to fact) **benar**

true (= genuine) **sejati**

true (= exact) **cocok**

true (= loyal) **setia**

true (= actual) **sebenarnya**

true (= real, not a lie) **betul**

to come true (= be granted, wish) **terkabul**

to be true to one's word **mematuhi janji**

It's true! (= not kidding) **Betul!**

true to life (= according to the facts) **sesuai dengan kenyataan**

true to form (= according to character) **sesuai dengan wataknya**

TURN

to turn ([intrans.], in a certain direction) **bélok** [more formal: **berbélok**]: to turn to the north **bélok ke utara**

to turn ([intrans.], = go round, e.g. wheel) **berputar**

to turn (= become) **menjadi**: It turned sour. **Menjadi pahit.**

to turn ([trans.], = turn over) **membalik**: to turn the page **membalik halaman**

to turn (records, tapes) **memutar**

to turn (the face) **memalingkan**

to turn (= point something in a direction) **mengarahkan**

to turn back (= return) **kembali / berbalik**

to turn down (= refuse) **menolak**

to turn into (= become) **berubah menjadi**

to turn off (tap) **menutup**; (electricity) **mematikan**

to turn on **memasang / menghidupkan**
to turn out (= end) **berakhir**
to turn over **membalikkan**; (in bed) **berguling**
to turn up (= increase sound) **membesarkan**; (= appear) **muncul**
a turn **giliran**; to take turns **bergiliran**
to turn the stomach **memualkan**

UNDERSTAND

to understand **mengerti**
(= to comprehend the meaning of) **memahami**
(= to be understood, intended) **dimaksudkan**
(= to hear, be informed) **menangkap**
(= to interpret as) **mengartikan / menafsirkan**

UP

up (= in an upward direction) **ke atas**
to go up **naik**
up the hill **naik bukit**
up to the top **sampai ke atas**
up in the sky **(tinggi) di langit**
up the street (= at the end of the street) **di ujung jalan**; (= along the street) **sepanjang jalan**
to add up **menghitung**
it doesn't add up (= not correct) **tidak cocok**
to give up **menyerah**
it's up to you **terserah**
Time's up! **Waktunya habis!**
What are you up to (= doing) these days? **Sedang apa sekarang?**
to walk up and down (= back and forth) **mondar-mandir**
to get up (from sleeping or lying down) **bangun**; (from sitting) **berdiri**
up the pole (= crazy) **sinting**

VERY

very **sangat** (placed before word modified): very satisfactory **sangat memuaskan**
very **sekali** (placed after word modified): very sweet **manis sekali**
very (superlative) **ter-**: the very best **yang terbaik**
very (emphatic) **juga**: that very day **hari itu juga**
very (exact) **tepat**: his very words **katanya persis**
not very **tidak begitu**
Very well! **Baiklah!**
to do one's very best **berusaha sebaik-baiknya**
the very first **pertama-tama**
at the very most **paling banyak / sebanyak-banyaknya**
at the very least **paling sedikit / sekurang-kurangnya**

WANT

to want to **mau** (also: willing; going to): What do you want (to do)? **Mau apa?**
ingin (= wish, desire, would like to): I want to see that film. **Saya ingin menonton film itu.**
to want (= require, need) **membutuhkan**: Wanted, a nightwatchman **Dibutuhkan, seorang jaga malam**
to want (= ask) **minta**: How much do you want for that bike? **Minta berapa untuk sepéda itu?**
to want (= desire, wish for, long for) **menginginkan**: The lecturer wants her students to make good progress with their language study. **Bu dosén menginginkan supaya mahasiswanya maju dalam studi bahasa meréka.**
to want (= wish for, desire, have in view) **menghendaki**, undesirable **tidak dihendaki**
wants [noun] **kebutuhan**
for want of (= lacking) **karena kekurangan**
wanting (= missing, lacking, not enough) **kurang**

WAY

way (general) **jalan**; (= street, road) **jalan, Jl.**); (= method) **cara**
in a … way **secara**: in a regular / orderly way **secara teratur**
all the way (= completely) **sepenuhnya / sampai selesai**
by way of (= via) **léwat / melalui**
to get one's way **mendapat apa yang diingini**
to get in the way (= obstruct) **menghalangi / merintangi jalan**
to give way (= surrender) **mengalah / menyerah**; (= collapse) **ambruk**
to go one's own way **menurut kemauan sendiri**
to go out of one's way **merépotkan diri / bersusah-payah**
in a way (= somewhat) **sedikit banyak**
in no way (= not at all) **tidak…sama sekali**
to know one's way around **tahu jalan / mengerti seluk-beluk**
to lead the way **memimpin / merintis jalan**
to look the other way (= pretend not to know) **pura-pura tidak tahu**
to lose one's way **tersesat**
to make one's way (= advance) **berhasil maju / naik pangkat**

to make way for **melapangkan / membuka jalan untuk**

out of the way (= isolated) **terpencil**

to see one's way (clear) to **mendapat kesempatan**

to stand in the way of **menghalangi / menentang**

under way **dalam perjalanan** (journey, voyage); **sedang dikerjakan** (project, work)

ways (= customs) **adat-istiadat / kebiasaan**

ways and means **akal dan siasat**

a long way off **jauh** (distance); **masih lama** (time)

way ahead **jauh di muka**

way off (= very inaccurate) **salah benar / berselisih banyak**

way out in the country **jauh di pedésaan / di udik / di pedalaman**

by the way,… **ngomong-omong,…**

Have it your own way! **Terserah! Biarin! Sekarepmu!**

on the way (= going to happen) **akan terjadi**; (= going to be born) **akan lahir**

to have a way (= special talent) with **berbakat untuk**

on the way out (fashion) **mulai tidak mode lagi**

the other way round (the reverse) **sebaliknya**

WHEN

Question words: when? **kapan?**

(= at what time of day?) **jam berapa?**

(= in what period?) **jaman apa?**: When was that? **Jaman apa itu?**

(= if) **kalau**: Ring me when you get home. **Bél kalau sudah tiba di rumah.**

(= at the time, in the past) **waktu / ketika**: When I was young… **Waktu saya masih muda**

(= at the moment when) **saat**: When I was about to board, I was called to Information. **Saat saya mau naik ke pesawat, saya dipanggil ke bagian Informasi.**

(= the time when) **waktunya**: That was the time when the Arts Faculty was still in the Wijilan (the residence of Prince Wijil). **Itu waktunya Fakultas Sastra masih di Wijilan.**

WHERE

Question word: where (= in which place?) **di mana?**

(= to which place?) **ke mana?**

Relative: where **tempat, di mana**: She visited the house where she was born. **Dia berkunjung ke rumah tempat dia lahir.**

WHICH

Question word: which (= which one, out of several?) **yang mana?**: Which one do you want? **Mau ambil yang mana?**

Relative: which (= that) **yang**: I want a book which has photos. **Saya mau buku yang ada foto.**

WHILE

Conjunction: (used to join two sentences which have the same subject) **sambil**: …he said while laughing …**katanya sambil tertawa**

(= during the time that) **sementara / selagi**: While the teacher wrote, the pupils made notes. **Sementara pak guru menulis, murid-murid membuat catatan.**

(= whereas, joining two sentences with different subjects, expressing a contrast) **sedangkan**: Indonesian rice tastes nice, while Australian rice doesn't. **Nasi di Indonesia énak, sedangkan nasi Australia kurang énak.**

while [noun] (= a period of time)

for a while **beberapa waktu**

a little while **sebentar**

in a while **sebentar lagi**

once in a while **sekali-sekali / kadang-kadang**

a while ago **beberapa waktu lalu**

to be worthwhile (= useful, beneficial) **bermanfaat / berfaédah / bernilai**

while [verb] to while away the time **menghabiskan waktu / bermalas-malas**

WILL, WOULD

will [future tense] **akan** We'll meet tonight. **Kita akan bertemu nanti malam.**

It's going to rain. **Akan hujan.**

Not likely! (= not going to happen) **Tidak akan!**

Also 'will have' **akan**: We will have paid it off in another six months. **Akan kita lunasi enam bulan lagi.**

NOTE: 'would' is past tense of 'will', and also a conditional, indicating the consequence of an imagined event: also **akan**. We would have paid too much, if you hadn't told us this. **Kita akan membayar terlalu banyak, kalau anda tidak memberitahu.**

Mau (= want to): The engine won't start. **Mesinnya tak mau hidup.**

'Would' in polite requests:

Would you please... **tolong / minta / mohon /**

silakan: Would you please be seated. **Silakan duduk.**

In plain requests:

…would you …, ya: Wash these clothes, would you? **Pakaian ini dicuci, ya?**

Will do! **Baiklah! / Oké!**

WITH

with (= together with) **dengan**

(= by means of) **dengan**

with pleasure **dengan senang hati**

with white hair **berambut putih**

with respect/regard to **mengenai**

with the exception of **terkecuali**

to have nothing to do with **tidak berurusan dengan**

to do (something) with (something) **Diapakan?** What do you do with it?

with all one's strength **sekuat-kuatnya**

coffee with milk **kopi susu**

WORK

to work (at a job) **bekerja**

to work (= go) **jalan**: My watch isn't working. **Jamku tidak jalan.**

to work (= make move) **menggerakkan**

to work (= be effective) **mujarab**: The medicine works. **Obat itu mujarab.**

to work on/at **mengerjakan**

to work off (debt) **melunasi dengan bekerja**

to work on (= influence) **mempengaruhi**

to work out (a puzzle) **memecahkan**

(= determine) **menentukan**

(= exercise) **berolahraga**

to work it out (= understand) **mengerti**

out of work (= be unemployed) **menganggur**

a work (artistic, scholarly) **karya**

the works (machine, engine) **mesin**

to be worked up **bergairah**

Translations

Please note that the following translations are only suggestions – other wordings may be possible as well. An example is the use of tense; for the earlier lessons we use present tense, and then switch to the past tense, to indicate what happened at a particular time.

LESSON 1 Getting To Know Each Other

SARI	I am Sari.
	I am a student.
	I am a student of the University of Indonesia.
	This is my house.
	Welcome!
	This is my mother.
	This is my friend, Joel.
JOEL	Good morning.
SARI'S MOTHER	How are you, Joel?
JOEL	Fine, thanks.
SARI	And this is my father.
JOEL	Good morning.
SARI'S FATHER	Please come in, Joel.
JOEL	Thanks.
SARI	My father is a lecturer, and my mother is a doctor. And this is my elder brother.
SARI'S BROTHER	My name's Agus.
JOEL	Hi, Agus!
SARI	And this is my younger sister.
SARI'S SISTER	My name's Ratih.
JOEL	Hi, Ratih!

LESSON 2 At the Campus

Sari was born in Jakarta.
Sari's family live in Pasar Minggu.
Sari goes to the UI campus in Depok.
She goes with her father.
Sari's father has a car.
At the campus Sari is studying International Relations.
In the afternoon she goes home from the campus.

At the canteen Sari drinks Pepsi.
At home she drinks tea.
Her sister likes to drink cold orange juice.
Her brother likes drinking Bintang beer.
They like eating fried rice.

Sari has lunch at the campus.
At the campus she eats fried noodles.

LESSON 3 Lectures

Sari has finished eating her breakfast.
Now she is ready to leave for the campus.
Yesterday she forgot her umbrella.
So today she is not going to forget it.

Sari has arrived at the campus.
She is going to follow a lecture.
The lecture is going to begin.
She enters the room, and then she goes out again.
"I'm stupid", she thinks.
"What's wrong, Sari?" her friend asks.

Today there's no lecture!
The lecturer isn't there.
He's away.
The students are chatting:
"Come on, let's go home!" they say.
"There's no use staying at the campus."

But Sari wants to go to the Law Faculty.
"I guess I'll be able to meet Joel again", she thinks.
Usually Joel will come out late in the morning.

LESSON 4 At the Mall

SARI Would you like to go out to Mangga Mall?

JOEL Yes, I would. I like going around shops like that.

SARI Good, let's go now.

JOEL Can I ask you, Sari – what's that man doing?

SARI He's asking for money. He's what you call a beggar.

JOEL What sort of shop is this?

SARI This is a motorcycle / shoe / flower... shop.

JOEL What's that smell?

SARI That's the smell of fried peanuts. Do you like fried peanuts?

JOEL Yes, I do. Do you like them?

SARI Let's just keep going, okay?

JOEL Is there something to drink in this café?

SARI I think there is. What do you want to drink?

JOEL What's that?

SARI That's cold orange juice. Try it!

JOEL Thanks, Sari. What do you want?

SARI I'll have the same.

JOEL Well now, do I have any small change...?

LESSON 5 Prices

Joel needs to go to a bookshop.

He goes by taxi to Gramedia Bookshop.

How much does it cost?

It costs about Rp 50,000 to take a taxi to the bookshop.

Joel buys a ruler. It costs Rp 1,500.

He buys a notebook. It costs Rp 25,000.

Joel looks for a dictionary of legal terms. It costs Rp 450,000.

He buys a newspaper. It costs Rp 2,000.

There's a magazine in English too. It costs Rp 350,000.

Finally Joel buys three Tin-Tin comics and a novel in Indonesian. They cost Rp. 40,000.

Everything is fixed price. What is the total?

LESSON 6 What Time?

JOEL When do you have some time, Sari? I would like to meet you again.

SARI I have time tomorrow. Ten o'clock?

JOEL Sorry, I have an appointment with the lecturer at 10. Can you make it at 11?

SARI Okay. I'll wait for you at the corner of the Law Faculty building, right?

JOEL When is your birthday?

SARI 10 April. I was born in 1987.

JOEL So you'll be 22.

SARI Yes. What about you?

JOEL My birthday is 11 September. I was born in 1986.

SARI So now you're 23. We're almost the same!

JOEL What time is it now?

SARI It's almost 12. Today is Friday. Muslims will be going to the mosque for Friday prayers. They finish at 1. Then they go home.

LESSON 7 Where?

Excuse me, where is the Law Faculty?

Over there, at the side of the Faculty of Psychology. From the railway station, turn left. It's located on the right-hand side of the road. To the south of it there is the Campus Mosque.

At the centre of the UI campus there is the Central Administration building.

And at the back of that there is the Library building.

Between the buildings there are trees, grass and gardens.

Students eat their lunch outside or in the Student Activities Centre.

Joel is going for a walk beneath the trees.

"Where are you going?"

"I want to go to the Arts Faculty. Where is it?"

"From here, keep on going, then turn left. The building is located on the right-hand side of the road."

LESSON 8   In the Street

JOEL	Excuse me, is there a post office here?
PASSER-BY	Yes, there is. Over there. Across the road.
JOEL	Thanks.
P.	Wow, you speak Indonesian fluently…
JOEL	Yes, I can a bit.
P.	It's great! How many times have you been to Indonesia?
JOEL	This is just the first time.
P.	Are you happy in Indonesia?
JOEL	Yes. It's very interesting. But it's hot!
P.	What's your name?
JOEL	Joel.
P.	Do you have a family?
JOEL	Sorry?
P.	Um, are you married?
JOEL	Oh, no.
P.	You mean, 'not yet', don't you.
JOEL	Oh yes, I made a mistake.
P.	You're from America, aren't you?
JOEL	No, I'm an Australian.
P.	From kangaroo country! Do you want to find a girlfriend here?
JOEL	Yes, I'd like to. But it's quite difficult.
P.	Why?
JOEL	They're all pretty! Bye!

(Joel goes to cross the road.)

P.	Careful! See you again.

LESSON 9   Buying a Fan

Joel is sad.

He is feeling tired.

But it's not because he has been studying too hard.

Outside the air is hot and humid.

The traffic is very noisy.

As a result, it's hard to sleep.

Joel is thinking, "I had better just go home. How can I study in Jakarta?"

Knock, knock! (a sound at the door)

"Who is it?"

Sari enters, with a sweet smile.

She says, "I was thinking just now. I think you need to buy a little electric fan. Come and we'll look for one at an electrical goods shop!"

They get a fine fan. It is blue. Well, now it feels cooler.

"That's cool, Sari!"

"Fresh, isn't it, Joel."

Now Joel is feeling strong again. He's full of new vigour.

"Thanks, Sari. You're very kind."

"You're welcome", says Sari.

LESSON 10   Clothes

What should we wear in a tropical region?

It's clear that we don't need to wear thick clothes.

It's better to just wear thin ones.

As well as that, cotton material is much more comfortable than synthetic.

Yes, it has to be pure cotton, not a mixture.

So we need to buy clothes that fit the climate.

If we don't, we may possibly get sick!

People who have just arrived in Jakarta can get sick because of the climate.

We have to be careful.

But our clothes also have to be decent.

It's not allowed to wear short pants outside.

At home of course we will wear a sarong, especially when we want to go to sleep.

It feels cool!

Joel once tried it, and then he got used to it.

Who is it that washes Joel's clothes?

Joel wants to wash his clothes himself.

He's not very happy if someone else washes his underclothes.

But it's quite troublesome, in particular if it's a rainy day!

How can they get dry?

LESSON 11   In the Kampong

From the main road there are alleyways that head into the kampong at the back of the shops. The alleyways are narrow. Cars can almost not get through. Some children are playing kites there. Now is the season of sea breezes. There are kites high in the air, and there are kites that come down fast, and then get stuck in trees in people's yards or on electric poles. From the window Joel can see that there are naughty boys climbing onto the mosque roof with kites in their hands.

Now it is evening. There is the sound of '**Allahu akbar, Allahu akbar**' coming from the mosques again and again. Then the children go into their houses, because in a moment it will be dark. The sun is soon lost in the grey gloom in the west, and lamps are burning in the streets. Joel is feeling homesick. He thinks, "I wonder how my family at home in Australia are. I hope they're all well!"

LESSON 12   Law Lectures

According to the plan, Joel is going to stay in Jakarta for six months. He is diligently following lectures in the Faculty of Law, all of them in Indonesian. It doesn't bother him, as his Indonesian is quite good, since he studied it in Melbourne. It is only the legal terms that are still difficult. It is the lecturers who help Joel.

In Joel's opinion, the legal structure in Indonesia is very interesting, because it differs from Australia. The systems of civil and criminal law originate from the law of the Dutch colonial era. In Indonesia there are also Islamic law and customary law.

Several classmates often ask Joel to practise their English. Some of them are fluent, and others are not very serious. In the beginning Joel is happy to chat with them in English, but sometimes he gets sick of it too, answering questions that are always the same. He says, "Some other time, okay."

LESSON 13   The Poor

While travelling around in the city, by taxi or by bus, Joel sees there are many tall and luxurious buildings in the centre of Jakarta, such as the BCA Tower at Jalan MH Thamrin 1, on the western side of the HI Roundabout. He is of the opinion that Indonesia is a developing country, because there are many big businesses.

But not far from there are also dirty districts with piled up garbage, for example on the banks of the Ciliwung River. The garbage smells bad. Poor people are living underneath the bridges and next to the railway lines, or sheltering under big trees.

After arriving at the campus, Joel asks his friends: "Why doesn't the government do anything for those poor people?" They answer: "Possibly the government regards the problem of street people as too difficult. That's their fate! And what about Melbourne? We suppose everybody there is rich."

Joel answers: "In fact, there are ones who sleep outside there too, in the doorways of shops or lying on benches in public parks, even in winter…"

"Oh, you must be kidding!"

LESSON 14   Smoking

At intersections there are often people who are selling cigarettes. When the lights are red and the traffic stops, they come running to offer their wares. There are various brands. For example, there is Gudang Garam Merah. It contains 12 cigarettes per pack. The price per pack is around Rp 7,500. There is also Gudang Garam International Merah, with its motto "Men's taste". In one carton there are 10 packs. Filter cigarettes and foreign cigarettes certainly cost more.

In Indonesia there are still lots of people who smoke. One day Joel and his friend Hanafi were sitting down. Hanafi lit up a cigarette. Then Joel said, "At my place there's a prohibition on smoking inside university buildings and around them. They say it's unhealthy." Hanafi was a heavy smoker. He often coughed. Hanafi answered, "Actually I agree with you. But after studying I want to enjoy the aroma, when the tobacco smoke rises in clouds on the evening air like this…" And Hanafi was still coughing.

LESSON 15   The "Taman Mini"

Sari already knew that Joel was going to celebrate his birthday. When the day drew nearer, Sari asked her father: "How would it be if we invite him to go out to Taman Mini? As far as I know, Joel has never been there."

Sari's father: "Yes, of course lots of tourists like going there. But in fact your Joel isn't a tourist…"

Sari: "Even so it's sure to be interesting for him too."

Right on time, they fetched Joel by car to go to TMII, or Taman Mini Indonesia Indah in full. On the way to East Jakarta, while wrestling with the traffic, Sari's father told the story:

"In the year 1970 Bu Tien Suharto got the idea of building the garden, as a kind of display, in particular for architecture, art and daily life from all the provinces of Indonesia. Then the Taman Mini was opened in 1973. At that time there were 26 provinces — now the number has increased!"

When they arrived at Taman Mini, the parking area was almost full. The cost of parking was Rp 10,000 for a car. Joel was amazed to see the buildings that resembled exactly the original houses, each one with a sign in Indonesian and English, for example "Sumatera Barat, West Sumatra" in front of a traditional Minangkabau house. Joel thought it must have been expensive to build the TMII.

Sari's father explained: "The Indonesian term for a building of this kind is **anjungan**. The English is 'pavilion', isn't it?"

Joel: "Yes, that's right. I understand."

They went on the cable car, and then watched some dances from the region of Riau. They were very thirsty! Well, where do we find something to drink that isn't too expensive?

LESSON 16   TV Dramas

When Joel arrived home it was already past 9 o'clock. As it happened, his landlady, Bu Tuti, was absorbed in watching her favourite TV series, **Cinta Fitri**, which is shown on SCTV every evening at 21.00. Fitri is a girl aged 19, originally from the village of Wonogiri. Firman, her fiancé, has died. Then Fitri lives in Jakarta and experiences various sad adventures.

Bu Tuti asked Joel to join her watching, because she was sure he would be interested in a story about rich people in Indonesia. The female character often cries, and then there is a male character who is good at soothing her. The plot moves slowly, but Joel still didn't understand what was going on. Each scene is constantly accompanied by touching music. There are always difficult problems.

The most interesting thing for Joel, as someone who has studied language, was the way the characters speak: full of emotion, quickly, and using words from everyday speech, such as "I'll certainly help you" and "There's nothing wrong with me". Clearly there is a special style of speech for this kind of drama. Joel was wanting to ask Bu Tuti why the characters always use the word **aku** and not **saya**. But he didn't want to disturb her. "Another time," he thought.

LESSON 17   Visit to an Expat Family

Through the network of students at the Faculty of Law Joel contacted a foreign American family who lived in Tebet, South Jakarta. He wanted to know what influenced their decision to work in Indonesia.

Joel was looking for their house. But the taxi driver got lost. Or did he deliberately get himself lost? Or was it the address that was unclear? There was a Jalan Tebet Dalam, Jalan Tebet Timur Dalam, Tebet Timur 1, Tebet Timur 2, Tebet Timur 3, and so on. Of course it was confusing, so that Joel was forced to call them on the phone. Finally the neighbours were asked for directions: "Where is the house of the American family Schroeder?"

The house that they occupied was not their own property. The house had been contracted by a big company. There were two floors, there was air-conditioning in all the bedrooms, there were two maids, even a swimming pool… Its water was clear, cool and tempting to dive straight in.

But the tiled floor was very slippery when wet. Joel fell over and hurt his foot. He was beginning to regret this plan of his. Only when he tasted the peanut sauce and cold beer that were provided by the maid with a cheerful face did he feel better. Ah, that was quite nice!

LESSON 18 The Interview

Several friends of Sari's wanted to meet Joel. Joel was going to be interviewed in Indonesian for a student magazine. But they felt shy, so they asked Sari, "How would it be if you asked Joel? He's sure to agree!"

Joel doesn't like being laughed at. "Don't just make jokes, okay? There have to be meaningful questions. I want to be given the themes of the interview in advance, if you can. I hope it goes smoothly."

The students crowded around Joel, led by Sari. His answers were going to be recorded. For example:

Sari: "What do you like most about Indonesia?"

Joel: "Yes, it's hard if you tell me to choose. Possibly it's the Indonesian people's nature, friendly and open toward outsiders…"

Sari: "What do you hate most about Indonesia?"

Joel: "Clearly it's the air pollution and the exploitation of the environment. We love nature, and don't like it if it is ruined for the sake of making excessive profits."

Sari: "Actually, there are some friends who want to continue their study overseas. Can you arrange this? What is the method?"

Joel: "Well, there are quite a few ways to go. For example, there is post-graduate research, under the supervision of an expert in Australia or America. But there is always the condition: their English has to be excellent, so that they can communicate freely."

Sari: "Probably that's enough. Thanks very much, Joel."

Joel: "You're welcome."

LESSON 19 What Will We Watch?

As usual, Joel wanted to get more complete information about the society around him. He was very interested in studying the lives of Indonesian people.

He said to Sari: "Sari, where do kids in Jakarta usually go out to, on a Saturday evening? Give me a bit of info, would you?"

Sari: "Some like going to a film, and others prefer a pop concert, such as…"

Joel: "I'm interested in seeing a contemporary Indonesian film. Please note the title for me."

(Sari wrote down film titles.) "Now, this story is very romantic. The title is **Ayat-Ayat Cinta**. This film is very well known at this time, in Singapore and Malaysia as well. Would you like it? But wait a moment, let me phone Mas Agus…

(Sari phones.) Mas Agus! Help me a moment, would you? When you go to Mangga Mall, have a look and see what films are showing there. Not action movies, right. Just romantic ones. Joel wants to see one, he says."

Agus: "Careful! Or he'll get stolen by girls crazy about white people…"

Sari: "Oh, in that case a concert by a pop singer would be better, like Citra Lestari. What on earth will I do?

(to Joel) Joel, you'll have to choose for yourself. I'll go along too!"

Joel: "I like both of them. But not at the same time. We'll go to the film first, providing you don't cry, and the next week we'll go to the pop concert. Please get the tickets for me. How many people? Just two, or the whole gang? I'm the one paying, right!"

LESSON 20 Twilight in Jakarta

After his afternoon bath, while drinking **kopi tubruk** on the veranda, Joel was having a read of the magazine *Gatra* that he had just bought in a bookshop. The price was Rp 24,500. There were articles of various kinds, such as politics and law, business, medicine and sport. The most useful ones for him were politics and law.

For example, there was an article on the process of electing the president. Its author was of the opinion that "the colossal general election needs well thought-out and careful preparation from those organizing it." All the regulations have to be ready in advance. If not, this can make the implementation difficult. "There has to be

an understanding of geographical conditions, the demographic character of…"

But Joel was already beginning to get sleepy. His eyes were tired. In a moment, suddenly it was dark, the hour at which cockroaches come out to play on the bathroom floor. He was getting interested in having something to eat. What will he eat? Fried chicken or pizza? Yes, fried chicken! So Joel went out and headed for the nearest KFC, on the corner of the main road. Their chicken was delicious, and in the restaurant it was more fun than sitting alone at home. Maybe he would be able to meet some new friends. Right, where's the list of foods?

LESSON 21   Going to the Doctor

One morning Joel was passing a bus stop, as it happened, right outside the Australian Embassy. There were lots of people waiting for the bus to come, and then when the red bus arrived they pushed each other while trying to get on. There were a few youths who came running, pushed Joel from behind and then got on the bus. Only when the bus had left did Joel feel his pocket: empty. His pocket had been picked. Luckily, he had not lost much, only a purse containing some small change.

But from that moment his feelings changed. He experienced feelings of fear, disappointment and failure, as if the incident had influenced his attitude toward his surroundings. Why was it like this? Sari was aware that something wasn't in order. She said to Joel: "Joel, I'm going to take you to the doctor, to have you examined, okay?"

Joel had no objections. The two of them were there at Dr Lim's consulting hour, at six o'clock in the evening. They didn't have to wait long. Joel explained to the doctor: "I always feel exhausted and tired. What do you think it is, doctor?"

Dr Lim said, "Yes, Joel, your face is rather pale. There is a possibility that you have **kurang darah**. That means the blood is lacking in iron. The English term is anaemia. It's caused by the climate, or a lack of nutritious food. If you can, my advice is that you take a holiday, to Puncak, for example. There you can have a rest in a cool place. As well as that, I'll write a prescription for tablets containing iron. Okay?"

Joel and Sari: "Thanks very much, doctor."

LESSON 22   International Relations

Ever since she was little Sari had been attracted to stories about far-away countries overseas, such as are found in children's books. She wanted to roam the world to see it for herself. Her parents suggested to Sari that she take the course in International Relations Studies, at least as a first step. After that a career path would be open in the Department of Foreign Affairs, or to the world of business.

While studying developments in East Asia, Sari got an assignment to read lecture materials including books and journal articles, the majority of them in English. She had searched for these books in the library, but rarely found them. Her frustration was indescribable! Finally she remembered: I have a friend, our Joel. Possibly he can help.

Sari: "By the way, Joel, I'm having trouble looking for sources for an essay my lecturer has assigned to me. Where do you think I might get those books?"

Joel: "Let's have a look at the titles. Well, that kind of book is certain to be available in Monash library. Hey, I have an idea! My sister's going to visit Indonesia very soon, amongst other things to see me. How would it be if she borrowed them, and then we photocopy the most important parts here? It's not allowed to photocopy all of them, so we'll just select the necessary chapters. Agreed?"

Sari's feeling of gratitude was incalculable. She kept kissing Joel on the cheek.

Joel: "This is what's called 'International Relations', isn't it?"

Sari and Joel laughed.

LESSON 23   A Trip to Yogyakarta

To his surprise Joel got an opportunity to visit the city of Yogyakarta, the famous centre of Javanese culture.

Sari informed Joel: "In the semester break we are planning to go to Yogya, because we want to see our grandmother, that is, the mother of my mother, who lives there. Would you like to come along? We won't be there long, only about five days."

Joel: "Yes, of course I want to. I've long wanted to see the archaeological remains there are in that region. But how are we going to travel there?"

Sari: "There's the night bus, the train, and there's the plane… The night bus and the train take a long time, and are very physically tiring. So we just choose the plane…"

Joel: "Yes, clearly it's quicker and more comfortable. Let's look for a timetable and ticket price, will we?"

Loudspeaker: "Passengers are invited to board the aircraft, flight number GA 210."

Flight attendant: "Fasten your seat belts, put your seats in an upright position, and stow your tray tables. Life vests are under your seat…"

Within 60 minutes they were near the destination. Mount Merbabu and Mount Merapi were visible on the left-hand side, and the Indian Ocean and the Menoreh Range were visible on the right. The aircraft turned to the north and then made a smooth landing at Adi Sutjip-to Airport.

The family from Jakarta were met by the family from Yogya outside the baggage collection area. They didn't need to go to a hotel, as there was plenty of space in grandmother's house. Joel was introduced to Sari's grandmother: "Grandmother, this is my friend, an Australian who is studying at UI. His name is Joel."

Grandmother: "Are you well?"

Sari: "Yes, Grandmother, by your blessing."

Joel was very impressed. This Javanese, how refined and melodious it sounded!

LESSON 24   To the Market

JOEL   Where are you going, Sari?

SARI   I want to call in at the Beringharjo Market. Come on!

In the market various fruits and vegetables were piled up. People were pushing each other, looking for the cheapest. Some were buying rice, spices, clothes, shoes…

SARI   In the market we can bargain. In fact you have to. It's not like the shops. In shops it's only fixed prices.

Meanwhile there were two old sellers who were quarrelling with each other.

SELLER 1   Look over there – there's a pretty princess courting with a giant. A giant with a red face!

SELLER 2   Don't go on like that! Or he'll punch you on the head, your brains will be scattered about, and then they'll be cooked with a hot sauce the Minang way…

SELLER 1   You're envious. I'm the one he's going to run away with!

SELLER 2   Out of the question! With that face of yours, like a fried potato chip!

SARI   Careful, please, Joel. Don't let your foot touch any of the goods on the ground there. Come on, it's a durian I'm looking for, so you can get to know that famous fruit. Ha, what's this… How much for the durian?

Joel looked at the fruit with a brownish green colour and a skin like thorns.

SARI   This is what we call a durian. It's very tasty! We like it.

Joel said nothing. His eyes met Sari's. Only then did Sari realize that Joel didn't like the smell much. Certainly the smell was pungent. Joel kept his distance from the pile of fruits.

SARI   Don't worry. When I've opened it at home, I'll give you a bit to taste. Just a little bit! They say it can make your blood hotter…

LESSON 25 National Days

Hanafi and Joel were chatting in the Espresso Coffee Shop in Margonda Street.

HANAFI By the way, Joel, does Australia have a national day, like our Proclamation Day on 17 August? Here there are big ceremonies everywhere each year.

JOEL Yes, of course it does. It's called Australia Day, on 26 January. We have ceremonies too, and there are fireworks. On that day, in 1788, a fleet consisting of eleven sailing ships anchored in Sydney Harbour. The first English arrivals disembarked from the ships and landed there. So what is being celebrated is the first European settlement, not a proclamation of independence, for instance.

HANAFI But wasn't there anybody living there before that, the people called 'original inhabitants' or Aborigines? They had been settled in the country for a long time, for tens of thousands of years, according to an article I once read.

JOEL Yes, that's true. The Aborigines must have been astonished when they saw those ships sailing in, and then spewing out hundreds of white-skinned people. And they were certainly not happy to have their land seized. Because they didn't build houses of stone, plant crops or herd animals they were thought to be primitive, so that they didn't need to be taken into account. Whereas their culture was to be found on the spiritual side…

HANAFI Weren't there any conflicts?

JOEL It was inevitable that disputes arose. As well as that, the diseases brought by the English spread to the Aborigines. They were unable to resist the diseases, so that many died. And so these days some people are of the opinion that Australia Day should not be celebrated, as it commemorates a disaster. It would be better for a nation that is truly united to choose another day, which brings together every social group, and which honours the achievements of each one, including the original inhabitants and all the waves of immigrants who have arrived since 1788…

HANAFI Wow, that's so interesting! I hadn't imagined there was a history like that. Maybe I should register for lectures in the Department of Australian Studies!

LESSON 26 Wall Lizards

In Jakarta Joel often saw the lizards that came out in the evenings and ran around on the walls of houses near the outside lights, chasing little insects attracted by the light of the lamps. He thought how sweet the animals were, friends sharing the same house with humans. From time to time their sound, cek cek cek, could be heard.

Sari told him: "According to what the Balinese believe, if we're in a state of uncertainty, and then hear the lizards sounding three times, then we are given certainty. The wall lizard is a manifestation of the goddess Saraswati, the patroness of speech and writing…"

Mas Agus interrupted her: "Ah, that's nonsense, superstition! Imagine believing in the sound of an animal! It's better to believe in your own reasoning, based on observation and an examination of the facts."

Sari's father added: "According to some Muslim groups, the wall lizard should be exterminated. This is because at the time when the Prophet Muhammad was being pursued by the Arab polytheists, and was hiding in the Hiro cave, suddenly a wall lizard informed them with its sound that there was someone in the cave."

Then the next day, at his boarding house, Joel had a surprise. There was a racket outside, as if struck by a great storm. What was that? It turned out that the neighbours had asked for fogging to eliminate mosquitoes. By coincidence Joel had just been reading a report in the paper *Kompas* that cases of dengue fever were on the rise in the Jakarta metropolitan area and there had begun to be deaths. The number of sufferers from dengue fever in Depok had risen by 29 percent at that time.

According to the Head of the Disease Control and Environmental Improvement Section of the Health Service of the Municipality of Depok, most patients were being treated at Bhakti Yudha Hospital, and totalled 55. In keeping with the rise in sufferers from dengue fever, there was also a rise in requests from residents for fogging to be carried out, according to the report.

In this way someone was taking responsibility for keeping an eye on the health of the inhabitants of the area. But Joel was reminded of the wall lizards. If all the mosquitoes were gone, where would they find their food? And if the wall lizards were also affected by the vapour, what would the result be?

LESSON 27 Demonstrations

One day Joel arrived at the campus early in the morning. He was surprised to see an unusual situation: hundreds of students had gathered in front of the main gate. There were pick-up trucks with microphones, and a number of banners had been set up along the road.

After meeting his friend Hanafi, Joel asked: "What's going on today?" Hanafi was confused for a moment, thinking "to die?" then answered, "Don't be scared. There's no danger. Nobody's going to die. This is what you call a "demo" in your language, right? The Indonesian for it is **unjuk rasa**. This means informing the authorities about our feelings, for example, a feeling of dissatisfaction. This is an aspect of freedom of expression. It's common in Indonesia, especially since the fall of the Soeharto regime in 1998. A demonstration happens almost every day, in particular in Jakarta. Just recently there were seven on the same day, in different parts of the city, so that the traffic experienced jams on the main arteries and it interfered with road users."

Joel: "Why are there so many demonstrations?"

Hanafi: "Usually they are carried out by students who oppose government policy, or the workers who are dissatisfied with their treatment by their employers."

Joel: "Do they have any use?"

Hanafi: "Yes, listen. The Rector has issued a decree, with the aim of charging admission fees of Rp 5 million up to Rp 25 million per new student. Our campaign demands that this decree be withdrawn. The opportunity to study should be open equally to all students who achieve, and must not be sold to anyone who is able to pay entry money!"

About 10.00 the crowd moved to block the entrance to the campus, so that they got a response from the local security. The leaders held speeches from the pick-up trucks for two hours, slogans were shouted, and everyone worked up a sweat. Joel was wondering whether there would be any result. There had been an announcement that the Rector's office had scheduled a dialogue with the students, to take place the next morning at the Salemba campus at 9.00 a.m. The only thing left to do was to await news.

LESSON 28 The Secret Trumpet

SARI Joel, at the weekend in the evening at home like this, what are you usually doing?

JOEL I rarely have time, but if I want to relax I play my trumpet. Sometimes I'm asked to play with a few friends. We have a little band. It's called 'Sticky and the Insects'.

SARI Hey, we've known each other as long as this, and only now do I hear you can play the trumpet! That means that the longer we know each other the deeper our friendship gets, doesn't it. So, what kind of music is it?

JOEL Oh well, funky jazz, and I did once play hip hop Jamaica style.

SARI Why didn't you bring your trumpet here?

JOEL I was afraid it would disturb the neighbours, and then I'd get a warning from Pak RT. Especially if I blow the trumpet to imitate the sound of a wild elephant. It's sooo funny.

SARI Mas Agus has a friend who owns a trumpet. Would you like to try it? I'm longing to hear what it sounds like.

JOEL Ah, some other time, okay?

SARI There's a program on RCTI called *Dahsyat*, where they invite bands. Their music is terrific. Not long ago they invited Hillary Clinton, at the request of the American Embassy. Unfortunately, Hillary only knew the names of The Beatles and The Rolling Stones.

JOEL What is RCTI?"

SARI It means **Rajawali Citra Televisi Indonesia**, the biggest private TV station in Indonesia.

JOEL By the way, Sari, what song do you like best?

SARI **Godai aku lagi** [Tempt me again], a single by Agnes Monica. If you like, I'll write down the lyrics for you. And then you can take them home, and sing them there.

JOEL Is *Dahsyat* only in Jakarta?

SARI No. Soon the Friends of Dahsyat living in Bali will be able to watch guest stars there, broadcast direct from the Hard Rock Café in Kuta. Oh, I'd love to go to Bali. Bali's close to Australia, isn't it?

JOEL Yes, it is. And I hope you'll go to Australia too, and go and see my parents in Geelong…

The time for Joel to go home was approaching. His program of study in Jakarta had finished.

SARI When will you come back to Jakarta?

JOEL I don't know yet. But for sure, I want to come again, as soon as possible.

SARI Parting…

JOEL Makes the heart grow fonder.

Listening Comprehension

These are the transcripts for the Listening Comprehension passages found in each lesson's Exercise B.

TAPE LATIHAN 1 | **Berkenalan**
EXERCISE TAPE 1 | Getting to Know Each Other

Orang tua Sari tidak lahir di Jakarta. Sari adalah nama yang dipilih oléh bapaknya. Keluarga Sari mempunyai seékor kucing yang bernama Biru. Biru berumur sepuluh tahun. Ratih suka sekali membaca, menari dan melukis. Setiap hari Minggu ibu Sari berkebun di belakang rumah. Sari bertemu Joel di kampus Universitas Indonesia. Karena orang tua Sari orang Jawa, di rumah meréka memakai bahasa Jawa dan bahasa Indonesia. Bapak Sari sudah bekerja menjadi dosén di Universitas Indonesia selama lima belas (15) tahun, sementara ibu Sari yang bekerja di Rumah Sakit yang dekat dengan rumah meréka sudah bekerja di sana kira-kira sepuluh (10) tahun.

TAPE LATIHAN 2 | **Di Kampus**
EXERCISE TAPE 2 | At the Campus

Sari, Agus dan Ratih suka minum téh dan jarang sekali minum kopi. Kadang-kadang Agus minum bir dengan Joel. Sépak bola, bulu tangkis dan mendayung adalah olah raga kegemaran Agus. Meskipun Ratih dan Sari suka sekali membaca, bacaan meréka berbéda. Ratih suka membaca novel, tetapi Sari lebih suka membaca surat kabar dan majalah. Untuk acara télévisi, Agus selalu menonton olah raga, Sari dan bapaknya selalu menonton berita. Hanya Agus yang menyukai game di komputer. Sari dan Ratih lebih memilih naik gunung atau naik sepéda daripada pergi ke gym seperti Agus. Tidak ada yang merokok di keluarga Sari. Tidak seperti Ratih yang suka melukis, Sari lebih suka memasak atau menyanyi.

TAPE LATIHAN 3 | **Kuliah**
EXERCISE TAPE 3 | Lectures

Hari ini ada lima puluhan mahasiswa di kelas Sari. Sari ingin menjadi seorang diplomat. Seperti teman kuliah Sari yang berasal dari luar Jakarta, Sari harus menguasai bahasa Inggris dengan baik. Setelah bertemu Joel, bahasa Inggris Sari menjadi lebih baik. Setiap seminggu sekali Sari dan Joel bertemu di café dekat Fakultas Hukum untuk belajar bahasa. Sari harus berbicara dalam bahasa Inggris dan Joel harus berbicara dalam bahasa Indonesia. Joel pikir untuk hidup di Indonesia dia harus menguasai bahasa itu dengan baik.

TAPE LATIHAN 4 | **Di Mall**
EXERCISE TAPE 4 | At the Mall

Diperkirakan ada ribuan mall di Jakarta. Konsép tersebut berasal dari negara maju seperti Amerika atau negara-negara Eropa lainnya. Masih banyak orang yang suka berbelanja di pasar tradisional. Nénék Sari dan générasinya lebih menyukai pergi ke pasar tradisional. Orang tua Sari juga sering pergi ke pasar tradisional. Bapak Sari selalu pergi ke toko buku di Mangga Mall. Ratih pikir musik di Mangga Mall terlalu keras dan bising. Banyak toko pakaian, perhiasan, mainan anak-anak, éléktronika, sepatu dan makanan yang memenuhi Mangga Mall.

TAPE LATIHAN 5 | **Harga**
EXERCISE TAPE 5 | Prices

Joel sudah lama ingin membelikan buku memasak untuk Sari. Ibu Sari sering membaca buku dan majalah keséhatan. Agus selalu pergi ke toko buku dengan bapaknya, karena meréka berdua tidak suka pergi ke toko lainnya. Ratih menghabiskan uang seratus lima puluh ribu (Rp. 150.000) untuk membeli sedosin komik Tin-Tin. Joel suka pergi ke toko buku di Mangga Mall karena pegawai toko di sana semua ramah-ramah. Salah satu pegawai yang menjadi teman baru Joel bernama Sunu. Hari Sabtu atau Minggu Ratih, Sari dan ibu meréka suka pergi ke toko buku. Sekitar tiga puluh lima (35) orang dipekerjakan di toko buku itu. Agus lebih suka pergi ke sana hari Senin karena tidak banyak orang.

TAPE LATIHAN 6 — Jam Berapa?
EXERCISE TAPE 6 — What Time?

Joel dan Sari sudah berjanji untuk saling membantu belajar bahasa dan kuliah meréka berdua. Joel sering mengajak Sari untuk berbicara dalam bahasa Inggris dan membaca majalah atau buku-buku yang ditulis dalam bahasa Inggris. Sari juga selalu mendorong Joel untuk berbicara dan menulis dalam bahasa Indonesia. Ada empat orang da-lam keluarga Sari yang lahir pada bulan keempat, yaitu April. Sari dan ibunya yang dibantu dengan Ratih dan bapaknya selalu memasak nasi kuning ketika ada yang berulang tahun. Nasi kuning itu biasanya dinikmati keluarga dan teman-teman dekat di rumah Sari.

TAPE LATIHAN 7 — Di Mana?
EXERCISE TAPE 7 — Where?

Kampus Depok adalah kampus Universitas Indonesia yang terbesar. Kantor Administrasi ada di tengah-tengah kampus, supaya mudah dicari oléh calon mahasiswa. Joel pergi ke Fakultas Hukum hampir setiap hari. Joel tertarik dengan bangunan Masjid kampus. Banyak mahasiswa laki-laki dan pegawai universitas yang bersembahyang di Masjid kampus. Cukup banyak mahasiswa asing yang belajar di kampus UI. Sari ingin sekali mengambil gelar master Hubungan Internasional di univérsitas di Australia, seperti Univérsitas Monash di Melbourne misalnya.

TAPE LATIHAN 8 — Di Jalan
EXERCISE TAPE 8 — In the Street

Joel perlu mencari kantor pos karena banyak kartu pos yang harus dia kirimkan kepada ibu, nénék dan anggota keluarganya di Australia. Dengan kakaknya Joel lebih suka memakai email atau Facebook untuk berkomunikasi. Ibu dan nénék Joel lebih suka menerima surat atau kartu pos dari Joel. Selain kakaknya, teman-teman Joel yang ada di Australia atau negara-negara lainnya sering berkomunikasi léwat email. Anak muda sekarang menganggap bahwa jasa pos terlalu lamban untuk berkomunikasi. Di Indonesia, Joel selalu membeli banyak kartu pos dengan gambar-gambar tradisional.

TAPE LATIHAN 9 — Beli Kipas Angin
EXERCISE TAPE 9 — Buying a Fan

Secara umum di Indonesia hanya ada dua musim. Keluarga Sari, terutama ibunya, lebih memilih musim hujan kerena kegemarannya berkebun. Akan tetapi jika terlalu banyak hujan di Jakarta akan mengakibatkan kebanjiran. Meskipun begitu keluarga Sari tidak terlalu kuatir karena tempat tinggal meréka lumayan tinggi. Kurang tidur akan menyebabkan Joel pusing. Musim panas di Melbourne yang kadang-kadang bisa mencapai empat puluh drajat sélsius (40 C) lebih sering menyebabkan Joel sakit kepala juga. Di musim panas, masyarakat Australia sering terancam masalah kebakaran besar. Menurut bapak Sari, AC tidak baik untuk keséhatan.

TAPE LATIHAN 10 — Pakaian
EXERCISE TAPE 10 — Clothes

Joel percaya bahwa musim dingin lebih baik daripada musim panas. Ketika musim panas tiba, Joel seperti anak muda Australia lainnya suka pergi ke pantai. Polusi menyebabkan penyakit yang diderita oléh banyak orang di Indonesia. Polusi di Indonesia diakibatkan salah satunya karena banyaknya jumlah kendaraan. Selain itu banyaknya penebangan hutan di wilayah Indonesia memperburuk masalah polusi di Indonesia. LSM atau Lembaga Swadaya Masyarakat peduli lingkungan merupakan bagian yang sangat penting untuk mengatasi masalah lingkungan di Indonesia. Salah satu mata kuliah yang diambil Agus berhubungan dengan analisa dampak lingkungan. Sari mulai membuat kompos dan prosés daur ulang secara kecil-kecilan di rumah, sementara ibu Sari selalu membersihkan got di sekitar rumah dan menanam banyak tumbuhan di kebun.

TAPE LATIHAN 11 · Di Kampung
EXERCISE TAPE 11 · In the Kampong

Pada dasarnya définisi 'kampung' tidak sama dengan définisi 'désa'. Kampung berarti daérah kecil dan sempit dengan rumah-rumah kecil yang dibangun di depan gang-gang kecil di perkotaan. Désa biasanya letaknya jauh di luar kota dengan fasilitas yang masih dianggap belum modérn, tetapi luas tanahnya masih lapang. Orang-orang dari kelompok sosial-ékonomi yang rendah biasanya tinggal di kampung-kampung. Suasana khas yang sering kita temui di kampung-kampung adalah kedekatan dan keramahan orang-orangnya yang sering duduk-duduk bersama di gang-gang depan rumah meréka tinggal. Satu hal yang sama antara kampung dan désa adalah banyaknya jumlah mesjid yang ada, karena lebih dari sembilan puluh (90) persén penduduk Indonesia beragama Islam. Kebanyakan hanya orang laki-laki yang pergi bersembahyang di Masjid. Pada awal kedatangannya di Indonesia Joel terkejut dengan suara-suara keras dari pengeras suara Masjid lima kali sehari. Setelah beberapa minggu dia menjadi biasa dengan suara "Adzan" itu. Keluarga Joel tinggal di Geelong, Australia dan meréka sudah pernah beberapa kali pergi ke Indonesia.

TAPE LATIHAN 12 · Kuliah Hukum
EXERCISE TAPE 12 · Law Lectures

Joel ingin belajar hukum di UI selama satu seméster karena di negaranya dia belajar hukum dan studi Indonesia. Selama belajar di Indonesia Joel juga ingin bertemu dengan para praktisi hukum, dosén dan ahli di bidang hukum Indonesia dan mahasiswanya. Joel sudah belajar bahasa Indonesia dari sekolah dasar. Ibu Joel mendorongnya untuk meneruskan belajar bahasa Indonesia di univérsitas setelah Joel selesai SMA. Ketika di SMA ada program pertukaraan yang diikuti oléh Joel. Joel tinggal selama enam bulan di kota Bandung dengan keluarga barunya. Bandung yang sering juga disebut sebagai 'Kota kembang' adalah ibu kota propinsi Jawa Barat. Joel masih sering berkomunikasi dengan keluarganya dari Bandung dan sudah beberapa kali mengunjungi meréka.

TAPE LATIHAN 13 · Orang Miskin
EXERCISE TAPE 13 · The Poor

Banyaknya jumlah kendaraan bermotor di Jakarta menyebabkan tingkat polusi udara yang tinggi dan menjadikan orang tidak suka berjalan kaki. Sudah ada upaya pemerintah lokal untuk mengatasi masalah kemacetan lalu-lintas, tapi masih banyak yang harus meréka lakukan. Jumlah penduduk propinsi Jakarta yang diperkirakan sudah mencapai 15 juta lebih menjadi masalah tersendiri. Kebanyakan orang-orang dari berbagai tempat di Indonesia ingin pergi ke Jakarta untuk mencari pekerjaan. Kebanyakan orang-orang yang hanya berpendidikan rendah sering tidak mendapat pekerjaan, lalu mengalami kesulitan ekonomi. Meskipun begitu meréka enggan pulang karena merasa malu. Masalah ini sering dihadapi kota-kota besar di seluruh dunia.

TAPE LATIHAN 14 · Merokok
EXERCISE TAPE 14 · Smoking

Iklan rokok ada di mana-mana di Indonesia. Targét utama iklan ini adalah para remaja, terutama remaja laki-laki. 'Pergaulan atau sosialisasi' adalah alasan yang sering diungkapkan oléh teman-teman Joel dari Universitas Indonesia dan suka merokok. Banyak penyakit yang ditimbulkan oléh kebiasaan merokok dan yang paling berbahaya adalah kanker paru-paru, tenggorokan dan mulut. Di negara seperti Indonesia banyak juga orang yang sering disebut sebagai 'perokok pasif'. Artinya orang ini tidak merokok tetapi hidup di lingkungan yang penuh dengan perokok. Pendidikan tentang bahaya merokok dianggap sangat kurang sekali di negara seperti Indonesia. Semua pihak, misalnya pemerintah, sekolah, média, keluarga punya tanggung jawab untuk mendidik masyarakat tentang dampak buruk kebiasaan merokok.

TAPE LATIHAN 15 Taman Mini
EXERCISE TAPE 15 The "Taman Mini"

Sari ingin sekali mengajak Joel untuk melihat Taman Mini karena Sari ingin tahu réaksinya Joel. Menurut bapak Sari pengunjung Taman Mini hanya turis saja. Taman Mini menggambarkan konsép yang disebut Bhinneka Tunggal Ika, yang berarti 'berbéda-béda tetapi tetap satu jua'. Dari keréta gantung yang dinaiki di Taman Mini kita bisa melihat kumpulan pulau-pulau mini di seluruh Indonesia. Di zaman pemerintahan Orde Baru semua anak sekolah diharuskan berkunjung ke Taman Mini. Joel tertarik untuk lebih tahu tentang pendapat pengritik Taman Mini yang mengatakan bahwa konsép persatuan, kesatuan dan identitas Indonesia agak dipaksakan dari pemerintah pusat yang waktu itu présidénnya adalah présidén Suharto. Sekarang ini Taman Mini agak sedikit pengunjungnya.

TAPE LATIHAN 16 Sinétron
EXERCISE TAPE 16 TV Dramas

Setiap harinya Joel sering tiba di rumah kosnya pada jam setengah lima soré. Joel pergi ke kampus dari hari Senin hingga Jumat. Joel mencoba pulang ketika hari sudah gelap karena sudah tidak terlalu panas. Sinétron atau sinéma éléktronik adalah drama télévisi yang sangat digemari terutama oléh ibu-ibu rumah tangga di Indonesia. Akhir-akhir ini sinétron di Indonesia tumbuh seperti jamur dan penggemarnya menjadi bertambah banyak. Ada yang mengatakan bahwa sinétron banyak digemari di Indonesia karena isinya banyak mengandung fantasi yang luar biasa, dan pengritik sinétron percaya bahwa fantasi ini adalah berbahaya karena dianggap sebagai 'anti realita' atau kenyataan. Hampir semua sinétron yang dipertontonkan di télévisi Indonesia memakai bahasa Indonesia dialék Jakarta.

TAPE LATIHAN 17 Kunjungan Ke Keluarga Ékspat
EXERCISE TAPE 17 Visit to an Expat Family

Ada ribuan ékspat yang tinggal dan bekerja di Jakarta. Meréka bekerja di macam-macam bidang seperti keuangan, pendidikan, property, média, perhotélan, pertambangan, pariwisata, dll. Para ékspat itu berasal dari seluruh penjuru dunia. Joel ingin sekali bertemu dan bercakap-cakap dengan salah satu ékspat di Jakarta, karena dia ingin mendengar pengalaman meréka. Menurut para ékspat itu fasilitas seperti pembantu, sopir, pelayan dan orang-orang yang bekerja untuk meréka sehari-hari merupakan salah satu aspék yang sangat dinikmati. Tentu saja keuntungan utama adalah kemampuan bahasa Indonesia yang menjadi semakin baik setiap hari. Naséhat penting Eric kepada Joel adalah 'nikmati saja semua aspék yang kamu alami di sini'. Joel sangat setuju dan dia berkeinginan untuk bekerja di Jakarta setelah dia lulus dari univérsitas.

TAPE LATIHAN 18 Wawancara
EXERCISE TAPE 18 The Interview

Ada berbagai macam kegiatan mahasiswa UI di luar kuliah meréka seperti misalnya baskét, bulu tangkis, silat, naik gunung, ténis, drama, puisi, radio, majalah kampus, diskusi antar agama, menari, débat, peduli lingkungan, karaté, music dan lain-lain. Orang tua Sari sangat mendukung anak meréka untuk aktif mengikuti kegiatan ékstrakurikulér. Seperti Joel, Sari percaya bahwa kegiatan-kegiatan tersebut sama pentingnya dengan kuliah meréka. Joel tertarik dengan satu kegiatan yang dilakukan oléh kelompok peduli lingkungan, karena menurut Joel meréka génerasi yang paling aktif dalam hal lingkungan di sekitar kampus. Sari aktif terlibat dengan majalah kampus dan olah raga karaté, sedangkan Agus mengikuti kegiatan débat dan olah raga bulu tangkis. Kadang-kadang dia juga menulis artikel untuk majalah kampus. Menurut Joel, mahasiswa di Indonesia lebih aktif terlibat dalam kehidupan kampus daripada mahasiswa di univérsitas di Australia. Agus dan Sari setuju bahwa majalah kampus merupakan alat ékprési mahasiswa Indonesia yang masih sangat perlu dilatih.

TAPE LATIHAN 19   Menonton Apa?
EXERCISE TAPE 19   What Will We Watch?

Joel yakin bahwa cara yang paling éféktif untuk memahami suatu budaya tertentu adalah léwat bahasanya. Menurut ibu Joel, cara yang paling baik untuk belajar bahasa adalah 'hidup dalam bahasa tersebut'. Ini berarti Joel harus tinggal dan hidup di Indonesia untuk benar-benar mempelajari bahasa dan budaya Indonesia. Tetapi sejak dia tiba di Jakarta Joel selalu héran mendengar bahasa yang dipakai orang-orang, karena sangat berbéda dengan bahasa yang dia pelajari di univérsitas di Austra-lia. Untuk memahami bahasa Indonesia dialék Jakarta, Joel sering menonton sinétron dengan Bu Tuti, pemilik rumah kosnya, berkumpul dengan teman-teman di kampus dan menonton filem Indonesia. Banyak filem-filem Indonesia yang memakai bahasa dialék Jakarta. Filem-filem yang dibuat sekarang ini sudah banyak yang dianggap berkualitas, seperti misalnya Ada Apa Dengan Cinta, Laskar Pelangi dan Berbagi Suami.

TAPE LATIHAN 20   Senja Di Jakarta
EXERCISE TAPE 20   Twilight in Jakarta

Kopi tubruk adalah kopi tradisional khas dari Indonesia yang berisi banyak ampas atau endapan sesudah diminum. Orang biasanya minum kopi tubruk dengan gula sehingga terasa manis dan kenthal. Joel suka minum kopi tubruk sambil membaca. Majalah Gatra bergaya seperti majalah berbahasa Inggris 'Time'. Bahasa Indonesia yang dipakai dalam majalah seperti Gatra biasanya bersifat resmi atau formal. Topik yang selalu menjadi bahan tulisan di Indonesia adalah politik. Salah satu manfaat yang diperoléh Joel dengan membaca majalah populer seperti Gatra atau Tempo adalah kemampuan menulis dan berdiskusi dalam bahasa Indonesianya semakin baik. Joel selalu membaca rubrik hukum dan politik karena kedua topik itu sering dibicarakan di kampus dengan dosén dan mahasiswa lain.

TAPE LATIHAN 21   Ke Dokter
EXERCISE TAPE 21   Going to the Doctor

Joel diberi tahu oléh teman-temannya yang pernah tinggal di Jakarta untuk mencoba naik bis. Sekarang ini lebih banyak orang memakai jasa bis di Jakarta karena naik mobil akan menambah kemacetan. Sebenarnya semakin banyak orang memakai bis semakin baik karena bisa mengurangi jumlah pemakai mobil. Dengan demikian polusi dan kerusakan jalan bisa berkurang. Banyak macam bis yang ada di Jakarta dari yang murah tanpa AC dan bis jenis éksprés dengan AC. Joel sudah mencoba bis biasa dan bis yang méwah berAC. Banyak sekali yang ingin dilakukan Joel, kadang-kadang dia lupa beristirahat dan memelihara keséhatannya. Setelah beberapa minggu di Jakarta Joel menderita anémia yang menurut dokter disebabkan oleh perubahan cuaca dan kurang makanan yang bergizi. Joel disarankan untuk beristirahat, makan secara séhat dan minum tablét zat besi.

TAPE LATIHAN 22   Hubungan Internasional
EXERCISE TAPE 22   International Relations

Fisipol adalah singkatan dari Fakultas Ilmu Sosial dan Politik. Setelah lulus mahasiswa jurusan HI bisa bekerja menjadi diplomat, binis internasional atau menjadi dosén. Mengikuti saran orang tuanya, Sari masuk di jurusan HI karena dia mempunyai cita-cita untuk berkeliling dunia. Karena bahasa Inggris adalah bahasa komunikasi internasional, mahasiswa seperti Sari harus menguasainya dengan baik. Tujuan penting studi Hubungan Internasional adalah menyiapkan calon-calon diplomat atau générasi yang mempunyai keahlian diplomasi antar negara. Sari sangat bersemangat kuliah di jurusan HI di universitas Indonesia.

TAPE LATIHAN 23 **Perjalanan Ke Yogyakarta**
EXERCISE TAPE 23 A Trip to Yogyakarta

Sari dan keluarganya sering pergi ke Yogyakarta karena nénéknya tinggal di sana. Ibu Sari lahir dan besar di Yogyakarta. Propinsi Yogyakarta sering juga disebut DIY. DIY berarti Daérah Istiméwa Yogyakarta. Jumlah penduduk DIY kira-kira tiga juta. Gubernur DIY sekarang ini dianggap sebagai tokoh yang istiméwa, karena dia juga merupakan salah satu Raja Mataram. Kota Yogyakarta terkenal sebagai kota budaya dan pendidikan. Bahasa yang dipakai penduduk asli Yogyakarta adalah Bahasa Jawa. Di sekitar Yogyakarta banyak sekali terdapat candi-candi seperti Borobudur, Prambanan, Mendut, Kalasan dan sebagainya.

TAPE LATIHAN 24 **Ke Pasar**
EXERCISE TAPE 24 To the Market

Siapa saja yang pergi ke Yogyakarta harus mengunjungi Pasar Beringharjo, karena pasar tradisional itu merupakan salah satu atraksi yang menarik. Orang selalu ingin membeli batik di pasar itu. Meskipun di dekat pasar dibangun pusat perbelanjaan moderen, orang-orang masih mencintai Pasar Beringharjo. Karena kabanyakan pedagang di pasar itu penduduk asli Yogyakarta, meréka biasanya berbicara dalam Bahasa Jawa. Aspék yang paling disukai pengunjung pasar Beringharjo adalah keramahan pedagangnya yang luar biasa. Menurut Joel suasana di dalam Pasar Beringharjo seperti suasana di dalam rumah sebuah keluarga besar ala Jawa. Karena Joel belum bisa berbahasa Jawa, para pedagang berbicara kepada Joel dalam bahasa Indonesia.

TAPE LATIHAN 25 **Hari Nasional**
EXERCISE TAPE 25 National Days

Biasanya sekitar dua minggu sebelum tanggal tujuh belas (17) Agustus orang-orang di Indonesia sibuk membersihkan lingkungan dan mengadakan lomba-lomba atau kompétisi. Pada tanggal 17 Agustus seribu sembilan ratus empat puluh lima (1945) Indonesia menyatakan kemerdékaannya. Untuk merayakan hari kemerdékaan itu, masyarakat biasanya membersihkan dan mendékor daérah di mana meréka tinggal dan melakukan kompétisi olah raga, menyanyi, memasak dan lain-lain. Suasana meriah pada bulan Agustus membuat Joel terkesan. Joel sendiri kurang setuju dengan dipilihnya tanggal 26 Januari sebagai Hari Australia, karena itu bukan hari kemerdékaan Australia tetapi hari ketika pertama kali bangsa Eropa masuk di Australia. Penduduk asli Australia juga kurang setuju dengan dipilihnya tanggal 26 Januari sebagai hari nasional Australia.

TAPE LATIHAN 26 **Cicak**
EXERCISE TAPE 26 Wall Lizards

Makanan utama cicak adalah nyamuk. Joel pernah melihat binatang yang sama persis bentuknya seperti cicak tetapi lebih besar. Binatang itu namanya 'Tokék'. Ketika orang datang ke Indonesia dan melihat banyak cicak di rumah meréka terkejut. Joel diperingatkan oléh orang tuanya tentang nyamuk yang banyak di Indonesia, tetapi meréka lupa memberitahu Joel tentang cicak. Selama sepuluh tahun terakhir banyak sekali penderita demam berdarah di kota Jakarta yang disebabkan oléh nyamuk. Pemerintah lokal biasanya melakukan pengasapan untuk membasmi nyamuk yang menyebabkan demam berdarah. Selain pengasapan nyamuk cara lain untuk mengurangi penyakit demam berdarah adalah dengan menghindari genangan air di sekitar rumah dan gaya hidup yang séhat.

TAPE LATIHAN 27 **Unjuk Rasa**
EXERCISE TAPE 27   Demonstrations

Di Indonesia démonstrasi di kampus-kampus merupakan hal yang sangat biasa. Pagi itu Joel melihat banyak sekali mahasiswa yang berkumpul di kampus dengan membawa spanduk dan mikrofon. Hanafi memberitahu Joel bahwa para mahasiswa itu sedang melakukan démonstrasi. Menurut Hanafi démonstrasi itu cara untuk menyampaikan perasaan, sehingga dalam istilah bahasa Indonesia disebut 'unjuk rasa'. Ketika Suharto masih menjadi présidén démonstrasi mahasiswa sering dilarang. Sekarang ini lebih mudah mahasiswa Indonesia untuk berdémonstrasi. Dampaknya pasti ada, terutama di kota seperti Jakarta, yaitu menambah macetnya lalulintas. Pagi ini mahasiswa menuntut univérsitas untuk tidak menaikkan uang pangkal kuliah. Meréka merasa kenaikan uang pangkal sangat membebani mahasiswa. Kegiatan-kegiatan yang biasanya dilakukan oleh para mahasiswa ketika berunjuk rasa di antaranya berpidato, meneriakkan yél-yél, bernyanyi dan membagikan pamflét.

TAPE LATIHAN 28 **Trompét Rahasia**
EXERCISE TAPE 28   The Secret Trumpet

Selain memainkan alat musik trompét, Joel juga menyukai olah raga seperti baskét, sépak bola, bersepéda dan berenang. Musik tradisional dan musik bergaya alternatif juga sangat digemari Joel selain Jazz. Menurut Joel musik pop di Indonesia sangat dipengaruhi oléh musik barat, sehingga dia lebih memilih musik tradisional Indonesia seperti misalnya gamelan karena unik. Sari bisa bermain gamelan Jawa sedikit. Selain itu Sari juga bisa menari tarian Jawa tradisional. Seperti ibunya ketika dia masih remaja dan masih tinggal di Yogyakarta, Sari ikut kelompok menari Jawa tradisional di kampus. Ayah Sari sering mendengarkan gamelan dan musik keroncong.

Glossary of Key Grammatical Terms

Abilitative: a verb with the prefix **ter-** that indicates that the actor has the ability to perform the action

Abstract noun: a noun that refers to an abstract quality

Accidental: a verb with the prefix **ter-** that refers to an unintended, agentless action

Active: a verb is said to be active when its subject is the one who performs the action; the opposite of *passive*

Adjective: a word which refers to a characteristic of a thing or person

Adverb: an adjunct to a verb or an adjective which tells us how or when

Affixation: the process of attaching affixes to a base-word

Agent: the person or thing that performs the action of the verb

Base-word: the part of a word which carries the essential meaning and to which affixes are attached

Benefactive: a type of verb with the suffix **-kan** which expresses performing the action on behalf of someone else

Causative: a type of verb which expresses bringing about a certain outcome

Cardinal number: a number which is used in counting

Classifier: a word which precedes a noun in order to place it in a particular class

Clause: a unit or group of words below the sentence, containing a subject and a predicate and introduced by a conjunction

Comparative: refers to an adjective that indicates possessing the quality concerned to a higher degree ("more")

Complement: a word which adds to or completes the meaning of another

Conjunction: a word that joins two clauses

Demonstrative: a group of pronouns that point to position: "this (here), that (there)"

Doubling: a process by which a new word is formed on the basis of another by doubling it

First person: a group of pronouns that refer to the speaker

Foregrounding: a process whereby a word or word-group is placed at the beginning of a sentence in order to receive more attention

Intransitive: refers to a verb that does not have an object

Locative: refers to a verb with the suffix **-i** and an object which is a place

Modal word: a word in the predicate placed before the verb which refers to concepts such as ability or necessity

Nominalization: the process whereby a verb or an adjective is enabled to function as a noun

Noun: a word that refers to a thing, person or concept

Ordinal number: a number that indicates where something comes in a sequence

Passive: a form of the verb where the subject undergoes the action of the verb; the opposite of *active*

Predicate: that part of the sentence which tells us about the subject

Prefix: an affix which is attached to the front of the base-word

Preposition: a word preceding a noun or pronoun and forming a word-group with it which provides information regarding the predicate

Pronoun: a word that stands for a noun; can be first, second or third person

Reciprocal: a form of the verb in which the actors perform the action "to each other"

Reduplication See *doubling*

Relative pronoun: a pronoun that refers back to an antecedent and attaches a clause to it

Second person: a group of pronouns that refer to the person spoken to

Split subject: a subject made up of a word-group which is split, and part of it placed at the beginning of the sentence in order to receive more attention

Stative: a group of words with the prefix **ter-** which indicate a state

Subject: that part of the sentence which indicates what is being spoken about

Suffix: an affix which is attached to the end of the base-word

Superlative: refers to an adjective which indicates possessing a quality to the highest degree ("most")

Syllable: a unit of pronunciation having one vowel sound, with or without surrounding consonants, and forming all or part of a word

Tense: with verbs, the indication of the time when the action occurs

Third person: a group of pronouns that refer to the person spoken about

Transitive: refers to a verb that has, or can have, an object

Other Titles of Interest from
Periplus Editions/Tuttle Publishing